BIODESIGN
OUT FOR
A WALK

BIODESIGN
OUT FOR
A WALK

Lowell Harrison Young

Outskirts Press, Inc.
Denver, Colorado

Edited by Linda Williamson

Outskirts Press, Inc.
http://www.outskirtspress.com

PB ISBN: 978-1-4327-7285-7
HB ISBN: 978-1-4327-7287-1

To Christie: for coauthoring Biodesign, this book, and my life.

To my amazing children:

> *Maureen*
> *Paul*
> *Nicole*
> *Bethany*

To Lettie for asking a simple question.

Contents

Foreword

His class was around the corner from mine. For years I was so engrossed with building my own curriculum that I didn't know or care what went on in Room 103.

An aura of mystery surrounded Lowell Young's class. We saw him carry in flowers. He grew a beard, and then one day, it was gone. Teachers started calling him "The Philosopher" behind his back. He lit candles ... definitely against the fire code. His kids sat in a circle, and his room was as full of camping gear as microscopes and Bunsen burners. Was Biodesign a real science class? What the heck was he doing in there?

Because we shared students (I was the AP English teacher), one day I asked an articulate lad that question, who stammered and finally blurted out, "We talk a lot in there."

I was furious. I was working my tail off trying to get my students prepared for college writing as well as scoring high on standardized tests, and all Young was doing was listening to kids talk?

Then around November when I was teaching Thoreau in one class and English Romanticism in another, I noticed that the Biodesign kids grasped the concepts easily and sometimes knowing looks passed between them. They compared Thoreau to John Muir. They could explain the importance of nature to their lives. Their thoughts were perceptive. I wrote in the margin beside Wordsworth's Tintern Abbey ... Biodesign!!!!

One February I tagged along on the Grand Canyon trip. What I noticed first was the maturity of the young people as soon as they left the high school. They took charge. They were helpful to each other … and to me. Climbing nine hours from Phantom Ranch up to the South Rim is no Sunday stroll. The strong ones helped the weaker ones (me?), and eventually, we all made it to the top where Christie met us with a smile.

I now realize that one of the great lessons of Biodesign was learning how a strong marriage works. Christie was, and is, the strength behind the scenes; the wind beneath Lowell Young's wings.

Lowell and I are retired now. From the distance, I look back at my frantic days of vocabulary acquisition, writing tactics, and information stuffing that was my life for 25 years. I wonder how much of the information was retained. I am certain that most of the facts are gone, although I believe that most of my former students play a heck of a game of Jeopardy.

I am also certain that most of the knowledge of Biodesign is still with them. I now admire Young's courage in breaking with tradition and silly state standards to teach what is more important than minutia. The design between science and human life, science and religion, and science and his students' own experience is not lost knowledge, but a circle not easily broken.

Linda Williamson
February 2010

In Thanksgiving

Every good story involves mystery, comedy, tragedy, and a hero. This story was written by over 700 high school students who had the curiosity and courage to enroll in an experimental, and therefore, controversial, advanced biology course. Each added her or his voice and collaborated in the creative and evolutionary process. This is their story simply because without them, the class would not have existed. They are the heroes.

They represent, however, only part of the mystery. One of John Muir's many critics proclaimed that Muir wasn't particularly talented, but merely in the right place at the right time. I scoffed at the assertion, and then realized that in the writer's ignorance, he was revealing something profound. After all, had every cell that ever existed not been alive at the right place and the right time? Do the Earth, Solar System, Milky Way, and even the universe, not exist at the right place and the right time? Is every human that ever lived not a once-in-a-universe creation resulting from the union of an "o-i-a-u" sperm with an "o-i-a-u" egg?

There may have been 700 stars in this drama, but they were supported by a cast of thousands, all of who had to be in the right place at the right time or the drama would have flopped. Three of my teachers played huge roles. Ralph Ingols, my high school civics teacher, took me to the Grand Canyon. Dr. Sweeney, a plant ecology professor (San Francisco State University) took me to the pygmy forest in Mendocino. Dr. Joe? biology professor (Sonoma State University) took me to Yosemite. Hundreds of scientists and sages, naturalists and poets freely offered support and guidance. Over a thousand parents entrusted their precious children into the care of an openly avowed disciple of John Muir, who, like him, was "preaching" the doctrine of the redemptive power of Mother Nature.

Over 400 parent/chaperones drove cars and vans, helped pitch tents, carry water, and chop campfire wood. They proved Shakespeare's adage, "One touch of Nature and all men are kin," by eliminating the generation/parent gap and blending in so well that at times they were naughty too. The kids laughed when I had to discipline their parents; I hated it; it was all part of coming alive.

I am grateful to numerous school board members and administrators who were often baffled by what I was doing, yet continued to let me do it. I owe a huge debt of gratitude to my fellow teachers who graciously allowed students to miss nine school days annually to go on the trips.

I contacted approximately 30 alumni and chaperones seeking verification of facts and tone. Distilling 24 years, 63 trips, 700 students, and 400 chaperones can not be done without making some errors. I have done my best to avoid as many as possible and hope that no one has been misrepresented. All of those contacted preferred that I use their real names; otherwise, I used fictitious names.

The smaller numbers became the most important. My four children, Maureen, Paul, Nicole, and Bethany, were more precious than any dad could imagine. They taught, molded and shaped me into a better human. When each took the Biodesign class, she/he was put in the awkward position of having his/her dad as "the teacher." I know that I embarrassed them, but they never complained. Not once! They did better than I did. Three sons-in-law all contributed key pieces. Evan planted the seed to write; Alex provided an "unwanted" computer at the perfect time; and Andrew proofread and spurred me on.

Along with our loss of contact with Mother Earth, we have lost our sense of childlike wonder and innocence.

"God and the fairies be true, be true!"
Louise Townsend Nicholl

And angels too...

When the idea of a possible book project began to emerge, six angels were perfectly positioned to guide me to the promised land of publication. Lettie, who asked the fateful question, wanted to hear the whole story that she innocently initiated. Heather, a previous student, now skilled editor, urged me to publish. Linda, an ex-colleague-English teacher, happened along at the right moment and volunteered to be my editor. When she offered, I broke into a cold sweat. She was affectionately known by some of her students as the "Mad Whacker," because of her demanding writing standards. Her love of literature, learning and language touched multitudes. It was, however, daunting to entrust this project into her care. I knew her reputation and feared that the manuscript would return looking like she ran it through her paper shredder. Without her guidance and encouragement, the project would have failed.

The fourth angel arrived just as Linda finished editing. Jodee, from Outskirts Press, appeared out of cyberspace to guide me through the maze of prepublication. There is no doubt that she arrived at the perfect moment. What were the odds?

The fifth angel was every author's dream. What was so remarkable was that she was our daughter. When the book was ready for printing she stepped up and created a Face Book page, designed our web-site, and planned every detail of enlarging the reader base. She is a highly talented sociologist, however, I had no idea she had all the other talents.

And finally, the omega factor is often the most important in a list. If readers are not able to see, or perhaps more importantly feel between the lines, and sense that Christie was the guiding light for the Biodesign Class and this book, I will have failed. Her quiet life of prayer and contemplation provided the unseen spirit that hovered over the hundreds of circles we formed each year to compare, communicate, and contemplate. Without her, I would likely have been like Ingrid (class of '84) who suggested that, "I could have been born, grown up, grown old, and died without knowing what life was really all about."

Introduction

Going for a walk should be fun. So should biology. After all, without it, we wouldn't be able to experience the rapture, sorrow, and mystery of the universe. The "strange and wonderful magic" that created the Velveteen Rabbit is not confined to nurseries; it occurred at St. Helena High School, in the heart of California's Napa Valley. A scattered group of rebels magically overthrew my teaching style and curriculum and created an advanced biology course with a spiritual component. Each year, they traveled to Yosemite, the Grand Canyon, and California's Mendocino Coast, discovering themselves and their role in the world.

The birth of the class was not unlike the birth of a baby. There were moments of elation and sorrow, triumph and frustration, hope and despair. No one, especially me, realized that the students were responding to an ancient call which predated Christianity, perhaps by 100,000 years. Like Henry Thoreau, they were seeking a spiritual rebirth. Bloody palms, horrifying fear, and a battered ego were not included in my job description. They were, however, prerequisites for entering the uncharted wilderness of the teenage soul.

Lettie was dissecting a fetal pig when she suddenly paused, looked up, and asked, "Mr. Young, is this really important?" I discovered later that her question was a matter of her spiritual life and death. While discussing evolution, and the now discredited story of the wolf/dog wandering into the ocean to become a whale, Matthew shouted, "Wait a minute! What the hell do we believe, anyway? Did they think their way back into the ocean to become whales?" I discovered later that he was asking the most profound question that a person can ask. The collective human response will likely determine the fate of mankind.

These educational rebels elected to sit in a circle and rejected the traditional learning method of massive memorization of minutiae. Instead, they replaced it with an emphasis on critical thinking, communication skills, and problem solving. The focus was always biology, but collateral topics of natural history, evolution, the wilderness ethic, politics, sexuality, and religion were open for discussion. They understood the gravity that many had died so they could study and grow in an environment without fear, bitterness, or humiliation. Some began to contemplate the immensity, horror, and glory of the human journey. Evolution, they discovered, often involved bloodshed, and they pondered over the hundreds of millions of people who were stoned, clubbed, burned, or nailed on crosses for what they believed.

Their class discussions were often lively but could not compare with the three, six-day field trips that they took. They tested Emerson's adage, "The whole of Nature is but a metaphor of the human mind," and often discovered wonders, even miracles, in Nature, themselves and each other.

The theme for the class was defined by John Muir; "I only went out for a walk … and found that going out was really going in." They were invited to read the accounts of scientists, scholars, sages, and saints to see how they viewed Mother Nature. Many learned how to cope with the physical, mental, and spiritual blisters that they encountered along the way. Some learned to look for Jungian synchronicities and found them to be amusing, inspirational, or frightening. Each year, hundreds of ideas were born, some resulting from close encounters with death.

I have selected nearly 100 quotations which include scores of ideas from seekers whose thoughts and deeds have improved humanity. I felt that my deepest calling was not to "teach" but to share these designs with young, curious, and flexible minds and let them decide which ones they wanted to incorporate into their personal biblioteca (library).

As for me, the epic journey ended when a modern-day Moses appeared on Yosemite's Half Dome with an answer to Lettie's question. For 24 years, students smiled knowingly when their teacher pictured himself as Ahab, steering his tiny boatload of students into the vast wilderness. They knew better and that he was merely Ishmael, going along for the ride.

"In God's wildness lies the hope of the world;
the great fresh, unblighted, unredeemed wilderness.
The galling harness of civilization drops off
and the wounds heal ere we are aware."

John Muir

1: Genesis: Lettie's Question

"WAIT A MINUTE! What the hell do we believe anyway?" Matthew's question echoed around the circle of astonished students and was one of the three greatest questions a human can ask.

1. Who am?
2. What do I believe?
3. What will become of me?

Although the question was provocative, riveting, exciting, it was asked in a class that was conceived in a state of utter boredom. Boring may be a strange way to launch a 24-year odyssey; boring, however, was the mood when the adventure was conceived.

The seed was planted on a warm spring day during a high school faculty meeting in the library. The air-conditioning unit was down, the windows were not operable, and the fetid air was an accumulation of teenage body odor, cheap perfume, and guys' cologne. The principal droned on and on, on various inane topics, to a dull and listless faculty. I was having difficulty staying awake and formed a pact with a colleague whereby we agreed to elbow each other if we happened to nod off. Then, something totally unexpected happened. The principal paused in midsentence, gazed up at the ceiling, and wistfully mentioned, "If any of you have an idea for a new class, this would be a good time to try it." There were a few snickers and groans, and the idea was generally dismissed. I was intrigued by his challenge; however, after the meeting ended, I drifted home, oblivious of the fact that a seed had been planted. If I had examined it, I'm guessing that I would have dismissed it as a "could anything good come out of Nazareth?" moment.

My wife, Christie, has always planted her garden using *The Farmer's Almanac*. I don't know if there is real value, scientific or other, regarding planting by the moon, but what happened the following week would suggest that there are "forces" out there. There is no explanation for what was about to happen.

I was teaching an advanced biology course called human physiology. The class included a 12-week unit in which each student dissected a fetal pig. One day, I walked up and down the rows of lab tables, wearing a freshly starched lab coat, looking very professional. The students were working out of lab guides and only had occasional questions. As I approached Lettie, a bright, highly motivated girl, she took her hand out of her pig, looked up, and asked, "Mr. Young, is this really important?"

I was professionally prepared to deal with her question at two levels. First, I had recently completed a master's degree in biology, and my head was crammed full of all of the latest knowledge. Second, this large head also contained a large ego, bordering on arrogance, which commonly happens to people who have survived intensive academic regimens. All of my recent learning was predicated on a college degree, which was predicated on a high school diploma. I was loaded for bear, even though I was facing a lamb. I seized the moment and launched into a minisermon on the merits of mastering all the parts of the fetal pig.

Challenging classes like this one, I suggested, would prepare her for college or university and eventually help her become a richer, fuller human being. Furthermore, I had learned in *Human Destiny,* by Lecomte du Noüy, that children are insatiable sponges of knowledge until the age of 10, thereafter, there is a protest. They also discover that learning about themselves and others often involves stress and pain as prerequisites of growth. Often, they react negatively to situations that they sense will be uncomfortable. One of the most demanding and exhausting aspects of teaching was dealing with these daily protests. I dismissed her question as normal teenage resistance to a challenge.

Loren Eiseley was a scientist who claimed that water has magical, if not miraculous, properties, without which life would not be possible. I have often experienced creative solutions to personal and educational problems during my morning shower. The next morning would be no exception. Lettie's question reoccurred to me, and a cold shiver stirred my soul. She was too polite and respectful to suggest that I had totally missed her point. I hoped that I would be given a second chance. Lettie was not questioning my authority; she was exhibiting a vestigial, childlike sense of curiosity, and in so doing, asking a profound question. Her question, I would discover later, was nothing short of a matter of her spiritual life and death.

The next day, as physiology students filed into class and dutifully went to the refrigerator to retrieve their pigs, I announced that we would have a Friday philosophy day. In order to break the monotony, tedium, or intensity of the week, sometimes I selected quotes, poetry, music, or artwork to facilitate an interdisciplinary discussion related to our studies. I began by stating that Lettie had asked a very important question, and I had handled it poorly.

I said, "I am sure that you were all so engrossed in your pigs (laughter) that you probably didn't hear. I would like her to ask the question again and expand on it. After that, feel free to respond."

Lettie blushed and said, "Well, as you all know, I live out of town and I find nature fascinating. Memorizing all the parts of a pig is a lot of work, and I was just wondering if it were really important in the big picture."

Her comment opened a floodgate. Students opened up and shared hopes, dreams, and desires to learn to be more loving, compassionate people. Some contributions evoked laughter, and some caused tears. They understood the discipline part but generally agreed that memorizing all the parts of a pig was probably not going to add greatly to their sense of humanity. If the class sensed that I was disturbed, they were correct.

The following Monday, after the students were settled in the lab with their pigs, I commented on the high level of the Friday discussion.

I asked, "Did you know, 2,400 years ago, a Greek by the name of Plato said that the essence of being human involved a continual search for truth, beauty, and goodness? Is that what you were talking about?"

They responded with a resounding, "Yes."

I glanced over at Lettie, and she was beaming.

Someone asked, "Does this mean that we don't have to dissect the pigs anymore?"

I was proud of their perceptiveness, but had to answer, "Sorry, nice try." This time they responded with boos. It was a bittersweet moment, but Lettie had planted a seed.

I left school that afternoon knowing that I had to do something, but had absolutely no clue as to what that something would be.

"I have a low opinion of books;
they are but piles of stone set up
to show coming travelers where other minds
have been ... One day's exposure to the mountains
is worth cartloads of books."

John Muir

2: Looking for a Map

MR. INGOLS, MY high school senior history teacher, led a field trip to the Grand Canyon, which was an important part of my education. Many of the college classes I took had questionable value and were soon forgotten, but there was one striking exception. It was a graduate course in field-biology that integrated ecology, botany, vertebrate, and invertebrate zoology. It included a massive amount of information, but it also included a field trip that would have a profound influence on my life and work.

We drove to the northwest quadrant of Yosemite National Park and set up our campsites at Crane Flat campground. Our plan was to visit various sites and hear lectures and discussions from our professors and park naturalists. The next morning, we drove into "The Incomparable Valley."

El Capitan stood huge and almighty on our left with Bridal Veil Falls on the right. Moving up-valley, Cathedral Rocks loomed on the right and Three Brothers soared to the left. The dazzling Sentinel spire appeared to be a huge sack needle made of rock, and Yosemite Falls splashed down in a two-tiered display of watery wonder. And then, one of the most photographed rocks on the planet appeared: Half Dome. At nearly one mile high, it stood like a god of creation surveying his finest efforts.

My left brain took notes; however, my right brain was in a continual state of awe. Years later, I wouldn't remember my professor's name or what he said, but my first images of Yosemite would last my entire life. On our final afternoon visit, I remember standing in a meadow at the base of Half Dome, looking up and thinking, "WOW! If I ever had a chance, I would love to bring a biology class here." I had no inkling that I would eventually stand in that exact spot with 24 biology classes.

As an undergraduate, I had taken a course in plant ecology that took a three-day field trip to the Mendocino coast of California. I was so impressed with the biology of the area that I later selected the pygmy-forest ecosystem as a focus for a master's thesis.

The many trips north would expose my family and me to an amazingly diverse ecology. Within a 15-mile radius of the pygmy forest, I discovered the following ecosystems:

1. Redwood forest
2. Fresh-water fen
3. Intertidal community
4. Sand dune

5. Fern canyon
6. Marine estuary
7. Sandy beach
8. Coastal headlands

The intertidal community alone is one of the most diverse ecosystems on the planet, so there was much to experience.

Because one of my wife Christie's best friends is a student of astrology, I often teased her about the validity of acting or delaying an action based on the alignment of the planets. Planting by the moon phases perhaps, but expecting things to go awry because of Mercury retrograde was over-the-top. Over the summer, however, after Lettie asked her question, something began to happen that would morph my skepticism into yet another mystery.

I don't know what the stars and planets were doing the next fall, but I do know that something cosmic was coming together in my head. I met with our principal and said that I was formulating the syllabus for my new course of study. The trips to Yosemite and Mendocino were both life-changing events that would form the foundation upon which the new class would be built. Therefore, the earliest goals would involve taking students on a four-day trip to Mendocino in the fall and a four-day trip to Yosemite in the spring. The Smithsonian Institute and National Geographic Society were selected as curriculum models of study because of their goals of integrating the activities of plants, animals, and humans. Thus, plants, animals, and man became the first of many triads that would be considered. The impromptu discussion of the physiology students clued me in that high school seniors were eager and capable of searching for truth, beauty, and goodness. The second triad had been adopted. A quote that I felt best described my goal was by John Muir, "I only went out for a walk and finally concluded to stay out till sundown, for I found that going out was really going in."

Prior to each trip, we focused on the plants, animals, and human activities of the respective area. On the Mendocino trip, we considered the previously mentioned ecosystems as well as conservation, fishing, and logging practices. We also drew freely on the poetry, prose, music, and artwork of the Pacific Ocean. For the Yosemite trip, we studied the life and work of the legendary John Muir. This included his role in the formation of the United States National Park system, wilderness conservation, and its value as a source of inspiration, recreation, and healing. We also considered the poetry, prose, music, and artwork of the mountains; especially that of Ansel Adams.

The students were given journals and expected to make daily entries, which provided the basis for descriptive papers that were required after their return. Their papers would be presented orally and become a forum for sharing, reflection, and contemplation. Students were also invited to critique the trips and offer suggestions, deletions, or additions. Early student suggestions required returns to the school board asking to extend the Yosemite trip from four to six days, the Mendocino trip to five days, and eventually, adding a six-day trip to the Grand Canyon. The first trip to Yosemite was in the spring, and the trails were still snowbound, necessitating swapping with Mendocino the following year.

The development of the course eventually reached a stage that a name was necessary. The natural choice might simply have been advanced biology. I was searching, however, for a title that did not evoke a continued emphasis on massive memorization of minutiae. I had read a poem about the infinite array of designs in nature and the name came to me: Biodesign. The class would be dedicated to seeking and exploring the biological designs of nature in general, but specifically, the designs of Yosemite, the Mendocino coast, and eventually, the Grand Canyon. Students were encouraged to contemplate Emerson's adage, "The whole of Nature is but a metaphor of the human mind," and consider their role in the grand scheme.

When the class began, it was a time of great enthusiasm and excitement. However, its birth was not without pain, some intended, but much not. The Braille method of learning would be an apt descriptor, and both teacher and students ran into many doors. There were times when I longed for the security, albeit drudgery, of following a textbook and lab guide. Often, our only hope was the promise of John Muir—"one day in the wilderness was worth cartloads of books" (if we could only get there).

Improvements were gradually made in curriculum, resource contacts, logistics, and equipment. Caring for, feeding, and "housing" a group of 30 in the field is a big task. Small groups of students were formed and expected to plan a menu, shop for food, prepare the assigned meal and cleanup. The goal was to accomplish this in 1.5 hours or less, to minimize in-camp time, and maximize field time.

As the idea of the class grew, so did some storm clouds. The students who read Muir diligently suggested that he clearly understood that man was not merely a physical being with a mentality but also capable of possessing a deep sense of spirituality. To them, the logical progression was to add the triad of physical, mental, and spiritual to the class. In fact, some of the students felt frustrated and intimidated about expressing discoveries that supported their religious beliefs. Those who regarded themselves as nonreligious resented what they called "Bible-thumping," and suggested that God did not belong in a biology class.

I suggested that Aristotle, Galileo, Newton, Gregor Mendel, and many scientists regarded their studies simply as discovering aspects of a very creative supreme being. These men, I suggested, were unable to separate their spirituality from their work. A standoff was avoided when the Bible-thumpers agreed to tone down their rhetoric and the nonreligious agreed to exercise restraint. We managed to coexist peacefully as we prepared to go to Mendocino. The trip was a resounding success and proved Muir to be right: One day in the wilderness was worth cartloads of books.

Just as a candle cannot burn without fire,
Men cannot live without a spiritual life.

Buddha

3: Firestorm

HARRY TRUMAN SAID, "The buck stops here." This quote applied to what happened in the Biodesign class. The four Greek elements of nature were commonly known: earth, water, air, and fire. I looked forward to exposing students to three—earth, water, and air—in new and exciting ways. After all, standing under a waterfall at Yosemite was not a typical class experience.

I was, however, not expecting to expose students to fire. The class of '78 would change that. The preparations for Yosemite went fine, and the trip was outstanding. They were the second class to make it to the top of Half Dome, where they witnessed a spectacular sunset and spent a hard-won night's sleep. The follow-up papers were excellent, but that's when the discussion heated up.

The tension between believers and nonbelievers returned with a vengeance. The same obstacles recurred, with an emphasis on the argument that God did not belong in a biology class. Several students pointed out that John Muir used the word *God* frequently while describing the beauties, mysteries, and wonders of Yosemite; so why shouldn't they be able to?

I was not able to reconcile the two factions and at the semester break, one-fourth of the class dropped. Those remaining made a decent attempt to prepare for the Mendocino trip, which turned out fine, considering the circumstances. The follow-up papers were good but lacked the brightness of the Yosemite papers. The circle had been damaged, if not broken, and we were all glad when June arrived.

The following summer, I did some soul-searching and discovered that many of the errors were my responsibility:

1. Because we were a Judeo-Christian nation, I thought it would be appropriate to use selected biblical psalms to describe nature. I was surprised and confused when I received a memo from the school administration that demanded that I stop referring to the Bible. When asked about my faith, I casually mentioned that I was a struggling Christian, but was not recruiting for any brand of religion. I kept a copy of *World Religions* (Huston Smith) in my library and invited students to borrow it if they wanted.

2. I was naïvely unaware of a growing movement in the United States known as secular humanism, which proposed eliminating all references to God and spirituality from our schools, government, Pledge of Allegiance, and even money.

3. I knew of the rapid growth of cults, including the Moonies and Hare Krishna, but I did not expect that Biodesign could be considered a cult.

4. I assumed that the local clergy would be open to our experiment, given the fact that teens had abandoned their churches. They were not and angrily suggested that the only path to spirituality was through their church doors.

5. I thought that if we were going to engage in an intelligent debate about evolution vs. creationism, that we should examine both sides thoroughly. A small, but very vocal, group of parents and students strongly objected to considering biblical stories and metaphors and demanded a purely scientific approach.

6. There was a flourish of "New Age" scientists who preached the doctrine that man's intellect, not God, reigned supreme. They professed that, not only was there no evidence of the existence of God, but science would eventually prove that God never existed. Evidently they didn't know, care, or agree with Isaac Newton, who said: "This most beautiful system (the universe) could only proceed from the dominion of an intelligent and powerful being." They also must not have appreciated the legendary comment of Albert Einstein, who supposedly, on his deathbed, smiled, and said, "But I still wonder how nothing can become something."

In astronomer Bob Jastro's book, *Until the Sun Dies,* he used humor and intellectual honesty to suggest: "For the scientist, the story of the Big Bang theory ends like a nightmare. Centuries from now, after scientists have scaled the last mountain of knowledge, they will be greeted by a band of theologians who have been sitting there for centuries."

What began as an innocent walk in the woods ended with me in a minefield without a map. I was reminded of Socrates, Bruno, Galileo, and countless predecessors who had been punished, even killed, for encouraging students to think. It was a very confusing and troubling time.

Nevertheless, as formidable as these potentially class-ending forces were, something more deeply was stirring from within. Most of my colleagues were politically left-of-center and many made little or no effort to mask their thoughts. I regarded this as unprofessional, although I didn't question them. Therefore, I concluded that it was inappropriate for me to reveal my personal faith to students. I was a member of a small, conservative Episcopal Church which regarded themselves as "God's frozen chosen" because of their disinterest in evangelism; however, it was obvious to students that I identified with many of Muir's ideas, including: "John Baptist was not more eager to get all his fellow sinners into the Jordan than I to baptize all of mine in the beauty of God's mountains."

I regarded myself as a teacher; however, I began to sense that despite my effort to stay religiously neutral, I may have been a "closet" evangelist. If this were true, then perhaps I was doing something that I should not be doing. It would also mean that if I could not separate my faith from my work, I would not only be violating the spirit of the law of separation of church and state, but the trust of every future Biodesign student. Thomas Jefferson predicted my dilemma when he stated that if any branch of our government were to cause the collapse of this great experiment called democracy, it would be the judiciary, because in the end, it would not be able to determine one man's freedom from another. Another way to present my dilemma would be to cite Solomon. How could I salvage the Biodesign class without severing it in half?

That summer, I determined that I was going to find a way to avoid another train wreck, or we would have to go back to the pigs. As I sat in my office in quiet contemplation, I glanced up on the wall and saw the lyrics of a Crystal Gayle song that someone had printed for me.

> "You gotta smile, even if it kills you
> It's the common thing to say.
> For there ain't no doubt, when you sort it all out,
> It's too good to throw away."

Therefore, it was back to the drawing board in search of a solution.

Kahlil Gibran was helpful:

> "The teacher who walks in the shadow of the temple, among his students, gives not of his wisdom, but rather of his faith and lovingness. If he is indeed wise, he does not bid you to enter the house of his wisdom, but rather leads you to the threshold of your mind."

The word "temple" jumped out at me. My first visit to Yosemite was awesome in the richest meaning of the word; however, I did not think of it as a temple. But after researching the life and work of John Muir, I realized that is exactly what he thought. Yosemite was a temple!

Little wonder all hell was breaking loose. Any biology teacher in a public school, leading his class off to a church or temple to study biology, would be considered delusional and dangerous. Things were suddenly getting worse rather than better. I was on the brink of ordering pigs for the fall semester.

Christie has an uncanny spiritual gift. She can walk into a bookstore, run her hand along a row of books, almost like using a divining rod, and select books that are timely and appropriate. When this happened this particular time, it truly felt like manna from heaven. She selected a small, unassuming book by Abraham Maslow, *Religions, Values, and Peak-Experiences*. It knocked my socks off! He wrote:

> "I want to demonstrate that spiritual values have naturalistic meaning: that they are not the exclusive possession of organized churches, that they do not need supernatural concepts to validate them: that they are well within the jurisdiction of a suitably enlarged science, and that, therefore, they are the general responsibility of all mankind. If all this is so, then we

shall have to reevaluate the possible place of spiritual and moral values in education. For, if these values are not exclusively identified with churches, then teaching values need not breach the wall of separation of church and state ... Sooner or later we shall have to redefine both religion and science."

I couldn't believe what I was reading. I thought, "Abraham, Abraham, where were you last year in my hour of need?"

I have discovered that sometimes stressful and painful experiences are followed by laughter. Suddenly, I began to laugh. The whole drama now seemed so silly, and I could see clearly what had happened. In Robert Capon's book, *Hunting the Divine Fox,* he stated that apparently seekers are given invisible flashlights with which "they point their mysterious light not only at God, but also at creation and, and in the process, discover movements, shapes and colors they never saw before."

That reminded me of an excerpt from a previous Yosemite paper:

"After dinner on Half Dome, we watched a blood-red sun sink into the western horizon. As we turned around to go to our tents, we noticed that a full moon had sneaked up behind us. Some of us thought it was the most beautiful thing we had ever seen; some of us saw nothing."

Evidently, I had unknowingly turned a bunch of kids loose, some of whom had invisible flashlights, and they were seeing movements, shapes, and colors they had never seen before. I was laughing because the firestorm had passed and I was ready to begin the next chapter.

Lettie's words echoed in my mind. Is this what she meant when she asked, "Mr. Young, is this really important?" I still didn't realize it yet, but she gave me a gift that would transform my life.

" I only went out for a walk"...
-John Muir

"i thank You, God, for most this amazing
day: for the leaping greenly spirits of trees
and a blue true dream of sky; and for everything
which is natural which is infinite which is yes

(i who have died am alive again today,
and this is the sun's birthday; this is the birth
day of life and love and wings: and of the gay
great happening illimitably earth)"

"100 selected poems," e. e. cummings

4: A Class Is Born

THREE MEN PACED the floor of a smoke-filled waiting room, while
their wives labored valiantly without them. Twelve hours of tedium
was suddenly punctured by a woman screaming in agony. Each one
of us silently prayed that the screams were not from our wife. A few
minutes later, a nurse opened a door and announced that our first
child had arrived. The delivery was archaic. Christie was allowed, or
even encouraged to push, before she was fully dilated. As a result,
there was considerable cervical damage that protracted her recovery
time. Our next two children would be blessed gifts that would arrive
via Pan American stork service from Korea. One of us thought that our

family was complete. The other thought we needed one more bundle of love. In 1973, the first thing Christie said when she found out that she was pregnant was that "we" were going to attend Lamaze training classes. I reluctantly agreed.

Maria was a wonderful nurse/midwife from Guatemala, and an excellent teacher. She explained every detail including the Lamaze triad: preparing, concentrating, and communicating. "These are critically important," she said, "but the real key to Lamaze is knowing when to push and when to relax. If you push before you are fully dilated (ten centimeters), it will cause unnecessary pain and possibly damage." During the birthing, when Christie had dilated six centimeters, she yelled at me to leave the room. I winked at Maria and left the room. I had been prepared. At eight centimeters, she asked for me to return. At 10 centimeters, she walked into the delivery room and delivered our fourth child on the second push. Her recovery was almost immediate.

I would experience a four-year-delayed eureka moment. The first five Biodesign classes had many wonderful moments; however, there was much unnecessary pain which reminded me of Christie's Neanderthal experience. Therefore, gathering Galileo, Gibran, Maslow, and Maria, I set out to totally revamp the opening day of the next Biodesign class. It seemed clear that I had to better prepare, concentrate, and communicate to incoming students not only the aims, goals, and objectives, but the hopes, aspirations, and dreams of a suitably enlarged advanced biology curriculum.

Fall came, and as the first day of school neared, I felt a renewed sense of vitality, enthusiasm, and confidence. Christie, the spiritual half of our marriage, and my team of silent cheerleaders, urged me on. The first day of school was normally an adrenaline rush for teachers; Biodesign '79 would be off the charts.

I began by telling the students that despite what they might have heard, Biodesign was an advanced biology class. Without biology, it would make absolutely no sense. Some of the reading materials were rated at the sophomore/junior level of college, and many of the ideas were challenging to adults. I added that it may be the only class of its kind in the country, and I was prepared to show them why it could be considered controversial. I read Maslow's introduction to *Religions, Values, and Peak-Experiences*, and suggested that if that sounded both scary and exciting, I understood; I often felt that way too. Furthermore, I suggested that although the class was based on biology, it was also based on a John Muir idea that "by going out, we were really going in." I borrowed the theme from a greeting card. "We can not own each other; we can not change each other; we can only discover each other."

Providing an overview of the units of study, the list of reference authors, and the two trips was straightforward. We would also consider three triads.

1. The plants, animals, and human interactions of Yosemite and Mendocino.
2. The search for the platonic values of truth, beauty, and goodness of those areas.
3. The consideration of man as a physical, mental, and spiritual being.

We would also study the wilderness as a source inspiration, contemplation, recreation, prose, poetry, music, and art. The focus would be primarily biological; however, collateral topics of natural history, evolution, politics, sexuality, and religion were open for debate and discussion. And, although this outline would be vital to the success of the class, understanding what the class was not would be equally important. Therefore, the following clarifications were made:

1. The class was not a philosophy class.
2. The class was not a religion class.
3. The class was not a spirituality class.

Any discoveries that may relate to these topics would be a by-product of biological studies and not a direct focus.

On an unscripted whim, I had them close their eyes and asked them how many of them had a soul? Every hand shot up.

"Hands down," I said.

"How'd we vote?" someone asked.

I answered, "One hundred percent positive. I guess this class has a lot of soul."

I continued, "I would like to illustrate what Maslow meant by using an excerpt from a previous Biodesign paper written by Jennifer":

> "While sleeping on Half Dome, I awoke around midnight. My mind was so excited I couldn't sleep. The air was icy-cold, and the stars seemed so close and so bright that I thought I could reach out and pick a basket of them. Then, I remembered the Merced River 2,000 feet below, flowing over Nevada Falls. I thought about the water that had been flowing for over 50 million years and wondered why people waste so much time hating each other?"

The new class sat in silence.

The second day of class, I mentioned that there were two related discoveries that had the most profound effect on the class. The first was Lettie's question, which led to the rejection of the massive memorization learning method. The second occurred after I read a passage from John Neihardt's *Black Elk Speaks*:

> "You have noticed that everything an Indian does is in a circle, and that is because the Power of the World always works in circles, and everything tries to be round ... Everything the Power of the World does is in a circle."

After reading the passage a student thoughtfully asked, "So why aren't we sitting in a circle?"

Their choice was not only rooted in ancient mysticism and symbolism, but practicality. By sitting in a circle, they could all see each other's eyes, which was absolutely essential to help them read joy, sorrow, laughter, anger, and an infinite array of emotions and responses. There was a sense of communal bonding that was simply not possible while sitting in rows. The classroom circles provided the daily bread, but the circles at Yosemite and Mendocino (eventually the Grand Canyon), often transformed classes into a state where what was real, imaginary, and symbolic converged and rendered words meaningless. Although the circles were not perfect, they greatly increased student awareness that the quality of the discussion depended heavily on how well they read assignments ahead of time.

On a whimsical note, one of the first designs the students adopted was the rainbow. It was not chosen for religious reasons but because of its beauty, mystery, and ephemeral quality. They intuitively knew that nature's colors added dynamics, richness, and more complexity than simply black and white. On a more serious note, classes discovered that the triangle was not only the strongest engineering shape, but that many scholars, sages, and poets used the triad to synthesize important concepts.

On the very first trip to Yosemite, a girl student had a hissy fit because someone had forgotten the salt and pepper for the meals. During the trip debriefing, students decided that Dale Carnegie's triad of not condemning, complaining, or criticizing should be added. In an essay, poet Maya Angelou suggested that Americans think that they are liberated thinkers; yet, they can not discuss politics, sexuality, and religion without become uncivil. That class decided that the three were an important part of their biology and proceeded with caution. St. Paul stated that faith, hope, and love were essential elements of life. They heard Descartes warn that every person must educate himself and not rely on others. They began to use Hegel's dialectic method of thinking and decided it was often difficult to embrace antithesis at the personal level. Emerson challenged them to make their own bible.

All of these ideas were offered with no strings attached and no forced marches. If students elected to add them to their personal library of knowledge, fine; if not, they would not be tested on them. I described the class as a grand smorgasbord of ideas, and if anyone didn't like pickled herring that was fine. However, they did not have the right to deny someone else the pleasure of consuming the pickled fish. One of Christie's discoveries was a powerful little book by John Powell, *Unconditional Love.*

"In the process of loving there are three important stages or moments: Kindness: Encouragement: Challenge."

Love, he claimed, always begins with kindness, moves on to encouragement, and graduates to challenge. If challenges become too stressful, lovers learn to retreat to encouragement or begin anew at the kindness level. This was yet another triad that most students were eager to embrace.

The difference between the previous physiology class and Biodesign was nothing short of the difference between spiritual life and death. Each day, physiology students trudged into class, doing their best to be cheerful, knowing exactly what to expect. It was cut-and-dried, pun intended. Sometimes Biodesigners would peek around the door and ask if it were safe to enter. One day, during a painful discussion of *On Death and Dying,* by Kübler-Ross, one by one, eight students left the room in tears. All eight had lost their dads and the discussion was too painful to bear.

One year, shortly after discussing Maslow's, *Religions, Values, and Peak-Experiences,* a student entered the room and asked if I knew that religion with a little "r" was a biology term. I guessed that I was being tricked, trapped, or baited but decided that I had no other choice but to bite. He whipped out a definition that surprised all of us. He read, "The word is Latin and derives from *re-ligare;* to re-ligament. Ligaments are the connective tissue which holds bones together, so apparently whoever coined the word thought that religion was what held individuals and cultures together." The response from the class was a collective "WOW!" Unlike the often threatening tone of Religion with a big "R," the biological kind of religion seemed to be pretty cool. After all, try climbing Half Dome without ligaments. I could imagine Maslow applauding.

After each trip, students were given two weeks to complete a descriptive paper. They had read accounts from many authors, and now it was their turn to describe what they saw, heard, touched, smelled, and tasted. Sometimes they would be encouraged by the words of Martin Buber:

> "Everyone has in him something precious that is in no one else. This precious something in a man is revealed to him if he truly perceives his strongest feeling, his central wish, that in him which stirs his inmost being."

The paper presentations often proved to be wonderful celebrations. Students shared lines that amazed, instilled awe, were uproariously funny, or reduced the class to tears. On many occasions, classmates blurted out, "That's exactly how I felt, but could not find the words to describe it." We were on a schedule, but sometimes after three or four papers, we felt like we had just climbed Half Dome or out of the Grand Canyon and needed a rest. Over the years, I would eventually hear and read over 1,500 papers, many of which could have been published in *Nature* magazines.

Toby wrote;

> "When we got to the top of Half Dome, we began to explore. I was drawn to the edge and amazed by the grandeur. I saw a slab of rock, known as The Diving Board, projecting out over the edge and into Yosemite Valley. The slab was about six-feet wide, twelve-feet long and about four-feet deep. I carefully inched my way out. Slowly, slowly, I decided to focus on the rock and not look down. When I got to the end, I very

carefully stuck one leg at a time over the edge. After I was settled, I leaned over and looked down between my legs into 4,800 hundred feet of free air. At first, I couldn't breathe, and then my balls jumped up into my chest. I was about to explode. My heart was pounding. I thought if an earthquake hits now, it's all over. I quickly got back on my knees, carefully pivoted, and crept back to safety."

When he shared this, the boys roared with laughter. The girls blushed, but only a little. One of them said, "Wow! I can't relate, but it sure sheds a new light on the term, *moving experience*. I was too scared to creep out on The Diving Board. I wonder, if I had, do you think my ovaries would have jumped?"

The Class of '79 was not utopian. There were miffs, tiffs, and spats, but they quickly learned that it was all part of what we call growth. They conquered the 10-mile hike from the stables at Yosemite to the top of Half Dome in one very difficult day. With boots and backpacks, they earned the privilege of sleeping a little closer to heaven. On all of our hikes we carried a first-aid kit, which included an ample supply of moleskin. Hikers were warned to stop and treat "hot spots" before they became debilitating blisters. The climb up Half Dome would become a metaphor for life, and most students understood that they would face many hot spots in order to reach higher ground. They quickly learned to anticipate and apply mental and spiritual moleskin, when to push, and when to relax, and thus, precluded much unnecessary pain. They responded to challenges over which wars have been fought and for which people were burned, hung, or nailed on crosses. They were able to see that religions have inspired, yet caused terrible mistakes, and that science has solved yet, created, problems. This class was able to negotiate many minefields and learned to prepare, concentrate, and communicate. In doing so, they not only created an incredible learning environment, but they built a foundation that would support nearly 20 more years of Biodesign.

The year proved to a banner year with the only major trauma coming at the very end. I had fallen in love with a whole class, and when it was time for them to graduate, I was heartbroken. I decided that it would have been much less painful dissecting pigs.

> "So the little prince tamed the fox. And when the hour of his departure drew near—
> 'Ah,' said the fox, 'I shall cry.'
> 'It is your own fault,' said the little prince. 'I never wished you any sort of harm; but you wanted me to tame you ...'"
>
> *The Little Prince*, Antoine de Saint Exupery.

Note: When I asked Toby if I had portrayed him accurately and if he wanted his name used, he said yes to both. Then he said, "I hope you described the stunning sunrise, coupled with the full moon setting in the west which we saw from the top of Half Dome. It was the most beautiful thing I have ever seen." I had not, and I also omitted the same phenomenon that occurred at the Grand Canyon.

"… but just as instinct may fail an animal under some shift of environmental conditions, so man's cultural beliefs may prove inadequate to meet a new situation, or, on an individual level, the confused mind may substitute, by some terrible alchemy, cruelty for love."

The Immense Journey, Loren Eiseley

5: A Very Bad Idea

SOMETIMES MY CREATIVITY got the best of me. I taught a little too fast and a little too loose. I used hundreds of quotes, sometimes from the hip, like an ego-crazed gunslinger. They were always well intended, often hit the mark, but sometimes they missed wildly or ricocheted into innocent bystanders. Once, when a class had excessively belabored a point, I said there was no sense beating a dead horse. The discussion took a new course and the class ended. I noticed one of the girls wiping tears from her face and asked if I had said something dumb.

"It's OK," she said. "It's just that my horse died yesterday and your analogy just kind of shocked me." I felt sorry and told her so.

I enjoyed using adages, aphorisms, and idioms, but I made a mental note to delete the dead horse expression. I've been told that care must be taken not to overload a flintlock rifle, lest it blow up in your face. This happened several times but never more painfully than "the very bad idea" event.

Maybe it was because Ben Nevis, at 4,400 feet, was the highest mountain in Scotland. Maybe, it was because the heather was the dominant flora and was rarely taller than three feet. Maybe it was because he was still rejoicing in his freedom from his father's fanatical religious oppression. Maybe he was prepared by his 150-mile walk from San Francisco to a strange and unexplored territory. Maybe these were a few of the qualifiers that resulted in John Muir's triumphant initial walk into Yosemite Valley.

He surely must have thought he had died and gone to heaven and would eventually write "No holier temple has been sanctified by man than Yosemite Valley; it is truly a place to pray and a place to play." The walk transformed his life and led to one of the United States' greatest accomplishments, the National Park System. Instead of Ben Nevis, he found mountains soaring to fourteen thousand feet. Instead of heather, he found firs, pines, cedars, and sequoias that rose to 250 feet. Instead of his father's harsh religion, he found a "gentle wilderness" which he described as "the clearest way to the universe." He was a wilderness lover and never more excited than during a lightning storm, wind storm, avalanche, or even an earthquake. To him, these, along with volcanoes, hurricanes, floods, and droughts, were all creative dynamics of Mother Nature. They were necessary forces, and if man, including himself, got in the way, then so be it. Every aspect of nature was right and true, including death.

All of these ideas were covered in the early weeks of Biodesign, in preparation for our trip to Yosemite. Muir thought that the Sierra Nevada Mountains in general and Yosemite in particular were the epitome of truth, beauty, and goodness. It seemed, to me a logical step to connect Plato's admonition that the search for these three was the purpose of human existence. I offered the class the challenge to consider and apply the discoveries of these men to their own lives.

One year during a class discussion, I used a quote from Anne

Frank, in which she suggested that even during the horrors of World War II, she thought that man was basically good.

Lisa's hand shot up and she said, "We don't know what the human potential for good or evil is, which means we have no baseline for comparison. Therefore, I think you are making an unverifiable assumption."

I commended her for her excellent critical thinking skills; however, I felt that there was much anecdotal evidence that suggested the contrary. I countered with the idea that it is a good thing that bad news is still news. If a time ever comes in our society when good news is rare, and therefore, newsworthy, and bad news is common, we will surely be doomed. The local newspaper, the *St. Helena Star*, had no comics page; however, readers were entertained by the "police log" column. All calls were reported and often included items like: Officer sent out to investigate noisy rooster; Teenager pulled over for riding skateboard without helmet; Irate woman called and reported tree in her front yard was covered with toilet paper.

I noted that St. Helena had about 5,000 residents. I thought the felony rate was about one every seven years, and aside from traffic violations, the misdemeanor rate was less than one per day. That meant that the crime rate was practically zero.

Lisa shook her head in vigorous disagreement.

"Well, then," I continued, "we have 500 students attending classes. You guys have to put up with a lot of grief. Teachers make all sorts of demands; you are expected to attend six hours of classes daily; you have homework, projects, papers, and have to prepare for exams, all of which can be very stressful. This process is unprecedented in the history of mankind. I once asked our vice principal, who is responsible for discipline, how many students he met on a typical day. His response was a shocking 'five.' This means that in spite of all the stress that is being generated on this campus, 1 percent of the students have minor problems with tardiness, attendance, inappropriate behavior, language, etc., on a daily basis. If this were not a testament of kids' innate, or learned, sense of goodness, I could not imagine what could be." Lisa was not convinced, and we agreed to disagree and returned to our studies of Muir's life and work.

The next morning in the shower, I had a great idea, or at least I thought it was great. During the morning break at school, I grabbed my coffee and wandered out to the quad where students were mingling. I nonchalantly approached five Biodesigners and asked if they would stop by for a minute at the beginning of the lunch break. I tried to pick a cross section of kids, including a cheerleader who had never mentioned an unkind word. They all agreed and showed up promptly. We gathered in my office, and I told them that I wanted them to be bad. They looked at me and asked collectively, "What do you mean?"

I responded that they knew what I meant, just be bad. "After class begins this afternoon," I said, "you may call me any anatomical part or product. You can call me a phony or hypocrite or any mean thing you want, and then get up and leave the class." They looked reluctant but agreed.

That afternoon, after class had begun, Mike stood up and said, "I keep expecting to have lists of plants and animals to memorize, and instead, all we are getting is philosophy crap." Then he exited the room.

Donna (the cheerleader) stood up and said, "I'm glad someone had the courage to say something." Then she exited the room.

Brian and Janie stood up and railed about the class, and left the room. Things instantly went from bad to horrid.

Finally, Tish stood up and said, "You all talk lovey-dovey in class, but out on the quad, you trash people just like all the rest."

After she left the room the class sat in stunned silence. Someone muttered, "What the hell was that all about?" Another started to cry. The tension was almost unbearable until Kevin blurted out:

"Wait a minute! Mr. Young planned this little skit to illustrate what he was talking about yesterday!"

Lisa's face flashed red with anger, and she said, "No, he didn't. He could not possibly be that cruel!"

It was the most bloodcurdling moment I have ever experienced.

There was no place to go and no place to hide. I raised my hand to speak and said, "This was obviously a very bad—"

Lisa cut me off and shrieked, "How could you be so cruel?"

My palms and brow were sweaty. I couldn't breathe. I had no idea what to do. I finally mumbled, "I'm sorry—" and someone cut me off quickly and said, "Will you leave the room?"

I got up and left the room with a very sad and heavy heart. When I got outside, the five "bad" students were quietly standing along the wall with their heads bowed down. As I neared, one of them said, without looking up, "We were bad, weren't we?"

"Yes, you were," I said, "but you were responding to a very bad idea at my request. You are not responsible for the damage that has been done. I can't imagine how this terrible drama will play out, but I am solely responsible."

After a very long 15 minutes, someone came out and solemnly invited us all to return to the classroom. The mood was mournful, not unlike a funeral. We all sat down and a leader began to speak.

"What happened today," he said, "was really horrible. Some members want to drop out immediately; some do not. We have reached an agreement that we will continue as a class if you agree to not discuss, mention, or refer to this event at all."

I responded by saying, "I just—"

The leader cut me off and said, "Not one word!"

"Well, then," I said, "I think we were discussing John Muir's childhood in Wisconsin."

I don't know if the infamous five or other class members ever discussed the event, but I was glad to move on and leave the lesson behind.

Months later, Lisa was hanging out in Christie's and my room in our Grand Canyon Lodge. We were involved in a lighthearted exchange when she elected to return to the scene of the "very bad idea" crime.

She said, "You know I was furious with you over the event."

I laughed and said, "You did a good job communicating your anger."

She went on, "When I told my mom about what happened, she said you were evil and she wanted to go to the school board and have you fired."

"I am glad she didn't," I said, "or we wouldn't be here."

We both laughed. Somehow, with two billion years of history as a backdrop, even our gravest grievances seemed to pale in contrast. Jennifer's words echoed from Half Dome, "Why do people waste so much time hating each other?"

The "bad idea" event was 26 years ago, and thankfully, nothing that severe ever happened again. In retrospect, however, I think the way the class handled the crisis was truly exceptional. They avoided a circle-destroying storm and managed to save every person's dignity. Ironically, and thankfully, their goodness prevailed over my cruelty. Lisa was expressing a legitimate question about mankind. After all these years, the question still lingers. I suspect that if man were not basically good, that he would have destroyed humanity many years ago. On the other hand, if we have missed opportunities to expand our goodness, we might be enjoying world peace and prosperity. One of the humbling aspects of teaching is that when I goofed, the whole class was watching. My path involved countless errors or assumptions that were either naïve or overly optimistic; nevertheless, I knew that I was in good company when I read Loren Eiseley's lines:

> "I have been accused of wooly-mindeddness for entertaining even hope for man. I can only respond that in the dim morning shadows of humanity, the inarticulate creature who first hesitantly formed the words for pity and love must have received similar guffaws around a fire. Yet some men listened, for the words survive."
>
> *The Immense Journey*

"Red exhaustion rips at your throat
And salt sweat spills off your forehead and mats
your eyelids and brows
And drips on the burning ground
And your legs start to turn to rubber and collapse
like a balloon.
'Pretty soon I've got to rest.
How much farther? What's the good of this God
damn work anyway?'"

On The Loose, Terry and Renny Russell

6: Cindy

WHETHER MAN IS the only animal that laughs may be arguable. What is not debatable, at this time, is that man is the only animal who prays or builds altars. My first order of business, after we moved into what became our family homestead, was to build an altar. It was not my idea. Christie was so overwhelmed with joy that she would be able raise her four children in such a beautiful, although neglected home, that she wanted to install a simple shelf that would hold a single burning candle.

She often teased me by saying that I needed to bulldoze my way through nature in order to find my altars; she was probably right. It is, therefore, not surprising that Yosemite's Half Dome became an altar that I would visit yearly for over 30 years. It was also not surprising that, having devoured much of John Muir's writing, I wanted to share my altar with curious, eager students.

Only a few ever learned about Christie's altar, but most came to know and love her. They also discovered that the class was not only guided by a team of teachers, but by hundreds of authors, scientists, poets, and naturalists.

Each fall, sitting in our first circle at the base of Half Dome, each class member received a carefully prepared journal with a laminated nature scene and appropriate quotation. (Many but not all from Muir.) During the first week of school, Christie visited the class and briefly got to know each member. She gathered a feel for each student and was able to write each one an encouraging note, including insights that she had gathered. It was not a given, but also not uncommon, for kids to come to me after the circle, with tears in their eyes and ask, "How did she know?"

I was usually busy multitasking and soon learned to laugh and simply say, "You will have to ask her when we get back home." They got to know her mostly on a spiritual basis. They would get to know me through our class circles and our boots on the trail.

In the earlier years, the Yosemite trip was four days. Students begged for more time, and I went to the school board on two occasions and shared their pleadings. On both visits, the board agreed and the trip eventually became six days. Before that, however, with only four days, we had to climb Half Dome in one day and return the next. Some would describe the hike as a marine's death march.

The chances of this ever reaching publication are remote and, therefore, the chances that Cindy will ever see this are highly unlikely. Even so, when I told Christie that I was giving Cindy a chapter title, she was shocked. She thought I should change her name. I considered, and then reconsidered and decided that a hero should not be hidden behind an alias. Most students knew that they were going to be challenged physically at Yosemite. Cindy could have either avoided the class or skipped the trip, but she chose neither.

The hike up Half Dome was divided into three legs. The two-mile walk from our campground to the trailhead was mostly flat and considered easy. Even so, for many kids, this would be their first backpacking experience and so they had to adjust to the additional weight. Essential items like a sleeping bag, foam pad, ground tarp, food, water, and personal items had to be carried. There were also shared items such as water filters, backpack stoves, and parts of tents that were required. They soon discovered that every pound carried on a level trail felt like two pounds going uphill.

The next four-mile leg was considerably more difficult, as we gained 2,000 feet to reach Little Yosemite Valley. During this section, the tidy line of happy hikers was stretched into an inchwormlike animal, with the faster hikers leading the way and the stragglers bringing up the rear. Hiking, by definition, is an individual sport, and so converting it into a team sport required sacrifices. Those in front had to slow down and rest more often than they preferred. Those in the rear felt the pressure to work harder to keep up. It was the only way the whole group could be assured of reaching the top. The next four-mile leg was the hardest, with an elevation gain of 2,700 feet. This put the greatest strain on our inchworm and required great cooperation. We had discussed the fact that a 1,500-pound mule could carry 200 pounds without overstressing. A 200-pound male carrying a 50-pound pack would be carrying 25 percent of his body weight, while a 100-pound girl would be carrying a whopping 50 percent of her weight.

I had given the girls a maximum of 35 pounds to help us achieve our goal. Typically, if one of the guys saw a girl struggling excessively, he would quietly approach and ask if he could transfer her sleeping bag or tent fly to his pack. There were no heroes and no victims.

Cindy started showing some signs of stress on leg two. By leg three, she was laboring with great difficulty. Before I learned that the best place for me to guide was actually from the rear, I would typically hike with the leaders to keep them in check. I later discovered that a responsible chaperone or even student could manage that position. Therefore, when word came up the trail that Cindy was in a distressed state, I grabbed my first-aid kit, shucked my pack beside the trail, and headed downhill to see what her problem was. She was about half a mile back, but I didn't have to reach her to guess about the cause of her stress. About two switchbacks above her location, I heard a terrifying "wheeeeeze-hawaaah" rasping noise. When I arrived, two of the chaperones were sitting with her trying to offer comfort. Cindy was a large girl. Actually at 18, she was a fully grown woman. She was not athletically inclined, partly because she was prone to severe asthma attacks that could be initiated by physical stress. I wasn't aware of this until it was too late, which may have been a blessing. I would probably have discouraged her from attempting the hike and deprived her of the experience. Unfortunately, I knew what was looming ahead, and it would be practically impossible for her to continue much farther.

The trail got steeper and about one-and-a-half miles ahead neared the shoulder of Half Dome. There is a very steep rock incline that forms a flank of Half Dome and involves stairs that have been carved out of granite. During the Great Depression, Civilian Conservation Corps crews hammered and blasted a fantastic set of steps that could be easily called a "Stairway to Heaven." The stairs were carved on the ridge of the Dome, and on either side the mountain drops away sharply into canyons. It was a challenge for able-bodied hikers and would surely be impossible for Cindy to manage. After the staircase, the infamous cables of Half Dome loomed. Here, two cables are suspended on paired pipe risers. The risers are spaced about 10 feet apart and feature a 2 x 4 cross-cleat attached at the bottom where hikers can rest their feet. Supposedly, the Dome gradient is never greater than 45 degrees, and supposedly the cables are only 400 feet long. When you are on the cables, neither of these statistics appears to be reliable. Knowing all of this, it was necessary to make a painful decision. By the grace of God or luck or chance, we had the luxury of having four chaperones that were alumni and had made the hike before. They were ready and willing to help wherever they were needed.

With great sadness, we agreed that we would have to continue without Cindy. Two of the grads would do their best to get her up to the shoulder of the Dome where there was an excellent campsite. They had several hours before nightfall, and they would likely make it. They would make camp there and wait for the rest of us to return the following morning. Tears were shed, but it was the best that we could do.

I returned to the head of the line, and we pressed on. We managed to ascend the stairway and reached the bottom of the cables. The intellectual of the class summed up the collective feeling when he announced, "I find this situation highly intimidating!"

Christie and I had prepared numerous poems and quotes and mounted them on brightly colored cards for future reference. I don't know where she found this one, but it summed up our hopes and dreams for the kids.

"May you always be inspired …
To stand tall in the sunlight,
    to seek out the bright face of Beauty,
To reach for the Dream, the Star,
    to see the World through eyes of tenderness,
To love with open-heartedness,
To speak the quiet word of comforting,
    to look up the mountain
    and not be afraid to climb,
To be aware of the needs of others,
    to believe in the wonder of life,
    the miracle of creation,
    the rapture of love,
The beauty of the universe,
The dignity of the human being."

Michaels

Looking up at the mighty dome and recognizing that this was usually a once-in-a-lifetime moment was a sobering experience. Someone asked if we could pray. I responded that they were free to pray, but because we were a public school we would not likely find a one-size-fits-all prayer that pleased all and offended none.

Instead, I referred them to Shakespeare who wrote, "A prayer is an idea that starts in the heart and passes through the mind on its way to Heaven." I didn't expect that anyone would object to that kind of prayer.

Hannah wept quietly and said, "There is no way I am going to be able to make it up there."

I assured her that she would be fine, but the decision would be hers. I suggested that if she decided not to try, that one of the chaperones would guide her down to stay with Cindy and the others.

She wiped her eyes, took a deep breath, and said, "You promise I'll be OK?"

"I promise," I said.

"Well, then, let's go," she said.

We strapped on our backpacks, alternated boys and girls, and began the ascent. Hannah was in front of me so I could watch her every move. I suggested that she focus on the cables in her hands and granite at her feet and not look to either side. She gained confidence with each cleat we passed, and soon, we were all safely at the top.

Now was a time for celebration. They dropped their packs and danced and gave each other hugs and high fives. They had faced their challenge head-on and prevailed. The sun was sinking, and so we moved over to the area where we would set up our campsite for the night.

We dumped our gear and explored the northern edge of the Dome. Some stood on "the Eyebrow" and looked down a numbing 4,800 feet. I showed them the "Diving Board" and one or two brave guys crept out, individually, on the overhang, and dangled their feet over the abyss. The sun was sinking in the west, which meant it was time to erect tents and heat water for dinners of Top Raman, instant soup, or freeze-dried meals. The sunset was one that took on a special alpine-glow, accentuated by the view from the top of the Dome. As soon as the sun set, the temperature started to drop and campers were soon snuggling in their sleeping bags, either in tents or under the stars.

I was exhausted from two very long days and expected a night of troubled sleep. I settled in and fell asleep but soon began to hear "wheeeeeze-hawaaah, wheeeeeze-hawaaah." I dreamed I was explaining to Cindy that I was sorry that she wouldn't be able to continue. Half-asleep, I rummaged through my pack and found some Benadryl allergy tablets and swallowed two of them with a swig of water. They usually helped.

I went to sleep, for I don't know how long, and the wheeeeeze-hawaaah came back. This time, however, I heard Wayne yell, "Where are you guys?"

I bolted upright and shook my head. Another wheeeeeze-hawaaah sounded in the night, and I blurted out, "OH-MY-GOD!"

I stood up and yelled, "We're over here!"

I flashed my flashlight in the direction of the wheezing, and they flashed back a response. Several other "Oh my Gods" and "You must be joking" emanated from the tents, and then a flurry of activity.

Within minutes, the three hikers staggered into our little campsite. There was room for one more in one of the girl tents, and they hustled Cindy's foam pad and sleeping bag into place. We quickly heated some water for a light dinner and hot tea. Within 30 minutes, everyone was resettled. As soon as Cindy was warm and rested, she was able to regain her breathing and get to sleep. On the other hand, I twitched and turned throughout the night.

The next morning, water was heated for oatmeal, coffee, or tea. We quickly packed up our gear and got ready for the long return hike. We formed a circle and all eyes were on the three latecomers.

Cindy, Wayne, and Jeff were glowing like three lightbulbs. Someone broke the silence and asked what all were wondering.

"OK, so how did you do it?"

Jeff and Wayne both laughed and pointed to Cindy.

"It was all her idea," they said. "She refused to quit, and so we just kept going."

Cindy started to laugh and said, "They're lying. I must have quit a thousand times, and they would say, 'Maybe we can make one more switchback; maybe we can make one more stair.' And finally, on the cables, they said, 'It would take longer to go back than to go forward.' But there is something that they will not tell you, and so I will. They didn't climb the cables once, they climbed them twice. Their packs were too heavy and too bulky to carry and push me up. So they took them off, pushed me up, got me settled with my sleeping bag wrapped around me, and ran down the cables to get their packs. In less than 30 minutes, they were back, absolutely exhausted. The rest is history, but I just have one question: Why did they do it?"

The question hung in the chilled morning air. After a pause, a shy female voice answered with a question, "Maybe because they love you?"

The circle collapsed into a group hug. We donned our packs and maneuvered down the cables, down the granite stairs, and the 10 miles back to base camp. We were hot, dirty, tired, and hungry, but we had seen our miracle.

Robert Frost wrote that "No poem can withstand dissection." The same can probably be said about spiritual experiences. But Cindy's question begs for the opportunity to describe young people in action. Wayne and Jeff's plan was risky. If I had been there, I probably would not have allowed it. However, what adventure, great or small, does not entail some risk?

In the process, I think they demonstrated what St. Francis of Assisi meant when he suggested that the purest form of love occurs when the giver and the receiver overlap so perfectly that the words become meaningless.

Cindy's dilemma offered a challenge for the guys to dig deep and in so doing became heroes. They, in turn, offered her the challenge to dig deep, rejoin the group, and see the coveted view from the top of Half Dome. Their combined efforts gave the whole class a glimpse into the depths of humanity and perhaps a peek of heaven.

On the way back down, one of the chaperones assumed the lead and agreed to stop and regroup at every trail junction. Wayne and Jeff joined me at the rear and were (half-seriously) pressed to explain their actions.

They laughed and said that it wasn't as dangerous as it sounded. The hike up to the shoulder was tedious but routine. When they got to the stairs, one led and held Cindy's hand and the other followed closely with his hand planted firmly on her back for support. The cables were a little trickier. Of course, they had divided her pack, which made their packs about 50 lbs each. As she said, they had to leave them behind.

They positioned Cindy with her hands on the cables and each of them took one cable firmly in one hand, stooped down and planted his shoulder on her appropriate butt cheek. She provided some help in the front, and they provided assistance from the rear.

"It was really quite safe," they said, "and besides, it was dark and what she couldn't see she couldn't fear." (Laughter)

John Muir climbed a hundred-foot-tall fir tree during a windstorm, crept behind a thundering waterfall to see the moonlight through the falling water, and rode an avalanche safely. Wayne and Jeff were following in his footsteps; I couldn't have been prouder.

We were sitting in the sunny meadow at the base of Half Dome in our final circle before returning home. One of the chaperones was an Army vet and with tears in his eyes said, "You kids have formed bonds that are usually only formed in the heat of battle; it has been an honor to climb that rock with you."

I thanked him, and said, "I guess that's why some students call it a marine's death march, no offense intended."

"No offense taken," he replied. We all laughed and headed for home.

"The mountains are fountains of men as well of rivers, of glaciers, of fertile soil. The great poets, philosophers, prophets, able men whose thoughts and deeds have moved the world, have come down from the mountains; mountain dwellers who have grown strong there with trees in Nature's workshops."

John Muir

7: Heather (Joy) & Nikolai (Sorrow)

Heather (Joy)

FED UP WITH the rat-race pace of California living, a young man moved his wife and three children to the Alaskan wilderness. They homesteaded a parcel of land 250 miles north of Fairbanks. After surviving five years, the man was interviewed by a television journalist.

The first question asked was, "What is the secret of your success?"

He smiled and said, "It's really quite simple. I quickly learned that whatever I had in mind, Alaska had something else in mind for me. I either had to accept her terms, move back to California, or die."

I smiled, knowing what he was speaking about. On a much

smaller scale, each of the 65 Biodesign field trips presented challenges that mandated that we alter our plans, go home, or die. Many of the mandates would involve minor adjustments, some would be life threatening. The '92 Yosemite trip would not be an exception.

September was always a hectic time in the school year. Seniors were adjusting to new and more demanding classes. Many would be applying for entrance to college or university. The Biodesign class was a beehive of activity. We had to establish our goals and objectives for the year, read as much as possible about the life and work of the legendary John Muir, and start planning for the Yosemite trip. Itinerary, menus, equipment lists, and driver/chaperones had to be arranged.

Students were told that the only way that they could achieve the Half-Dome challenge would be by working together. The key would be to travel as light as possible and be willing to help each other in times of need. Some people would likely be natural hikers, and some probably not, but it would not be an option to leave stragglers behind. The plans called for three days and two nights in the back-country, requiring seven trail meals plus water. There would be two springs available where water could be filtered, which would reduce the amount of water that had to be carried. The recommended pack weight for girls was not to exceed 35 pounds, and the maximum for guys, 45 pounds. There were hundreds of logistical details, but we had to get to Yosemite before mid-October or risk encountering early snowstorms. It always seemed like a minor miracle when we were actually driving into The Incomparable Valley.

When the class of '92 arrived, we encountered our first obstacle. A lightning strike had started a fire that would not be controlled and resulted in the closure of the trail we were going to use. The rangers rerouted our hike, starting us at the Lake Tenaya trailhead, which was 35 miles to the east. It would make the hike two miles longer, but we would start at a higher elevation, so it would be easier than starting from the Valley.

After dinner the first night, we were arranging our packs for the hike. One of the girls whispered that I might want to check out Nik's backpack. I sauntered over and tried to lift it. Trying to mask my frustration, I quipped that he would have to leave the kitchen sink at base camp. He grinned sheepishly and said he was an experienced backpacker and could handle it.

I was not convinced and said, "Let's have a look." I spread out his ground tarp, and we began to lay everything out. I discovered one #10 can of pork and beans, cans of smoked oysters and sardines, one large bag of "gorp," two or three bags of dried fruit, one dozen candy bars, several kinds of cheese and crackers, one dry salami, one large bag of oatmeal, and his crowning glory, one trail espresso maker with three blends of espresso. He also had clothing for a week. We ravaged his pack and reduced the weight by half. I relented and left the oysters, sardines, and espresso maker. After all, the hike was supposed to be fun.

The following day we drove to our new trailhead. The hike was moderate, with more down than up and so the marine's death-march element would be removed. At eight miles out, we found a suitable campsite and prepared for our first night on the trail.

The next day we covered the next four miles and were ready to approach the shoulder of Half Dome. The granite stairs were handled smoothly, and the Half Dome cables loomed and offered their normal blend of fear, wonder, and excitement. Bodies that in previous years would have been exhausted were better rested and able to manage the ascent without excess stress.

We arrived early enough so that students could explore the 13-acre dome, including the famous Eyebrow and Diving Board. After a brief orientation session, we proceeded to set up our tents and cooking center. Instead of 20 small backpack stoves, we carried three MSR, high-BTU stoves and three, six-quart pots to heat water. The stoves were noisy but heated a large amount of water quickly. Students were invited to add as much water as they would need to a pot, and retrieve it when it was hot. We always ended with surplus water, which was returned to water bottles.

Dinner was prepared and the class was treated to a sunset that can only be seen from the perspective of the Dome. The air was not chilly yet, so kids were free to relax, chat, journal, or dangle their legs off the 4,800 foot edge.

The pretrip effort, three 20-hour days (including a two-day hike) left me exhausted, and I was ready to turn in. Heather approached me and asked if we were going to have a "circle." I was surprised. These were great kids, but asking for additional class time was unprecedented.

I asked her if she had something in mind.

She said: "No, but maybe a circle would be cool."

I said it was fine with me and suggested that we meet in half an hour; it would be dark then and the students shouldn't be out wandering around.

The circle convened, and the students and chaperones were snuggled close together to ward off the chill that would be coming. Heather took out a brown paper bag and opened it to reveal a large, glass-enclosed candle, like some churches use to burn constantly. She lit the candle and paused. The combination of the candlelight and her inner glow made her look absolutely angelic.

She began, "Mr. Young, we understand that you don't like celebrating your birthday; however, we know that it is next week and we were hoping that you wouldn't mind if we shared some of our wishes with you."

There was a rustling of paper and journals that were being retrieved. After a pause, she read something beautiful that she had prepared and handed the candle to the person at her left. As the candle moved around the circle, I was flooded with a rush of complex emotions: Love, humility, embarrassment, humor, anxiety, disbelief, and an overwhelming sense of gratitude.

The birthday celebration was a one-in-a-million event, but it was only a prelude. When the candle returned to Heather, she stood and placed it in the center of the circle and returned to her place. How a small candle could illuminate each face was a mystery.

She began again by sharing a reflection, idea, image, or

experience that impressed her during the day. One by one, students shared thoughts, ideas, and observations from their first three days at Yosemite. The level of conversation seemed to soar, matching the mountains around us. By then, the stars were brighter than most had ever seen and seemed to draw the discussion heavenward. When the last person shared, Heather stood and gave me a warm hug, as did all her classmates and chaperones. Students and chaperones drifted off to chat, mingle, or retreat to their tents.

I needed some time to absorb what had happened, and so I went to the Eyebrow to think. Looking down, nearly one mile, at the tiny lights and campfires flickering in the night, I felt a million miles away from civilization.

A question occurred to me. Why would a person carry a heavy candle twelve miles up a mountain just for a birthday celebration? I have seen kids brush a loose down feather off of their jackets and say, "Get off of me; I can't carry the extra weight."

And then, there was a déjà vu moment. I had stood here in a circle before when a student asked the same question, "Why did they do that?" As I recalled, the answer had something to do with love. I wondered what it was about this place that seemed to release an outpouring of love every time we visited. Muir's words flowed out of me: "The mountains are fountains of men as well as rivers."

I remembered another book that Christie ferreted out for me, *Owning Your Own Shadow,* by Robert Johnson. In it, Johnson states, "Generally, the mandorla is described as the overlap of heaven and earth." He went on to say that it represented the process of healing and reconciling the great span between heaven and earth. Johnson's words hit me like a bolt. Heather and her classmates had assumed the leadership of the class. It was as if she had surged forward from the middle of a flying vee of geese to give the lead goose a rest or, more likely, help him reset his spiritual compass.

I was merely an observer. They either raised the earth up or brought heaven down. We were sitting in the middle of a mandorla. They were thinking and responding at a level that was simply otherworldly.

My wedding day and the arrival of our four children were mandorlas as well. This event, along with them, would be among the most important days in my life. I had attended various churches for 30 years. I had visited cathedrals in the United States and England, and I had never experienced a holier event than the one Heather led on the High Altar of Half Dome.

Nikolai (Sorrow)

I crawled into my sleeping bag, glowing from the light and heat of a single candle. I am not superstitious, and there was no wood to knock on, but perhaps I should have found some. I had often quoted Gibran's adage that, "Joy and sorrow come from the same cup." I didn't know that I would soon be drinking from the same invisible chalice of our last circle, and it would not be a joyful experience.

I had been sleeping about an hour when someone woke me and said that Nik was throwing up and had a stomachache. I was tired, groggy, and grouchy, and made one of my 10 dumbest remarks of all time.

"It's just those damned smoked oysters and sardines," I growled. "Tell him to take two aspirin tablets and call me in the morning."

As dawn broke, I rose and dressed quickly in the frosty air. I went to wake up Nik and tease him about the oysters. Instead, I was shocked down to my boots.

He was groaning in his sleeping bag and his tent-mates said that he had been vomiting all night. I put my hand gently on his abdomen, located his navel and right hip bone, and divided the distance. I had barely touched the spot when he winced with pain.

"I am so sorry, Nik." I said, "We have a problem, and we have to get you some help as soon as possible. Try to relax and let us take care of you."

The class was awakened and told to pack up as soon as possible. This was an emergency situation, and we would have to work harder and cooperate like no class had ever done before. As fate would have it, in 20 years of reaching Half Dome, we had three emergencies and on all three, we had extra chaperones with trail experience.

This situation was going to be complicated. The trail we needed to go down might still be closed due to fire. The trail back to the cars was 12 miles, mostly uphill, which would be nearly impossible. In order to lighten our packs, we left some of our gear at the previous campsite, and that had to be retrieved. But most important, we had to get Nik down off of the Dome, and I needed to run for assistance.

Three teams were quickly formed. We decided that we would have to wish, hope, or pray that the trail down would be open. If not, we would have to break the law and deal with the consequences. We had no other choice.

One group would backtrack four miles, grab the gear, and come down the John Muir Trail and meet us at Little Yosemite Valley. Another group would have to get Nik off the Dome, down the stairs, and down to Little Yosemite Valley. It was downhill all the way, but still, four miles would be a long, hard haul. I asked for a volunteer to join me to jog to the ranger station at Little Yosemite, and hopefully get help. We all wished each other well and went our separate ways.

Clay and I left immediately and scooted down the cables in record time. We hustled down the stairs, probably faster than we should have. When we tried to jog on the trail, our packs lurched awkwardly. We stopped and quickly restuffed them, creating a lower center-of-gravity, and hurried on. The solution was kind of a half jog, half speed-walk pace. Hindsight would tell us to have dumped the packs and dealt with them later.

Then we got our first bit of good news. Someone had miraculously removed the closed sign, meaning that the trail was now open. The four miles were covered in less than an hour, but then we got some heart-stopping news. The ranger station at Little Yosemite was closed for the winter.

Our next option involved racing another mile to Nevada Falls, where there was an emergency phone. Cell phones were not in use then, so this would be our only hope. I had seen the phone on every trip and never expected to use it. More important, I wondered if it even worked. It was mounted on a tree in a little wooden shelter.

As we approached, my heart was pounding due to heavy exercise, but also with the anxiety over the possibility that the phone would be dead. With exaggerated ambivalence, I picked up the phone. There was no dial, so I assumed that an operator, or ranger, would answer an emergency signal.

The phone clicked, made a strange crackling sound, and went dead. My heart sank, and I used language that I had learned while working on our family farm. I was almost ready to hang up when a friendly male voice answered and said,

"Backcountry emergency line, how can I help you?"

I looked at Clay and said, "Oh my God," and meant every word.

I proceeded, "We have a serious problem and need help. I am a biology teacher and leading a group down from Half Dome. We have a hiker who is seriously ill. He has been throwing up since midnight and is emitting yellow bile. Can you get some help for us?"

The voice said, "Roger that. I can dispatch a rider with a spare mule within 15 minutes."

I paused for a moment and said, "I have seen programs on TV, and I know that I am supposed to be calm, but this is really hard. It will take your rider two-and-a-half hours to get here and another two-and-a-half hours to get him down. I have done a field exam, and he has all the classic symptoms of appendicitis. I have seen med-evac helicopters in the area. Is there any chance of that?"

"Well," he said, "that decision would be made down the line, but wait a minute. Where is the sick boy now?"

"I hope they have him off of the stairway and are coming down the Half Dome trail," I said.

He asked, "Can you get back up to the junction of the Half Dome Trail?"

I gulped and said, "Yes," knowing that it was three miles, all uphill.

He proceeded, "We have a trail crew working on the Merced Lake Trail. The trail boss has a radio. I will contact him and have him scoot, hopefully only three or four miles, over to meet you. By that time, my superiors should have a plan, and we will contact you there. Did you copy all of that?"

"Yes, yes, and thank you, thank you," I gushed.

Clay and I quickly tied our packs to a tree and headed back up the trail. The first mile was a gentle incline. The next two would be the hardest we would face, even without packs. We arrived about 40 minutes later and what happened next was nothing but miraculous.

Shortly after we arrived, the trail boss arrived with his radio. Shortly after that, the chaperones arrived, with Nick stumbling along with one arm draped over each chaperone. Shortly after that, the group that retrieved the gear arrived. It was almost as if the whole scene had been scripted by a phantom writer. The radio crackled alive.

"Frank, do you copy?" the voice said.

"Ten-four," Frank responded.

"Have you reached the biology teacher yet?" the voice asked.

"Roger that," Frank responded. "It looks like we have the whole class here."

"Copy that and good work," the voice answered and continued. "Ask the teacher if they can get the boy down to LYV."

I nodded my head yes, vigorously.

"He says roger that," replied Frank.

"Copy," said the voice.

He continued, "Tell him we will have a chopper landing at LYV in approximately one hour. There is a large granite slab northwest of the ranger station that the pilot will use for a landing pad."

"Copy that," Frank said.

I mouthed to Frank, "Tell him thank you."

"Oh, the teacher says thank you," said Frank. (Laughter)

"Tell him he is more than welcome. It's all part of my job. Over and out," said the voice.

Clay and I left the group in order to be at Little Yosemite when the helicopter arrived. The rest of the group followed. It worked out that the chaperones and Nick and the rest of the class all arrived shortly before the helicopter landed.

The crew exited the craft and quickly approached Nick, who was sitting on a boulder. An EMT checked his vital signs and prepped him for the flight. They laid him on a stretcher and slid him into the rear of the craft. In less than 10 minutes, they were airborne.

The class stood watching, in a state of stunned wonder. Whatever happened to Nik was out of their control, and they knew that they had done their very best. It was a huge, cathartic moment.

It was decided that the chaperones would accompany the class and ensure that all would return safely to base camp. Clay and I would trot/walk the last six miles, in the event that I needed to sign any release forms for Nick.

About one mile down the trail, we reached the junction of the Mist Trail. I had forgotten that detail and was now concerned that the class might take it down to Yosemite Valley. The trail was shorter, but steeper, with several series of stairs that would be hard on tired knees and difficult with backpacks. We decided that Clay would stay and direct the class down the John Muir Trail, which was much more hiker-friendly.

I made good progress until I overtook a mule pack train returning from the backcountry. Mule skinners and hikers often have differing points of view regarding trail use. I knew it would anger the lead wrangler if I attempted to pass his train. Fortunately, he encountered a tight switchback and I was able to yell to him that I had a medical emergency to deal with.

He glared at me, but as soon as the last animal cleared the corner, he reined the train to a halt and motioned me to pass. Safely past the animals, I thanked him. He touched his Stetson with his gloved hand, which I regarded as right proper. It was about 1 p.m. when I reached base camp.

A bear had nearly torn the door off of our camp-trailer. Why he or she stopped I do not know, but I was grateful. He would not only have destroyed two days of food, but probably have cost us a fine for not securing our food properly.

I left the class a note that said, "Guess who came to dinner?"

The speed limit in the park is almost sacred among campers, but I cheated a little, trying to get to the Valley Medical Clinic. When I arrived, they were loading Nick into a larger helicopter. Hopping over the safety rope caused the supervising ranger to bark, "This is a restricted area."

Without slowing down, I lied and said, "That's my son you are loading up. Do you mind if I check on him before you take him away?"

I didn't wait for an answer. They had given Nick some pain relief medication, and he was partially sedated, but he was glad to see me.

I told him that some students will do anything to avoid hiking back to camp. He tried to laugh and said the ride off the mountain was neat.

The big blades began to rotate. I shook his hand and said, "Good luck." In three minutes, the helicopter was airborne and headed for Modesto.

By 3 p.m., everyone was safely back at base camp and settling back in. During one of the earlier planning sessions, I had mentioned that the Friday dinner would be the hardest because everyone would be trail-weary and not eager to prepare food. This class had proved to be exceptional in many ways, and they did not disappoint here. Extra hands volunteered without being prompted. I don't recall what they served, but I am betting that it tasted better than the dinner that they ate the next evening at the Ahwahnee Hotel.

After dinner, while the crew was cleaning up, I drove to the nearest pay phone and called Memorial North Hospital in Modesto. Nik's dad had arrived, and the surgery went very well. The chief surgeon indicated the appendix had numerous perforations and was likely ready to burst. Returning to camp, I announced the news which was greeted by a loud cheer.

That night, the sharing period around the campfire included comments and reflections from nearly every student and chaperone. Their compassion, sensitivity, and appreciation of Yosemite would have brought tears to John Muir's eyes. With all that they had been through, it was not surprising that the recurring theme throughout the evening was one of profound thankfulness.

The first circle the next morning was abbreviated, to allow students an hour or two to organize their thoughts. Two weeks after our return home, they would be expected to present a paper describing what they had seen, heard, touched, tasted, and smelled during their week at Yosemite. During the circle we contemplated the mystery, wonder, and power of human hands:

> Strong hands that grasped the cables;
> Working hands that pumped water filters;
> Compassionate hands that carried other backpacks;
> Happy hands that shared lots of hugs;
> Humble hands that clung to life;
> Skillful hands that could fly a helicopter;
> And, the most important pair of hands involved with the trip were not in Yosemite, but in a Modesto hospital, where they saved Nick's life.

The class was released with instructions to begin to gather their thoughts and sum up their experience. Two hours later, we gathered together for our final circle. The students were intensely engaged; however, I did not fault them if they glanced up at the Half Dome that towered one mile above their heads.

A month after we returned from Yosemite, I felt a nudge to call the Yosemite backcountry office and leave a thank-you message for the ranger that helped us out of our crisis. A voice answered and I explained that I was the biology teacher that had the student with appendicitis on Half Dome. Would he leave a message that I called?

He started to laugh, which I thought was odd. Then he paused and said, "I don't think that will be necessary. You are talking to him."

"Wow!" I said. "What are the odds of that?"

He replied, "Was it Muir that said, 'Great things happen when men and mountains meet'?"

"Roger that," I said, and added, "Did I get that right?"

"That's an affirmative," he replied.

Nick's dad mentioned later that he had seen a breakdown of the expenses, and the rescue operation totaled nearly $10,000. I gulped and wondered who would pay the bill. He quickly mentioned that the National Park Service covers accidents when there is no negligence involved. I was glad that we were fully permitted.

I said a prayer of thanksgiving to St. John of the mountains, the patron saint whose foresight established the National Park Service.

One of the lines from one of the posttrip papers asked: "How many angels can fit on the head of a pin?"

The answer: "I don't know, but the entire Biodesign class of '92 can, with room to spare."

"But, according to Genesis, God made Adam responsible
for looking after the Garden of Eden on His behalf, and now
it seems as if He expects us to be responsible for the whole
universe, which means that as workers, we have to regard the
universe *etsi deus non daretur*: God must be a hidden deity, veiled
by His creation."

W. H. Auden introduction to,
The Star Thrower, by Loren Eiseley

8: Storm Brewing

BIODESIGN WAS NOT a pro-God, anti-God, or ostrich-head-in-the-
sand-about-God class. This book is not about my spiritual quest, but
about a class that for some mysterious reason allowed students the
opportunity to consider the possibility of their own spirituality. Teens
are naturally inquisitive and whether or not they would eventually
ask the three most profound questions a human can ask was their
business and not mine. Unfortunately, we teach curiosity out of them
with an overemphasis of facts, which is why trips to the wilderness
are vitally necessary.

After I realized that it was spiritually incorrect to share my personal walk with students, it dawned on me that believing in God was
a lot like catching poison oak. Some people did and some didn't, and

no amount of word making would change much. It was a liberating discovery. I was not responsible for their spirituality; they were. Thereafter, when I was asked about what I believed, I often borrowed a line from the folk song "Today." "You'll know who I am by the songs that I sing." The songs that I sang often involved several ideas, concepts, or biological principles each day. Some of them referenced God, but not as the subject, but rather as an adjunct of the conversation about nature. When distinguished men or women naturalists, scientists, poets, and philosophers were studied, we focused on their work and not their spiritual persuasion.

One time early in the year, I feigned reading from my lesson-plan book and casually mentioned that on Day 23 we would discover God. I quickly moved on to the next item, while reading their response.

They looked puzzled and glanced around for confirmation. "Did he *really* say that?" And then titter morphed into laughter.

"Gotcha," I said.

I tried to keep our discourses light. It didn't always work. Many heated discussions were resolved with humor. The class of '92 got into serious debate as to whether dogs could smile or not. Both sides were entrenched. I didn't have a dog in the fight, and I watched with amusement.

Finally, Adam shouted, "Time out! Do you people know what you are arguing about?"

The entire class erupted in laughter. The argument reminded me of many of the God arguments I had heard, or even worse, participated in.

I revealed earlier my bias against the secular humanist movement, not only because all of the authors that we were using contradicted their beliefs, but they represented the epitome of egoism. Does the clay have the right to tell the potter that it could build a better universe? With that in mind, there is no way I could claim credit or responsibility for the wonders that students and chaperones witnessed over 24 years.

In Robert Capon's book *Hunting the Divine Fox,* he probes many mysteries and credits them to the Divine Fox. Although this was a more playful description of God, it was certainly not new. Native Americans often referred to the fox, raven, and coyote as tricksters involved with creation. Capon's metaphor wasn't a theme or even always referenced; however, it was an important reminder for me that The Fox was responsible for providing an endless supply of inspiration, creativity, enthusiasm, and surprises. I was never sure what The Fox would do next, but I was sure that students and teacher would have many special opportunities to look at, or possibly through, the veil of creation.

The surprises ranged from heavenly to horrible, and included every imaginable emotion and some that weren't imaginable. Often surprises would appear disguised as coincidences or synchronicities. This was the case when my neighbor discarded a book titled *The Treasure Chest*, edited by Charles Wallis. I rescued it from his trash heap and found a wonderful poem, *Bag of Tools*, by R. L. Sharpe:

> "Isn't it strange
> That princes and kings,
> And clowns that caper
> In sawdust rings,
> And common people
> Like you and me
> Are builders for eternity?
> Each is given a bag of tools,
> A shapeless mass,
> A book of rules,
> And each must make,
> Ere life is flown,
> A stumbling-block
> Or a stepping stone."

This poem would not only become the theme for the Yosemite trip, but for the entire year. For five days, students would hike on trails, often hewn out of granite, by men working during the Great

Depression. These men worked long, hard hours for a dollar a day and the meager rations of bread and soup. Without their effort, there was simply no way we could have reached the base of Half Dome, let alone scaled to the top. They converted thousands of stumbling blocks into stepping-stones for many generations and millions of hikers to walk on. Hundreds of miles of trails were blazed for purely recreational use. Summertime crowds are now so great that as many as two thousand hikers can reach the Half Dome cables, and some have to wait for hours to take their turn to reach the top. What are these people looking for? I am hoping that all or nearly all Biodesign alumni would have an answer.

The beginning of each year was hectic. Students had been warned the previous spring to get in shape by the fall. Mentally, we were absorbing Muir's work and learning how to "prepare, concentrate, and communicate." There was much to learn quickly. One of the many handouts included an equipment list for camping and the backpack hike. One line was printed in capital letters: DO NOT USE BUNGEE CORDS TO FASTEN YOUR SLEEPING BAG TO YOUR BACKPACK. As for spirituality, I left that up to Yosemite.

The class of '90 arrived at Yosemite and set up their base camp. The fact that I have no memory of this indicates that everything went smoothly. The next day, they donned their backpacks and handled the hike up to the base of Half Dome without a hitch. They maneuvered the granite stairway and ascended the cables with relative ease. As one of the foreign exchange students said, "This trip is going to be a piece of cake."

As usual, by the time our tents were pitched, dinner was consumed and we either shared a circle on top or not. I was exhausted and crawled into my sleeping bag. I wadded up my down jacket to use as a pillow and lay a very weary head down. Just as my head hit the pillow, I caught sight of something in the corner of my eye. Or, at least I thought I saw something, and it was not good. I kept my eyes shut tight, afraid to open them. After a long pause, I decided I had to face the possible problem.

Slowly opening them, they confirmed my worst fear. What happened next was a result of over 60 million years of evolution. The early mammals developed what is known as a pilomotor reflex. When they were threatened, their autonomic nervous system would trigger a release of adrenaline that prepared the body for either the fight or flight response. The process is known as horripilation and in humans can result in an elevated heart rate, goose bumps, or the hair on the nape of the neck becoming erect. In my case, it was all of them. My heart was pounding. My body shivered with goose bumps, and the hair on the back of my neck was bristling. Horripilation is rooted in the word *horrible*. The scientific name for the grizzly bear is *Ursa horribilis,* and a species of rattlesnake is named *horridus*. But I was not seeing either a bear or a rattlesnake, but something much worse: lightning. I estimated the flashes to be about 200 miles to the south, in the eastern Sierra Nevada Mountains. They were rhythmic, and after watching for a while, I confirmed that the storm was moving north.

I had religiously followed the weather maps before we left home and rechecked the forecast the morning that we began our hike. The forecast was for clear and sunny weather, with occasional high clouds in the afternoon. This was a classic fall weather pattern and offered no reason for alarm.

Ruthanne, one of the chaperones, was an experienced backpacker, and I immediately went to confer with her. She had seen the lightning and was wondering what I was going to do. We discussed waking the students and moving down the cables immediately. However, only one or two of us had headlamps, which meant that hiking down the cables at night would be extra treacherous. I suggested that southern storms were common in the summer and fall, and many crept north along the eastern Sierra and often wandered east into the Nevada desert.

The decision to wait it out would be one of the most monumental decisions I would ever have to make, and the pilomotor reflex would make sleeping impossible. We agreed to get as much rest as possible. We would monitor the storm and hopefully be spared the trauma. It was the longest night of my life, punctuated with flash, pause, flash, pause. By about 4 a.m., the storm had tracked up the eastern Sierra and seemed to be veering east toward Reno.

Feeling a modicum of relief, I settled down and hoped for an hour or two of sleep. I had just dozed off when a thunderclap boomed over our heads. It sounded like a bomb had exploded directly over the Dome. After that, things got very, very quiet. Someone muttered from a tent, "What the hell was that?"

And then it started: All Hell Broke Loose. More precisely, hail began pelting down and caused those of us who were sleeping outside to scurry for cover or retrieve rain flies to cover sleeping bags. I hoped that the spate would be brief and we would be all right. The kids and chaperones in the tents were warm and dry; the rest of us would have to cope.

After about an hour, it was clear that the storm was more than a spate. The chaperones huddled in the cold and discussed our only options. We could hunker down and wait out the storm or wait until daybreak and risk descending the cables. It was another monumental decision that I regretted having to make.

Our logic was that if the storm lasted all day, the group would be tired and cold and may have to spend another night. It wouldn't be impossible, but if anyone got seriously cold and developed hypothermia, it could become critical. We decided to get everyone up, move over to the top of the cables, and wait for daylight.

The storm continued, and we hunkered under rain flies to ward off the freezing hail. Dawn finally broke, and we prepared to descend. We alternated boys and girls hoping that the generally more muscular guys would be able to assist any girl having difficulty. Kaarin was a trail-experienced hiker and volunteered to lead. I opted to stay in the middle of the line in order to move up or down, if anyone needed assistance. A discussion ensued as to whether they should descend frontward or backward, and it was decided that watching where they were placing their feet trumped backing down. It would be a huge mistake. Girls typically lack the upper body strength that guys have. Their arms, deltoid, and pectoral muscles are not as large or as well developed. Due to the icy footing, when their feet slipped out from under them, all of their body weight, including backpacks, was transferred to arms and shoulders.

Shortly after we began, one of the girls in the rear lost her footing and started sliding down the rock. Thankfully, the boy in front of her heard her scream, spread his legs and clamped her body as she slid between his legs. She grabbed his legs with her arms and shouted, "Thank you, thank you!"

I immediately realized my error, and passed the word up and down the line for everyone to turn around and inch down backward. The line started to inch slowly downward.

The wind and hail came in waves, beating down, and then easing off. It was not unlike a cat playing with a mouse before it devoured it. About halfway down, the line stopped for longer than usual and word came up that Kaarin was frozen and couldn't go forward. I checked with my partner, a Swedish exchange student, to see if she would be all right if I left. Amazingly, she wasn't concerned and seemed to be enjoying the ordeal. I lowered my pack under one of the cables, and did a hand-over-hand maneuver down to Kaarin. She was frozen stiff, and her body was not responding. She did the wise thing by not taking a foolish risk.

In the meantime, I was in trouble. While packing my backpack, I made two critical decisions; one would save my life and possibly others and the other would cause foolishly unnecessary pain.

Christie purchased a wonderful Land's End down jacket for me, which was nice but often too warm for the autumn weather of Yosemite. While counting ounces, at the last minute, I decided to include it. I am convinced that without that jacket, I would have suffered debilitating cold and probably hypothermia, creating perhaps a tragic event on Half Dome. Unfortunately, I omitted my gloves, which were now badly needed. My hands were bitterly cold, and I needed help. I told Kaarin to hang on a little longer; that I would be back and be able to help her. I scooted and slid down the slippery rock surface.

The mind thinks at triple-time during trauma, and this was no exception. I pictured a lawyer, questioning me in a courtroom, saying: "Just what were you thinking when you led these innocent, ill-equipped, inexperienced youngsters up that dangerous mountain?"

When I reached the bottom of the cables, I quickly shucked my pack and in the process looked at my hands. They were so cold that I hadn't noticed that the cables had worn several layers of skin off. They were oozing blood, but pretty much numb. I knew there was a pile of gloves left by previous hikers, and I dove in. I don't know how it was possible, but the first glimmer of hope would come when I spotted a brand-new pair of leather gloves on top of the pile. They had never been worn and still had the tag on them. It was a great, although not joyful moment.

What I was doing was not heroic and, in fact, could be construed as just the opposite. Under different conditions, I might have invoked John Muir and said, "Let us make haste to join the storm and see what treasures she has in store for us." I was not in danger scaling down the cables, but certainly some of the kids were, and the burden of the situation was nearly overwhelming. I was shaking in my boots, not only because of the cold but the enormity of our crisis. There must have been some adrenaline remaining in my body, because, before I knew it, I was talking to Kaarin.

"OK, you," I kidded, "let's get you off of this goddamned mountain. My hands are warmer now, and I can hold on. I will plant my feet on the rock and you should use them as steps."

She was bitterly cold but somehow found the strength to carefully pick up her foot and lower it down to my waiting boot. It was painfully slow at first, but then we got a little rhythm going.

The line was inching along when suddenly a strong burst of wind blasted us. As the wind abated, the voice of a terrified chaperone screamed, "We've been tested enough!"

Somehow, if we were not all scared already, the terrified voice of a man pleading with God for mercy was enough to make the blood in our veins turn icy. The lull cued us to continue downward.

I looked over my shoulder and saw the pile of gloves and with them, a ray of hope. I remembered that my mom loved to say when things were going poorly: "A little bird landed on my shoulder and said, 'Cheer up; things could be worse.'" So I cheered up, and she was right. Things got worse.

It must have been a premonition. Moments later, I caught another glimpse of something that made the lightning flash seem like child's play. For the second time, I clinched my eyelids, only this time, I thought, or maybe said, "Oh, God, tell me this is not happening."

I opened my eyes, and for the second time, my worst fears were confirmed. Down through the cloudy mist, a small body, probably female, tumbled and careened wildly, headed for certain death. She had gained tremendous speed. When people say that we can review our whole life history in the moments before we die, I can see how. An incredible number of events flashed instantly through my mind.

A millisecond later, I recovered and thought, "You fool; you will need to know where the body was headed in order to aid the search-and-recovery team."

Meanwhile, I felt like I was going to vomit. My heart leapt into my throat, and I was unable to breathe. During the next microsecond, however, I saw the most beautiful sight I have, or will ever, see. It was a sleeping bag, not a body, tumbling out of control.

I was emotionally spent. In addition to the cold and wet, I now had legs that had turned to rubber. I had been in a pilomotor reflex state for 10 hours and there was not an iota of adrenaline left. I was ready for a stretcher, but we had miles to go before we could sleep.

Miraculously, everyone got down safely, and immediately, Dana ran over with tears in her eyes and said, "Mr. Young, I am so sorry. My brother packed my backpack, and he always uses bungee cords because they are so convenient. He didn't know that the ends could get caught on the cables."

I threw my arms around her and hugged her, and we did the dance of joy.

"Oh my God!" I said. "I've never been so happy to lose a sleeping bag. We have a spare at base camp. You'll be fine."

In the early '70s, Eric Ryback completed the first known solo hike of the Pacific Crest Trail, from Canada to Mexico. *National Geographic* magazine covered the story, and as I recall, the cover read, "Adventures like this are the source of triumph or tragedy." I could not have agreed more.

The walk down the stairway was treacherous because there were no cables; however, the footing was mostly flat, and by working together, the kids were able to progress smoothly.

When we reached the campsite area at the shoulder of the Dome, we were presented with a final ironic twist. The clouds parted, evaporated quickly, and were replaced by brilliant sunshine.

We built a fire and warmed frozen fingers, toes, and bodies. Steam rose from the earth, trees, and hikers. We were all in a state of shock and awe. They had climbed down the icy cables of Half Dome, in the shadow of death, and would, hopefully, live to tell their grandchildren about it.

Note: When Kaarin proofed this chapter, she said the tension, tone, and details were authentic. But she also said, "You omitted the two or three times I slipped and crashed into you." I have no memory of that, but assuming it happened, we were not alone. Both guys and girls had anxious moments when they also slipped on the frozen rock, and it was only an extreme act of teamwork that averted a catastrophic event.

"A single grateful thought toward heaven
is the most complete prayer."

Gotthold Lessing

9: Gratefulness

PLODDING ALONG THE next nine-and-a-half miles back to base camp allowed ample time to reflect and ponder. The three greatest questions reappeared. Who is God and why and what was the extent of my relationship (if any) with Him during our extraordinary event? I didn't know whether to praise, condemn, or simply blow the experience off. The bloody hands were of my own doing, but I was not responsible for the storm. While I was sorting out my mental snarl, the clouds cleared for the second time. This time, it was a Buddha sunshine that was warming my soul. I recalled that he warned that many perfectly sublime moments are ruined by our selfish desire to understand concepts that are beyond human comprehension.

"… and clowns that caper in sawdust rings."

Suddenly, my whole body erupted in laughter. Not a titter or giggle, but trail-rocking, belly laughter. This was not new, but it was a surprise. It happened on nearly every trip, usually after I was broken, or nearly so. I don't remember who was walking with me; I hope I was alone. Surely anyone would have thought that I was possessed by the devil, when I was really laughing at a very sly Fox.

Without being glib, the funny part was that the danger we experienced on the cables was illusory. Regardless of our religious belief, we were all going to die. Most people believe that the time of our death will be ordained by fate or other forces. The fact that none of us died confirmed that it was not our time. Therefore, the danger was illusory. Christie would later say, "Try telling that to the parents."

The Fox was playing with us, or in the kids' vernacular, "messing with our minds." John Muir could have died a hundred times in the wilderness, but he didn't. He died at home of old age. There is a 20-mile stretch of highway known as Blood Alley which we had to travel to and from Yosemite. There are multiple fatalities each year, while deaths at Yosemite are very rare. I would later discover that the weather event we encountered on Half Dome was highly unusual and, unpredicted.

The pace down was moderate, and gravity positive, so avoiding turned ankles became more important that exerting energy. Some of the girls broke into a song that carried up the trail. It reminded me of an Eiseley story. He had observed a raven catch and devour a nestling. He was intrigued that even birds of different species shrieked in protest. After the death, there was a period of silence, and then all the birds began to sing:

"They sang because life is sweet and sunshine is beautiful.
They sang under the brooding shadow of the raven.
In simple truth, they had forgotten the raven, for they were the singers of life, and not of death."
The Immense Journey, Loren Eiseley

The girls were singers of life, and although I doubted that they would forget their trial by ice, they were happy to be heading back to base camp, with the prospect of warm food and snug tents. Before each trip, I would say that I could not predict what they would experience. I could predict, however, that they would experience things that would be impossible to imagine from the comfort of their beds with their electric blankets turned on.

Thoreau believed that walking was really a kind of sauntering or venturing onto holy ground. He also stated that he went to the woods to live deliberately. He returned with a message that has had a global impact. His writing inspired Mohandas Gandhi, who would play a major role in liberating the subcontinent of India from British rule. Gandhi's writing, in turn, encouraged Martin Luther King Jr. to nonviolently address the scourge of racism that plagued millions of Afro Americans.

While reading about the life and work of Gandhi, I was intrigued that he intentionally visited Rome and St. Peter's Basilica. His biographer stated that he stood at the base of the large crucifix and wept. I have no idea what caused his tears, but I'm guessing that it had something to do with gratefulness. I know of few books that can be explained by their title. One of them is *Gratefulness, The Heart of Prayer*, by Brother David Steindl-Rast.

A feeling of warmth washed over me as I realized that all, or nearly all, of the great people we had been studying expressed a profound sense of gratefulness, including Galileo, Newton, Muir, and Eiseley. Albert Einstein said:

> "A hundred times every day I remind myself that my inner and outer life depend on the labors of other men, living and dead, and that I must exert myself in order to give in the same measure as I have received and am still receiving."

I was nearly overwhelmed by the things that I had to be thankful for. I was grateful that someone had not died on Half Dome and that I would not have to notify his/her parents. I was spared the humiliation of being responsible for that death and have the program that I loved, cancelled. A chill shuddered through my body. As soon as it passed, an epiphany exploded in my mind. I realized that the amazing journey I was experiencing would not have happened were it not for a three-minute "chance" conversation.

I was completing my requirements for a master's degree with the hope of transferring to a nearby community college. There would be an opening, and I knew the biology department chair and was practically assured of getting the position. The pay would be higher, and the hours would be fewer. During a lunch break one day, I casually asked a fellow biology teacher why he had not applied for the job.

He said, "Several years ago I taught one class at the college for one semester. The students were rude, inattentive, unappreciative, and only interested in a grade. But most disturbing was that they lacked curiosity and spontaneity. High school kids are much more creative and fun to work with."

So here I was, in a place that Muir called a temple and Thoreau would have called holy land. I came to live deliberately because of the people who guided me. How could I not be grateful?

I was down to the top of Nevada Falls, and I was grateful for the unspeakably rare privilege of being invited to share this spot with 19 previous classes. Students had shown and taught me things that were simply impossible for me to discover on my own. Students like Jennifer, who walked by here many years earlier and later wondered, "Why do people waste precious time hating each other?" The tumbling molecules splashed and danced, and I had to resist the urge to plunge over the 600-foot brink and join them on their mystical journey back to the sea.

Scientists claim that if a quart of water is collected, and each molecule is marked, and the molecules are then equally distributed around the waterways of the globe, every subsequent 8 oz. cup of water collected would contain 400 of the original molecules. I knelt down, cupped my hands, and splashed the cold water onto a hot and sweaty face. It immediately dawned on me that I had just been baptized by some of the same molecules that John the Baptist used to baptize Jesus. I cupped my hands again and scooped up a refreshing drink. What happened next was shocking. The water instantly electrified my body. Some of the same molecules that Socrates, John Muir, and Jennifer had borrowed were now surging through me. It was suddenly crystal clear why Muir regarded Yosemite's waterfalls as fountains of champagne.

> "... and each must make ere life is flown,
> A stumbling block,
> Or a stepping-stone."

We were sitting in the warm, bright sunshine on the meadow, below the watchful eye of Half Dome. The cars were packed, and we were nearly ready to head back home. One of Muir's all-time favorite stories involved a little mutt of a dog named Stickeen. The dog loved to hike and would not let Muir go abroad without him. They went on what became a 20-hour trek that nearly cost Muir and Stickeen's life. Muir was convinced that the dog was well aware that their lives were in the balance, and expressed as much. They would eventually prevail, but not before Stickeen's paws were bloodied and sore. After that, Stickeen was a changed dog. Near the end of the story Muir says, "And after that as he caught my eye he seemed to be trying to say, 'Wasn't that an awful time we had together on the glacier?'"

As we sat quietly in the circle, I noticed that the students had changed. I didn't know how or why, but they looked different. I didn't need to know; it felt good. I scanned the circle and saw Kaarin gazing up at the Dome. I thought I saw, or perhaps only imagined, a shiver shudder through her body. She lowered her eyes and looked over at me. I winked in affirmation. I wondered if she were having a Stickeen moment.

The final words of Muir's story are, "To me, Stickeen is immortal." Paraphrasing his line: To me, these kids are immortal.

"Prevalent people believed that they prevailed by virtue of the struggle for existence, in which the strong and cunning got the better of the weak and confiding. And they believed further that they had to be strong, energetic, ruthless, practical, egotistical, because God was dead and had always, it seemed, been dead—which was going altogether further than the new knowledge justified."

The Outline of History, H. G. Wells

"Perhaps there also, among rotting fish heads and blue, night-burning bog lights, moved the eternal mystery, the careful finger of God."

The Immense Journey, Loren Eisely

10: Matthew I.

A HUGE STEP in the evolution of man was the discovery of agriculture. The two great benefits were a more reliable food supply and the ability to put down community roots. Two subsequent discoveries were the invention of books and libraries to store and protect them. It has been said that armies move on their stomachs; that great civilizations are moved by their books. I have always believed that if a book had a single transformative idea, it was a good investment in time and energy.

When I discovered Loren Eiseley's *The Immense Journey*, I thought I had discovered the mother lode of biological and anthropological knowledge. It would become a vital component of the Biodesign reading list. Like John Muir, Eiseley was a multigifted scientist, naturalist, poet, talented storyteller, and theologian. He would deny the last designation; however, he not only saw Shakespeare's "sermons in stone," he saw and described sermons on a spider, fox pup, hawk, and most of all, in anthropology, which meant human evolution.

Eiseley was a quiet, humble protagonist who, according to a *Time/Life Books* editor, "was less concerned about man conquering nature than nature, in the form of God, conquering the human heart. Furthermore, if this happens, man is in danger of losing the essence of being human."

Eiseley properly identified and challenged post-Renaissance scientists who had thrown God out with the baptismal water, in an overzealous, overreach, which aimed at establishing science as the new salvation of mankind.

Like Muir, Eiseley was not overtly religious, which probably worked to his advantage. However, like Descartes and St. Paul, he insisted on testing all theories, ideas, and information, including his own observations, before arriving at conclusions. He received over 36 honorary degrees and countless awards and citations, both nationally and internationally, including the Le Comte du Nouy award, granted to writers who described unifying themes of science and religion. He was a major contributor to the body of anthropological knowledge, but I think his greatest gift was as a stalwart proponent of the fact that every branch of science is cloaked in mystery.

One day, in the early '80s, after completing *The Immense Journey*, some students suggested that we travel "somewhere" to experience what Eiseley was talking about. Yosemite, the mountains, and Muir's wilderness message had deeply impressed them, and they were eager to experience time, change, and evolution.

The next day, the school librarian brought a newly released book by the biology lab that she thought would interest me. It was a magnificent book published by the Smithsonian Institute titled, *The Thread of Life*, by Roger Lewin. I opened the book to a full-color picture of the Grand Canyon. The supporting text read:

> "And where better to grasp in one panoramic sweep
> the reality of time and change but on the rim of the
> Grand Canyon, the world's greatest geological gash."

The students were certain it was an omen; nevertheless, it was too late to make plans for their year. The idea was intriguing; however, the obstacles seemed too great. The school board would have to approve two more release days, and the 1,000-mile distance would necessitate air travel. Moving a group of 30 to San Francisco, Las Vegas, and on to the Grand Canyon seemed like an impossibility. Then, another one of the many mysteries associated with Biodesign occurred.

Later that week, two girls were standing by my teaching table at the front of the room. They were discussing the upcoming prom, the dress they would buy, who they were going with, where they would go for dinner, and who would pay for the limo. One of the girls mentioned that she had invited her date and felt obligated to pay all the expenses. The other said, "Wow! How much will that cost?" The answer was about $400. I was shocked. That seemed like a lot of money to spend on one night, but a seed was planted.

That afternoon, I stopped by the local travel agent and said that I had a crazy idea that I knew would be impossible, but would she crunch some numbers for me. Airlines and motels at the Grand Canyon were instantly contacted by computer, as she did her best to help the kids. I was not hopeful. The total estimate for five nights and round-trip airfare, mysteriously, came to $400. It seemed like great news, but how could we possibly earn $400 for each student?

Christie and I were a single-income family, with four kids, living on a teacher's income. We had no idea how we could afford to go. Nevertheless, a few weeks later, I called a meeting of the next year's prospective Biodesigners and presented the orientation talk.

"Oh, and by the way," I said, "this year's class has suggested that you should go to the Grand Canyon to complement Loren Eiseley's studies. Are any of you interested?" Every hand shot up.

The rest is a blur in my memory, which is probably a good thing. I had to go before the school board, and miraculously, they approved two more days of leave. I had to approach my colleagues and sheepishly ask for their approval of having students miss nine days of their classes the following year. Amazingly, they generally approved. The students made concessions, too, by agreeing to travel over President's weekend, thus, giving up four days of vacation. The school district agreed to pay for my substitute teacher, which was helpful. At the time, I was younger, more idealistic, and not afraid to dream, but realizing that all of the factors had to align was nothing less than astonishing.

Somehow, someway, we managed to complete the first trip. We arrived at the Grand Canyon, hiked to the bottom, spent two nights at Phantom Ranch, hiked out, and flew home in five days. It was a whirlwind trip with myriads of discoveries, which left me amazed but also confused. It was simply too huge to wrap my mind around. I was bewildered. The only meaningful note in my journal seemed pathetically inadequate. I wrote, "I am not certain why, but if possible, you should return next year."

We not only did that, but returned 14 more years, totaling 15 trips. They were never easy, and each year seemed financially impossible. Our annual budget, for all three trips, totaled $15,000, with no endowment or assistance from the school. I approached each class with the admission that I had no clue as to how we could afford to go. Furthermore, state law properly prohibited leaving any student home for financial reasons. Nevertheless, I assured them that we could all go if everyone did his very best to achieve the goal. The school secretary in charge of finances rolled her eyes each fall and said, "I've never seen a nonbudgeted program work before. Are you going to try again?" She knew better than anyone that if we ended the year in the red, we would have to cancel future trips. Miraculously, for 15 years we ended each year in the black. Sometimes when we seemed to be doomed, a parent, service club, concerned citizen, or foundation would appear with just enough support to achieve our goal.

In 1989, in preparation for our upcoming canyon trip, we were reading passages out of Eiseley, where he described the evolution of a wolf/dog mammal into the sea to become a whale. The fossil record, he claimed, suggested that they were very recent immigrants, having lived there only 50 million years.

There was nothing unusual about the discussion until Matthew bolted upright in his desk and shouted, "Wait a minute! What the hell do we believe anyway? What did they do, think their way back into the ocean?"

The classroom was quiet. All eyes shifted to Matt, and then to me. They expected an answer, and I had none. More importantly, I realized that I had committed the scientific sin that Eiseley warned me to be aware of. For six years, previous classes had read the same passages without a whimper. Class and teacher blindly followed Eiseley and the wolf/dog back into the sea. In a flash, Matt changed all that. His questions were profound, probative, and courageous. He was also revealing frustration or anger or a mixture of both. I had seen this type of behavior before.

Two years earlier in a biology class, we were discussing Hubble's discovery of the "red-shift" theory, which led to the "Big Bang" theory. I suggested that scientists now seem to agree that the universe had a beginning. We were setting the stage for considering conditions that had to occur before life could begin.

Unbeknown to me, a quiet, thoughtful Latina girl went to church the following Sunday. After the service, she approached her priest and asked, "Father, if God made the universe, what made God?" The priest's face turned red, and he stooped down and whispered sharply in her ear, "We don't ask questions like that!" Then he turned sharply on his heel and stomped away. She asked me, "Why would he get angry over a simple question?"

At the height of the "steady-state theory" era, Albert Einstein stated that the idea of a universe with a beginning was very irritating to him. Charles Darwin described the flowering plants as an "abominable mystery" because his theory could not explain how they appeared so quickly and spread so rapidly. He was also angry with Alfred Wallace, who pointed out that Darwin could not explain how an organ (the human brain) developed so far beyond the needs of its possessor. And finally, Wallace dealt Darwin a demoralizing blow by suggesting that chance and competition could not explain the emergence of man's musical, mathematical, and artistic abilities. In one explosive moment, Matt connected with H. G. Wells, Alfred Wallace, and Eiseley and questioned the completeness of Darwin's theory of evolution.

In the early '80s, I was eager to show my students the video series of Carl Sagan's book titled *Cosmos*. The series was going fine until we got to the segment on evolution, which was outside Sagan's field. At one point he stated, "Evolution is a fact."

He stated it with such conviction that I sensed a hint of anger in his tone. Perhaps it was because he was too brilliant to not know that for him to say that evolution was a fact would be like me going out on a clear night, looking up at the stars, and declaring that "astronomy is a fact."

Astronomers have made many amazing discoveries, yet they have failed to describe how the universe began (the first nanosecond), where in the universe we are now, and where we are going. Probably, not coincidentally, that is an appropriate description of evolution. For many years, scientists have been looking for "the missing link," as if there were only one. There are probably thousands of missing links, in both the sciences of evolution and astronomy, and there are currently infinitely more questions than answers.

Matt had not only acted on Eiseley's advice, he inferred that perhaps I could have done a better job of preparing the class by doing a brief background survey. Over the following years, I would offer different scenarios, each with the disclaimer that they were subject to personal interpretation and I was merely providing students with information to help them make as informed decisions as possible. I assured them that I was not concerned with "what" they thought, but deeply concerned "that" they thought. This was not always easy, for teacher or students, but it was the antithesis of massive memorization and seemed to be an important lesson in learning how to learn.

Therefore, what do we believe?

We used to believe that the universe was made in six days with God resting on the seventh. God threw Adam and Eve out of Eden because they were naughty. Eventually, the sons of Adam got even by throwing God out and by inventing the "steady-state theory." Obviously, the universe had "always" been there. However, Edwin Hubble, using a large telescope, discovered the red-shift theory, which led to the Big Bang theory, and suddenly, the universe, indeed, had a beginning. However, scientists were either too reluctant or too angry to discuss this beginning because it involved a being, power, or process that was beyond their realm of comprehension.

We used to believe that God created plants and animals on the fifth day. Then, biologists threw God out. Instead, they said, plants and animals spontaneously appeared out of mud puddles or in tidepools. This was called spontaneous generation. Then biologists discovered that this was not true, that all life came from previous life-forms. They named the new theory biogenesis. Unfortunately, for biogenesis to occur there had to be at least one act of spontaneous generation, which they did not believe in. Therefore, the origin of life must have occurred through a being, power, or process that they could not comprehend, but they were too reluctant or too angry to consider the possibility.

We used to believe that God created man on the sixth day. Then, anthropologists threw God out and suggested that ontogeny recapitulated phylogeny, which proved that man and his ultracomplex brain had evolved from fish, amphibians, reptiles, mammals, primates, and finally, "ape men."

Like the steady-state theory, this seemed scientifically logical until rebel scientists began to suggest that Darwin's theory could not explain the origin of man's brain. The cerebral hemispheres had tripled in size in a very short time period, rendering a brain that modern men are still not fully utilizing. The brain is so complex that many neurologists suggest that it will never be able to comprehend itself. Scientists estimate that each human has over a hundred billion neurons, comparable to the number of stars in the Milky Way galaxy. Many neurons have thousands of connections with neighboring cells, resulting in a human cerebral cortex that may have a hundred trillion interconnections. Some scientists have estimated that our brains have a potential capacity to handle a mind-boggling one hundred trillion words.

Nobel Laureate Dr. Roger Sperry also challenged the use of Darwin's model of evolution to explain the existence of the human brain. He suggested:

> "One of the great unresolved paradoxes of science involves consciousness, free will and values, three long-standing thorns in the hide of science. Materialist science couldn't cope with any of them, even in principle. It's not just that they're difficult. They're in direct conflict with basic models. Science has had to renounce them—to deny their existence or to say that they are beyond the domain of science. For most of us, of course, they are among the most important things in life."
>
> *Omni* Magazine

I don't know if there is an ultimate irony; however, secular scientists appear to have taken the gifts of consciousness and free will and used them in an attempt to disprove or discredit the very process by which they were created. I can imagine a group of them gathering on a mountaintop, on a brilliantly starry night, shaking their fists at the heavens, and chanting, "There is no God! There is no God! There is no God!" Afterward, they share high fives and walk down the hill, laughing and boasting, "Guess we showed him!"(Or her)

Eiseley noted that Wallace's challenges of Darwin were soon forgotten, and a "great complacency" settled down upon the scientific world. There are countless examples that suggest that scientific complacency is more prevalent today than ever. We still use the term "gifted" to describe people with rare mathematical, musical, artistic, and intellectual talents, knowing that they cannot be explained by either genetics or evolution.

Scientists estimate that the earliest prokaryotes needed about 100,000,000 bits of DNA information to survive. The odds that one of these could form spontaneously, as a result of a bolt of lightning, are astronomically low, if not impossible. Scientists, confronted with these odds, smile sheepishly, shrug their shoulders, and parrot, "Given enough time it could happen."

In the midfifties, a team of scientists from Cornell University filled a glass globe with ammonia gas, zapped it with a simulated lightning bolt, and created some simple amino acids. They boldly proclaimed that they were on the verge of proving how life was created. Upon further review, however, it was determined that they created some brown guck that was not unlike photochemical smog, not remotely related to the creation of life. That misinformation is still commonly taught in schools.

Perhaps the Cornell scientists had forgotten that in 1870, T. H. Huxley, the eminent supporter of Darwin, named a gelatinous goop, dredged up from the Atlantic, *Bathybius haeckelii*, and pronounced it to be the origin of all life. It was later shown that the goop could be produced by adding alcohol to seawater and had no resemblance to protoplasm. They had falsely assumed that life began at the bottom of the sea and were determined to prove it. They would later admit that deep-sea life was more highly evolved than life-forms near the surface.

Matt's question prompted me to research my library on evolution, which meant rereading Carl Sagan's *Cosmos*. I was stunned to read the following line:

"Some molecules reproduced themselves inefficiently, competed for building blocks and left crude copies of themselves."

In one terse line, Sagan not only trivialized the second-greatest miracle of nature, the creation of life, but he did so in violation of the laws of inorganic chemistry. To my knowledge, there is no evidence that inorganic molecules have ever "reproduced" themselves, "competed" for building blocks, left crude copies of themselves, or miraculously sprang to life. If they had, we would have discovered new life-forms popping up all over creation. The current genetic information suggests that all of life came from one source. Essentially, Sagan inferred that the miracle of the beginning of life happened when molecules randomly joined, eventually forming the first cell. He opined that the incompatible solutions of oil and water "drove" early lipoproteins into forming the first cell membrane. Estimates indicate that over 300,000 molecules would have to be organized for each cell membrane, without a plan or template. He failed to mention where the original organic oils and proteins came from. This was yet another poorly veiled version of spontaneous generation. The extension of his logic suggests that human beings are spiritless, random accidents resulting from chance and competition.

But that was only part of the problem. I was suddenly horrified that I had read the passage the first time and given him a pass. In essence, I had succumbed to the spiritual disease of complacency, and now I was hopping mad. How many millions of students would annually be taught that the origin of life was a random, plan-less event? What about Eiseley's "careful finger of God"? I decided that if even if I were the only public high school biology teacher in the country willing to take the risk, the sense of mystery had to be persevered.

Unfortunately, Loren Eiseley died four years before Sagan's *Cosmos* was released. If he had lived, he surely would have said that history repeated itself. Yet another wave of complacency washed over the land. Furthermore, he would have cited his own *Immense Journey*:

"It involves one of the most peculiar and fantastic errors ever committed in the name of science. It is useless to blame this error on one man because many leading figures of the day participated in what was, and remains, one of the most curious cases of self-delusion ever indulged in by scholars. It was the product of an overconfident materialism, and a vainglorious assumption that the secrets of life were about to be revealed."

Did no one suggest that a bolt of lightning would generate a massive burst of heat, light, and electrical energy, which would more likely have vaporized molecules than created life? How many lightning bolts have hit the Earth in its 4.5 billion-year history, resulting in only one start of life? The DNA molecule appears to be the smallest unit that can not only replicate itself, but direct protein synthesis and the thousands of tasks required by a living organism. Did Sagan really believe that the first DNA molecule "organized" itself out of inorganic matter? Furthermore, DNA can not live without RNA which presents us with the quintessential example of *the chicken and egg* dilemma.

It is widely theorized that the minimum odds of a DNA molecule spontaneously forming are in the range of 40,000,000:1. I would ask students if they would take those odds, knowing that they would have to flip a coin 40,000,000 consecutive heads without flipping a single tail. There were no takers.

I recalled that in Lewis Thomas's *Lives of a Cell*, he suggested that a single cell is so complex that we may never be able to completely understand its workings. Perhaps as many as 2,000 enzymes, coenzymes, vitamins, and minerals must work in perfect synchrony in order for cells to survive.

Eiseley would be the first to suggest that there is great fossil evidence, and the sciences of paleobotany, paleozoology, anthropology, comparative embryology, and genetics have offered mountains of knowledge about plant, animal, and human evolution. He would also be the first to suggest that evolutionists have miles of mysteries to go before they can sleep. "We teach the past," he says, and warns that scientific thinking alone is by definition anthropocentric and therefore extremely limited. Biology teachers encourage students to mock and ridicule our predecessors who believed mice "sprang up" out of piles of rags. They fail to note, however, that we have no logical theory about the origin of life and that future scientists will surely mock us.

The evolutionists' problem is related to that of the astronomers. We are not certain where we are now, and we have no clue about where we are going, especially since man has altered the evolutionary course through selective breeding, genetic engineering, agriculture, the use of pesticides and herbicides, as well as thousands of other, possibly disruptive, activities. Modern medical practices of disease prevention, corrective surgery, organ and tissue transplants, overriding genetic abnormalities, and using life-saving drugs have rendered Darwin's law of survival of the fittest moot. Human evolution should have slowed or stopped; it hasn't. The mysterious forces that Alfred Wallace alluded to still exist. Child prodigies are unexplainable. Mozart wrote symphonies, note perfect, on the first draft. The human face is getting flatter, resulting in no room for wisdom teeth; people of the future will not have them. A show of hands in my classes revealed about 25 percent of the students had less than four and some had none. Scientists have no clue why. Our little toes are disappearing, again no clue. I offered one theory that girls with smaller little toes have greater sex appeal that attracts more boys, thus passing their genes along. It was a poor attempt at humor to illustrate that evolution can and has occurred without our fully understanding the mechanism.

All of these thoughts amazed me. However, what was most amazing was that teenagers were capable of thoughts and questions that would not only challenge but prove adults, including me, or even experts, to be wrong. Lettie's question began this epic process, and now Matthew was following her lead. At first, I didn't realize it, but later discovered that Matthew was asking one of the most profound questions a human can ask: What do we believe? Our collective response may determine the fate of mankind.

"Mind is the Master power that moulds and makes,
And Man is Mind, and evermore he takes
The Tool of Thought, and, shaping what he wills,
Brings forth a thousand joys, a thousand ills:—
He thinks in secret, and it comes to pass:
Environment is but his looking glass."

As A Man Thinketh, James Allen

11: Matthew II.

PARAPHRASING MATTHEW, "WHAT did man do, think his way out of the ocean, or what?" The power of thought may have been overlooked or underestimated as an evolutionary force in the development of man. A proverb in the Bible states, "As a man thinketh in his heart, so he is." In yet another powerful little book, *As a Man Thinketh*, James Allen suggests that our thought patterns control our physical, mental, and spiritual health and destiny.

William James, considered by some as the father of American psychology, described Allen's book as the greatest revolution of the nineteenth century. He was referring to the fact that Allen rejected the "smite thyself thy wretched worm," religion of John Muir's father and replaced it with the belief in man's innate goodness and divine rationality. Muir and Allen were born 26 years apart and 250 miles from each other, but Muir emigrated from Scotland before Allen was born. I don't know whether they knew about each other, but Muir emulated what Allen was describing. In fact, Muir "lived" what Emerson and Thoreau were merely describing. In a paradoxical way, Muir's father's harsh Scottish Protestantism may have prepared Muir to see the beauties of the Yosemite wilderness.

I used to ask students, "Of all the knowledge, wisdom, and intelligence in the universe, how much did you think modern man possesses?" Common answers were, "Are you kidding?" "Is that a joke?" "We have no clue, but whatever it is, it must be such a small percentage that it would barely register on a scale."

I would press, "What if there were a bell curve of universal knowledge; where would we rank?"

One responded, "There is so much we don't know, how could we possibly guess? But for the sake of discussion, let's place man in the average range. It would have to be a huge curve, which would mean that there are beings, powers, or processes that are inferior to us. However, there must be beings, powers, and processes that are trillions of times more powerful and more intelligent than we are."

I laughed when he said that because it reminded me of a friend who holds a PhD in physics. When he heard that one of our space probes was carrying a map of our location in the Milky Way galaxy, he became irate.

"Stupidest thing we ever did," he said. "They are going to find the map and come and kick our ass."

I smiled and didn't ask why alien energies, that could travel trillions of light-years across space, would bother with an insignificant grain of sand on a spatial beach of "gleepillions" of other miniscule grains of sand.

After I had been through this a couple of times I decided to ask students if they had any ideas.

"Sure," they would answer, "there are no limits! UFOs! God! Galaxies or universes that have nothing in common with us! Four, five, ten dimensions; totally different kinds of matter/energy. Time travel? It's elementary." Sometimes they would make my head spin with delight. On more than one occasion, students suggested that what we perceive as reality may simply be an advanced-energy-state's version of a high school science project. On numerous occasions, they agreed that we know so little that it is ludicrous, arrogant, and presumptuous for us to assume that we actually know what we are talking about. Some of the students were keenly aware of the probability that compared to universal knowledge, we were still in the "stone age." Some agreed with Einstein's opinion that, "Science without religion is lame; religion without science is blind." Some suggested that his "formula" was reversible: Religion without science is lame; science without religion is blind. Over years, several students thoughtfully challenged Maslow and suggested that science and religion can not be defined and share a common bond of mystery.

One of our great spiritual gifts is that we never know what will happen next. I have often heard chemists describe the motion of gas molecules as random, or even chaotic. If Newton's laws of conservation of matter/energy are correct, then their contention is absurd. If we knew the mass and direction of every atom or molecule, then we could predict the direction that each would take as it caromed off the others. A good example of this is a billiards table, where pool professionals who understand this concept often make remarkable shots. A possible exception to the "no chaos rule" would be me playing pool. I like the metaphor because I have found that a person, idea, event, or news article can redirect my path in a totally unsuspected, sometimes fantastic, new direction. This was true when I read the following vignette written for the *San Francisco Chronicle*, by Art Hoppe.

The Landlord's Slime

Scene: The Heavenly Real Estate Office.

The Landlord, humming to himself, is craning forward to hang a medi-ocre-sized galaxy of a hundred billion suns on the far edge of the cosmos. His business agent, Mr. Gabriel, enters, golden trumpet in hand.

Gabriel: Excuse me, sir. A noisy debate's broken out on that planet Earth. The tenants are fighting over how the place was made.

Landlord: (frowning) Earth? Let's see ... Is that the one I patched together out of drifting stardust, rainbow wisps, and a few million snatches of birdsong?

Gabriel: No, that was Arcturus 4673-a.

Landlord: Good me! After a couple of zillion, it's hard to recall exactly how ...

What do the tenants say?

Gabriel: Well, the fundamentalists say that you created the whole shebang in six days with sort of a wave of your hand.

Landlord: (nodding) Yes, yes, I could have done it that way.

Gabriel: But the scientists claim that it evolved over 4 billion years.

Landlord: Six days? Four billion years? What's the difference, Gabriel?

Gabriel: That's easy for you to say, sir; you're not in a hurry. But to their finite little minds, it's an eternity.

Landlord: How do the scientists think life began?

Gabriel: The scientists say it could have started when some free-floating chemicals, perhaps in a tide pool, were zapped by a bolt of lightning.

Landlord: Ah! That sounds like me.

Gabriel: This created microscopic one-celled life-forms, which soon evolved into a thimbleful of green slime. Really, sir, why would you create green slime? It sounds sacrilegious.

Landlord: If it's my green slime, it's divine green slime.

Gabriel: Yes, sir. Anyway, you apparently told the green slime to go forth and multiply.

Landlord: "Go forth and multiply, green slime!" I like the ring to that.

Gabriel: Well, it certainly did multiply. According to the scientists, it multiplied into paramecia and sea worms and oysters and fish and great whales.

Landlord: How wonderful!

Gabriel: And at long last, the scientists say, the fish crawled up on the land to become the fowl of the air and the beasts of the field.

Landlord: How dramatic!

Gabriel: Finally the beasts stood erect as hairy, apelike creatures who ...

Landlord: (thoughtfully) Perhaps I should have stopped there.

Gabriel: ... in the end became man.

Landlord: What a lovely, lovely story, Gabriel. When I think of all the fish of the sea, the beasts of the land, the fowl of the air in all their shapes so singular and strange, in all their myriad colors, dappled and striped and iridescent, swimming and slithering and soaring ... All this emerging from a thimbleful of green slime! I ... What was that argument about again, Gabriel?

Gabriel: Basically, sir, it's over whether children in school should be taught to believe in cold, scientific facts or you—ordained miracles.

Landlord: I know that, Gabriel (frowning), but what's the difference?

I have lost contact with Matt, and so I don't know if he has forgotten his questions or burst out laughing when it was announced in 2000 that science was throwing out the wolf/dog theory and suggesting that the ancestor of the whales was really a hippopotamus-like animal. I don't know if the semihippo "thought" its way out of the mouth of some African river and out to sea or not, but it does seem more plausible than the wolf/dog wandering into the surf and never returning.

During the interval between Matt's class of 1989 and 2000, I began to see his questions as igniting a wonderful pyrotechnic canister. There was a tremendous BOOM! Millions of sparks exploded into the night, and each one represented a species of life on planet Earth. Each one was an absolutely unexplainable miracle, infinitely more complex than our finest computers, because they can grow, repair, and reproduce themselves. A bristlecone pine can live over 5,000 years. A sequoia can grow to 350 feet tall and mysteriously pump or suck over 600 gallons of water each day. A unicellular, microscopic paramecium, that surely "knows" nothing, can eat, excrete, breathe, reproduce sexually, and use its cilia for motion and tactility. Most of my students got to see them under a microscope and noted that when they encountered an obstacle, they would back up and try a new path. More than one student commented, "Hey, they are smarter than some people I know who keep making the same dumb mistakes over and over again."

Matt was asking about a, now discredited, wolf/dog, but he was also an advocate for every kind of life on our planet. What did they do, think their way into their respective niches? If we stretch the word "think" to include information encoded in the DNA of every living thing, then "thinking" is exactly what they did. This, of course, opens a cosmic can of worms that we call instinct. In Benjamin Hoff's wonderful little book, *The Tao of Pooh*, he suggests "instinct is just another word for something we don't understand."

Who can comprehend a submicroscopic, life-enabling molecule of information that can guide an ant or bee or elephant into making millions of yes/no, life/death decisions? Every one has its miracle story, none of which is humanly comprehendible. An Arctic tern egg hatches and grows into a bird that can fly 12,000 miles, without guidance, to an exact location, with its internal biological GPS unit. Salmon eggs hatch, the fry swim downstream thousands of miles, and are able to return to the exact gravel bed where they were spawned. Mutualistic bacteria found their way into the human large intestine and "learned" how to produce vitamin K, which is necessary for proper blood clot formation. The origin of the human liver fluke remains totally enigmatic.

There are countless examples of mutualism where each species cannot survive without the other, which puts a whole new spin on the ancient riddle, "Which came first, the chicken or the egg?" If we cannot understand one cell, how can we possibly understand the trillions of cells working cooperatively in each human being, as well as the cosmic numbers of their interactions?

And perhaps most baffling of all are the viruses. These are subcellular organisms that apparently can "turn life on and off." After they do their thing, they can crystallize themselves and remain "dead" indefinitely. When conditions are right, they can resurrect themselves and attack more host cells. They are all parasitic, which means their host organisms had to evolve first. Can they form spontaneously? Does God make them?

I don't believe that any educated person would doubt that the human brain is both structurally and functionally the most complex creation on our planet; however, how it was created/evolved remains the most vexing, perplexing, and wonder-filled mystery in the history of biology. Adapting Matt's perceptive question, did man get his brain by thinking it into existence?

Humans rely on a gene bank of knowledge as well as learned knowledge. Trillions of genetic instructions control heart rate, breathing rate, optical dilation; in brief, the command and control of 11 systems, made up of organs, made up of tissues, which are made up of cells.

In terms of learned behavior, Matt's question about going there by thinking may just be the tip of the iceberg. The most compelling mystery of the human brain is that we are currently only using a small percentage of its capacity. We have all heard that the average usage is 5 percent and that Einstein was using 10 percent. Whatever the number, it appears that there is growing room for a few thousand years.

Several years ago, after a thorough analysis of the Hawaiian language, a highly respected linguist theorized that the only way the new language could have emerged so rapidly would have been if pregnant mothers passed information on to their fetuses, predisposing them to be able to acquire the new tongue. Perhaps after our wisdom teeth and little toes are gone, and our faces look like something from the movie *E.T.*, we will discover that pregnant women will be able to "communicate" genetic information to their fetuses. The human brain remains mostly wilderness waiting to be explored and includes the mysteries of prophecy, prayer, ESP, clairvoyance, dream analysis, hypnosis, collective consciousness, healing, and others.

It has been 150 years since Darwin published *The Origin of Species*, and scientists are no closer to squaring his theory with the emergence of human cerebral hemispheres than he was. Perhaps they have forgotten Socrates's admission, "The more I know, the more I know I don't know." Isaac Newton acknowledged the riddle when he wrote, "I was like a boy playing on the seashore and diverting myself now and then, finding a smoother pebble or a prettier shell than ordinary, whilst the great ocean of truth lay all undiscovered before me."

And so grown-up little boys with huge scientific egos (edging God out), pounce on a never-ending line of mythical wolf/dogs, and proclaim they have found yet another missing link. Galileo knew that Michelangelo had symbolized the ultimate missing link on the ceiling of the Sistine Chapel by the gap he painted between Adam and God's index fingers. Two of the world's greatest scientific minds and the greatest artist, contemplating the works of God, have been trivialized by "progressive humanists" as regressive thinkers. Surely, proclaiming that ammonia molecules randomly organized themselves, eventually becoming a human brain, is as intellectually irresponsible as proclaiming that the same ammonia molecules formed themselves out of nothing. Little wonder Newton proclaimed, "Atheism is so senseless and odious to mankind that it never had many professors." Now, who is regressive?

In Africa, there is a widespread expression that is commonly used when people find themselves in unknowable situations: "God is playing with us." Perhaps the miniature worlds of astronomy and evolution are merely tiny playgrounds of God.

The mystery child knows that she is riding in a celestial cart, drawn by a magical pony that is being lured by a cosmic carrot. The child knows that the faster the carrot travels the farther behind the cart becomes. At this rate, she will certainly never "get there." She is not only OK with that, she celebrates it. She is on a fantastic voyage into eternity. The secular humanists wait restlessly at tide pools around the world, hoping for a bolt of lightning that will somehow prove that God does not exist. They may have a very long wait. There is no scientific evidence that in four-and-a-half billion years, life was started by a lightning bolt or any other spontaneous event. The mystery child senses that what we call real, imaginary, and symbolic are three-in-one and the words *evolution* and *creation* are one and the same.

At age 18, Matthew was in the twilight of his childhood. Perhaps, before his brain settled into the concrete rigidity of adulthood, the last vestige of innocent curiosity leaped out of him and yelled, "What the hell do we believe anyway?" Thanks, Matthew. You made my life richer.

"Up, up, the long delirious burning blue I've topped
The wind-swept height with easy grace where
Never lark or even eagle flew. And while with silent,
Lifting mind I've trod the high, untrespassed sanctity
Of space … put out my hand and touched the face of God."

Jon Gillispie Magee Jr.

The Miracle of Flight

IT HAS BEEN written that man is never more creative than when he designs tools of war and toys of play. Taking off and landing on a moving, pitching aircraft carrier deck is one of the most difficult tasks a pilot will undertake. The navy has long been interested in developing an aircraft that could fly at supersonic speeds, yet take off and land vertically.

Many years ago, I read an account that revealed that the United States Navy allocated $500,000 to an aerospace company to determine how bumblebees take off and land. They are the biggest and heaviest bees, and the navy was hopeful that the research might lead to a new aircraft design. After a thorough study, the research team concluded that it was scientifically impossible for bumblebees to fly. Man has been fascinated with flight, from the dawn of humanity up to Icarus, da Vinci, the Wright brothers, Charles Lindbergh, Amelia

Earhart, Chuck Yeager, and countless others. Even in cultures that lack a mystical or spiritual connection to birds, people have envied the freedom that birds exhibit.

Christie and I were making our annual dump run with tree clippings to be recycled. The dump is located seven miles out of town in a chaparral/oak woodland. While I was un-tarping the load, Christie noticed a dozen or so ravens acting in an unusual manner. They were diving, soaring, cavorting, and using several of their 30 known forms of vocalization.

Suddenly, two of them separated from the flock, spiraled up to an elevation of 1,500 feet, locked together, and plummeted down in a feathery freefall. Not to be outdone, another pair followed and took their turn at the prenuptial dance in the air. Reflecting the birds' excitement, Christie exclaimed, "What are they doing?"

I mentioned that she was watching a mystery that began over 100 million years ago. Ravens mate for life, and each spring, the unpaired birds engage in an aerial acrobatic display. It is kind of a coming out party for ravens seeking a mate, not unlike some of our courtship rituals.

The rich folklore of many of the indigenous tribes includes ravens as omens for being bearers of light, magicians, pranksters, and the bird of death. In Alaska, when the wind speed and direction are optimal, there is a mountain that forms a natural wind tunnel. When this occurs, ravens will dive into the current at the base of the mountain and be blown to the top, like being shot out of a cannon. The turbulence thrashes and tumbles them, sometimes dislodging feathers. After being exploded out of the top of the tunnel, they glide downslope and repeat the ride. What rational, even coldhearted, scientist could resist the urge to conclude that they are simply flying for the joy of it?

One Biodesign class that made it to the top of Half Dome was treated to a prenuptial flight by two Peregrine falcons. They were about 100 yards apart and flying upward. They arched over at the flight apex of 9,000 feet, passed each other, and stooped into respective power dives. They reached speeds of well over 100 miles per hour, pulled out of their dives at 7,000 feet, shrieked as they passed within inches of each other, and powered up only to repeat the the spectacle again. With a little imagination, they seemed to be forming invisible wedding rings in the sky.

After the first aerial tango, students gathered to watch the second. I suggested that we might see them mate, which is typically done at the top of the arc, allowing them enough time to copulate before reaching the ground. The guys began to cheer for the male and the girls were properly disgusted. After three attempts, the pair soared to their cliff-side aerie and settled down for a rest. One of the girls suggested that perhaps the female had a headache.

Christie always took the responsibility of making travel arrangements and getting us to and home from the Grand Canyon. We preferred to fly from Las Vegas to the Grand Canyon Airport, and return on Scenic Airlines. They had been flying tours since 1939 without an accident. They were obviously very safe, but could it mean that they were overdue for an accident?

On one of the trips, the weather was iffy, and we were told that there was the possibility we would have to lay over at Las Vegas for one night. When Christie heard the news she marched quickly up to the Scenic ticket counter and said, "We realize that safety is of utmost importance, but can you imagine being stuck overnight with 30 teenagers in Las Vegas?" The ticket agent's eyes widened to the size of Las Vegas silver dollars; she shuddered and said, "I'll do my very best." Thirty minutes later we boarded a de Havilland Twin Otter with the rainbow logo painted brightly on the tail rudder. The weather was an issue, and our pilots picked their way through scattered snow flurries. And then it happened. The plane in front of us banked to the right into a sunny opening in the clouds and was immediately encircled by a resplendent rainbow. When all of us on the right side of the plane whooped and applauded, those on the left hopped over to our side to see the event. The plane must have responded to the weight shift because the pilot looked over his shoulder through the archway and said, "Yea, it's pretty cool, but the plane would be easier to fly if you don't mind returning to your seats."

"Oops, sorry about that," someone said. We learned later that what we saw was rare but not unknown.

Another year we were surprised to discover that a Japanese travel company bought all of Scenic's tickets for the month of February, which is the month we had to travel. We were forced to book with a smaller company with smaller planes. We chartered three small, twin-engine planes that each carried nine passengers. I should have known that the flight was going to be "different" when I was assigned the copilot's seat. Matters became a little tenser when our pilot read through his preflight checklist, which he held on his lap. This is standard procedure for large commercial jets, but most commercial pilots are able to easily memorize the abbreviated preflight procedures of smaller, propeller-driven planes. I was wearing a headset with a microphone and was able to communicate with the pilot.

We took off safely and ascended to 9,000 feet which was 2,000 feet above the Kaibab Plateau. About 20 minutes out, the pilot asked if we wanted to take the direct flight or the scenic flight. I was always up for an adventure, so the decision was automatic. Over the next 15 minutes, I noticed that we were losing altitude. I could see the canyon rim looming and had no concerns. I didn't know what the Federal Aviation Administration minimum altitude was for commercial flights, but I glanced at "my" altimeter and saw that we were slightly less than 300 feet above the Plateau. I could clearly see cones on the piñon pine trees.

At any rate, I was totally unprepared for what was about to happen. In a flash, the rim and trees were gone. I swear that the pilot nosed the plane down into the canyon. Christie, who hates to fly, claimed that the vanishing cliffs gave the illusion that we were nosing down. It didn't matter. If you think you are going down, you think you are going down. I quickly calculated that at 300 feet per second, we would hit the esplanade in 10 seconds or the Colorado River in 15 seconds. It flashed through my mind that our pilot was wearing jeans and a flannel shirt, not the spiffy uniform of the Scenic pilots. The image of him reading the flight manual flashed through my mind, and I was convinced that he was probably a ticket agent filling in for the regular pilot. I don't remember him pulling up, so I presume that he did not have to do so.

When we arrived at Grand Canyon Airport, the other two planes were already there and we discovered that their pilots took the direct flight path. Neither Christie nor I slept well that night. We both had recurring visions and troubled dreams of hurtling into the Grand Canyon in a plane with seven high school students, piloted by an inexperienced prop-jock. At two hundred miles per hour, the borders had instantly shifted, and it was scary. I decided that flying was best left to the birds.

"It is a commonplace of all religious thought,
even the most primitive, that a man seeking visions
and insight must go apart from his fellows and live
for a time in the wilderness. If he is of the proper sort,
he will return with a message. It may not be a message from the god
he set out to seek, but even if he has failed
in that particular, he will have had vision or seen a marvel,
and these are always worth listening to and thinking about."

The Immense Journey, Loren Eiseley

13: Canyon Visions

THE EARLIEST TRIBES that resided within and around the Grand Canyon regarded it as a sacred place. They believed that The Great Spirit opened the Earth to allow humans to emerge. Whites have generally discounted Native culture, wisdom, and religious beliefs. Ironically, hikers who can decipher the fossil record as they ascend the Colorado River up to the canyon rim can replay the triumphant march of life from the first living cell to opera diva. Well, not quite; the layers of rock that would have included mammal fossils have eroded away. Understanding this, it is not surprising that students often emerged from the canyon using Jonahesque metaphors that described being egested from some wonderfully bewildering process.

Many scientists regard the Grand Canyon as the greatest single page of natural history on planet Earth. When scientists began to study it, it became as important to them as the Dead Sea Scrolls were to theologians. Interestingly, many theologians regard the Grand Canyon as the greatest single example of God's creation on planet Earth. And then there are the synthesizers like Thoreau, Emerson, Muir, and Eiseley who saw only harmony and not discord in the two points of view. Perhaps it should not be surprising that something that evokes such hyperbole would also generate conflict and confusion as well as inspiration.

My barber and I are a small, but classic example of this tension. Over the years, he became aware that I took high school seniors on three six-day field trips each year. One day he casually asked, "So, where are you planning to go on the next trip?"

I enthusiastically responded, "The Grand Canyon."

He snorted, "Jesus! Why in hell are you going there? I know that I'm a bigot, but I read *National Geographic*. So, after the umpteenth article, I told the wife we better go and see what all the fuss is about. Well, we drove to hell and gone and got there and couldn't see a damn thing. We couldn't even see the river at the bottom; we hightailed it to Las Vegas. Now, *that's* something to see."

Therefore, with malice toward none, I cite John Bradford, "There, but by the grace of God go I." It's not that I like the quote. I do not! Whenever I read or cite it, I get the disquieting feeling that God plays favorites. As a science teacher, however, I must confess that the awesome privilege of leading 15 classes down into the Grand Canyon revealed marvels that could have only happened by divine ordination. The inner and outer discoveries, even epiphanies, were simply not humanly possible. Most students saw visions and marvels, even if they were at a loss to explain them.

Anna was bright, curious, and wrote an excellent paper following her Yosemite experience. She was deeply moved, even a little frightened, by the spirituality that she perceived, especially at the bottom of the canyon. Her father was a vet, and she had a strong affinity to the animal world. The students knew that they had two weeks after they returned home to complete their descriptive papers. The deadline arrived, and she arrived at my office in tears. "I can't write the paper," she said. "You'll have to give me an F." At first I was shocked and disappointed. She continued, "It's not that I haven't tried. I have never tried harder to write a paper. It's just that the experience was too overwhelming to put down on paper. I don't know what to do."

I indicated that I was not going to give her an F unless she couldn't come up with something. Nearly all of the other students met the deadline so we had at least two weeks for presentations. Hopefully, I said, something will have clicked by then. The presentations began and included work that was generally at the college level. Often, students sought help from their English teachers to improve their work. On a Tuesday morning of the second week of presentations, Anna arrived before school and raced to my office. She looked tired but ecstatic at the same time. "You won't believe this," she blurted out. "I woke up at 2 a.m. and wrote nonstop until 7:00. The words seemed to pour out of somewhere deep inside of me. I almost thought that I could kick back and simply let my pen do the writing." I shared her elation but was somehow not surprised that the canyon was beguiling her. Her paper was outstanding and, interestingly, the other students did not feel that she should be penalized.

It would be impossible to record one day's images and events of 30 people interacting with each other and the canyon. Over six days, the number would explode exponentially. Multiplying this number by 15 years would create Google-ish numbers that would be impossible to Google.

A great irony, however, was that in the place where the clock ticks in million-year seconds, the demands of leadership were such that I had little time to maintain my own journal. I realize that this is only a worldly lament, and I am assured that John Muir was correct when he penned: "No earthly chemicals are so sensitive as those of the human soul. All that is required is exposure and purity of material. The pure in heart shall see God."

Therefore:

1. After staying 90 days at the Grand Canyon, including 30 nights at Phantom Ranch,
2. Viewing over 10,000 color slides,
3. Listening to over 500 descriptive essays, poems, and prose,

I have recorded some of the events that I was directly involved with at the Grand Canyon.

"We use mules rather than horses on the trails
because they have better endurance, are more sure-footed,
their hooves are smaller, and they founder less often."
Grand Canyon Mule Skinner

14: The Mule Skinner

THE EARLY MORNING sun created an expansive mural of orang-
es, blues, and purples over the chasm known as the Grand Canyon.
Twenty-four students and six chaperones shivered in the icy cold at
Yaki Point as they peered over the rim into something ominous, foreboding, almighty. Mr. Anderson, our advanced math teacher, had
volunteered to come along as a chaperone. He approached the rim,
held up his small Kodak camera, and began to laugh. "This thing is
worthless," he said. "That view is impossible to capture on film." He
reminded me of the many native tribal elders who refused to be photographed because they feared that their spirit would be captured.

We were about to descend the seven-mile South Kaibab Trail on
our way to Phantom Ranch. The trail is a ridge trail and drops nearly one mile, offering views that can be mind-expanding, yet mind-
numbing. We would be traveling back in time to a place that marks
the beginning of life and renders the argument of creation vs. evolution silly, even childish.

Each year our local chapter of The American Field Service provided us with one or more foreign exchange students who lived with a host family and studied for the school year. They were a wonderful addition to the Biodesign class and produced a form of socioeducational hybridization. We discovered that words were incomplete symbols that failed to communicate the deeply seated ethos of respective cultures. The classical example of this involved adages and idioms that defied word-for-word translation. We were hiking in Yosemite, and Claudio (from Italy) asked, "What are we going to do when we get to Little Yosemite Valley?"

I responded: "We will play it by ear."

He replied: "We will play it by ear? What does this mean?"

I answered: "It means that we will cross that bridge when we come to it."

"Oh," he said, "I see. There is a bridge there that we need to cross."

"Well," I said, "there is a bridge there, but that is not what you were asking about."

There are a precious few nurses who can administer a hypodermic injection without the patient's awareness. There are even fewer math teachers who can make learning advanced math relatively painless. Gordie Anderson is one of those gifted teachers.

Andrea, a foreign exchange student, arrived from Italy in the fall of '93. He promptly informed Mr. Anderson that he hated math. Gordie conjured up his magic and within the first week, math not only became Andrea's favorite subject, but a hobby as well.

Andrea, and his newly discovered friend Barry, brought calculators along on the canyon trip and proceeded to wonder how many years back in time they would be traveling with each step. They knew the trail length, the altitude drop, and the years of geological history. They each solved the problem in a different way but both arrived at the number of approximately 150,000 years per step.

They were both interested in computers and marveled that computers could "think" in nanoseconds.

Barry exclaimed, "That is over a billion times faster than people can think!"

"That eeze nothing," Andrea said. "Deo, he can make five billion conversations in each second."

We all laughed. Lofty thoughts and the deepening canyon conspired to make us feel microscopic.

The trail is moderately steep, gravity-positive, and is only a threat to those with weak knees. We stopped at Cedar Ridge for a rest, snack, and to view a fossil display. While there, a mule train laden with tourists emerged from the lower canyon. The sweep quickly dismounted, tied her mule to the hitching rail, and hurried to tie all the other mules. The riders dismounted and wobble-walked on bowed and shaky legs. The lead wrangler was grizzled, weather-worn, and remained mounted on his mule.

High schoolers are naturally curious, and Jason eased over and engaged the cowboy in a conversation:

Jason: "Do the mules get tired going up and down?"

Cowboy: "Heck, this trail is only seven miles long, and they hardly break a lather before they reach the rim."

Jason: "How often do they work?"

Cowboy: "They go down one day, up the next, and get the third day off. Not that they need it; animal rights, you know. Truth is, tomorrow morning these mules will kick up a ruckus when they are not chosen. It seems like they enjoy the walk rather than loafing in the paddock."

Jason: "How often do you ride?"

Cowboy: "We ride 10 days and get four days off."

Jason: "Do you ever get bored?"

The cowboy flinched in his saddle like he had been poked with a cattle prod. His forehead wrinkled, and his eyes narrowed, and then he barked: "Are you kidding or just a little loco?"

He swept his arm across the expansive canyon and said, "Look yonder. Do you call that boring? The sun and seasons are always changing, the weather is always different, the animals and people are never the same. I've been riding these trails for 25 years, and no two days have been the same. How many jobs do you know that can offer that? Have you seen the IMAX movie?"

Jason: "No, I think we will stop there on our way home."

Cowboy: "Well, if you do, just remember, while you are watching it, I am living it. Don't get me wrong; for a movie it's a damn good one. The problem is some folks think it's better than the real deal, and that's a lie. Hollywood had to use helicopters, boats, rafts, amped-up music, and special effects; cheating is what I call it. But here's the sad part. Folks will sooner or later forget that movie. Now if they was to come along with Banjo here and me, mosey down Bright Angel to Phantom Ranch, spend the night and come out this way the next day, they would have an experience that they would never, ever forget; kinda like what you'll be doing. But, I guess I got a little rankled and started preachin' to the choir. Sorry about that, and anyway, thanks for asking. I appreciate that."

Jason: "Well, no, I mean you're welcome, and thanks for the information."

Jason wandered away a little dazed but realizing that he had just heard a priceless lecture that he would likely not forget. The cowboy must have guessed as much because he looked over at me, touched his hat, smiled, and winked. It was a champagne-bubble-bursting-moment in one of the most timeless, amazing classrooms on Earth.

Barry and Andrea graduated. Andrea returned to Italy, and Barry went to college and majored in computer science. During his sophomore year he wrote:

"Mr. Young, our college just installed a new computer mainframe that can handle 20,000 functions simultaneously. Is this getting closer to the speed of God?"

I laughed to myself and marveled over the teenage mind, and then recalled Eiseley's line, "We are now in a position to see the wonder and terror of the human predicament." My mood suddenly turned melancholic. What oxymoronic abomination would allow, even dictate, that a man should kill a fellow human in the name of

God? Was this part of evolution? Was this part of God's plan? Was Lisa right? Do we have no baseline for good and evil? For the second time I suspected I knew why Gandhi wept.

And then, something wonderful happened. Those thoughts occurred in my office. I remembered that every step we took up Half Dome resulted in leaving a worldly care below in the valley. With each 150,000-year step we took down into the Grand Canyon, the cares, horrors, injustices, and contradictions of the world remained above the rim. The natural history of time, change, and creation were so vast, so timeless, that worldly issues became inconsequential.

There must be blueprints in the universe that make the Grand Canyon look like child's play. I am eager to discover the next plane. However, if C. S. Lewis is right, I am pretty sure I will be shocked and dismayed by all of the wonderful opportunities I missed at this level.

"For thousands of years Australian Aboriginals have known the importance of a walk-about. For thousands of years native Americans have known the importance of a vision-quest. Aristotle developed the peripatetic school of philosophy. A branch of Zen Buddhism incorporates walking and meditation. There is an ancient Zen Koan that states that you cannot enter the same river twice. Likewise, no human can enter the Grand Canyon and emerge unchanged."

Author.

15: Ingrid

THERE IS A story about a woman stopping a ranger at Yosemite Valley and asking, "Sir, if you only had one day to spend in Yosemite, what you would do?"

"Madam," he responded, "if I had only one day to spend in Yosemite, I would weep."

On numerous occasions I have seen tourists drive up to the rim of the canyon, look out the car window, and in as little as 30 seconds drive away. They saw the Grand Canyon. I was conflicted. I even thought of running after them, shouting, "Stop! Wait, you are missing it!" When we began the Biodesign program, we were alone on Half Dome. Now, thousands wait in line to climb the famous rock. I think this is a good thing. Thousands of people tour the famous French cathedral of Chartres, I suspect, for similar reasons. When the world discovers the treasures hidden below the rim of the Grand Canyon, there will be a 10-year waiting list for permits to hike to the Colorado River.

As much as I admired John Muir and Loren Eiseley, I never envied them. I am, however, deeply indebted to them for guiding me into worlds that I had no idea existed. Muir and Eiseley spent most of their working hours alone, in the wilderness. They regaled and excelled in what they did and offered the world the fruits of their labor. I, on the other hand, opted to work with high school students. During any break in classes, I would sneak out to the rim to absorb whatever mysteries the canyon had to offer. Often, the faces of students from previous trips would emerge, carried on the updrafting breezes.

Shakespeare said, "One touch of nature and all men are kin," and he was spot on. The canyon walks and talks provided the opportunity to enter the scary but fantastic wilderness of the teenage mind. Although the students were generally appreciative, at the spiritual level, neither they nor I really knew what we were doing. It was a little like being a late-night radio disc jockey asking, "Is there anybody out there?" Then, an event or discovery would occur, always by surprise, and we knew that we were on a path with a heart.

On the '84 trip, I was walking with Ingrid, who was an exchange student from the former Yugoslavia. We were sauntering along the Colorado River, and then made the necessary turn up the Bright Angel Trail toward Indian Gardens. As the trail got steeper, our words got fewer. We had eight miles and 4,500 feet of "up" before we could rest. After several switchbacks, I noticed tears streaming down her face. We hadn't been talking so I was hopeful that I had not said anything to upset her. A quick check confirmed that I had not.

"I was just thinking about my papa," she said. "Five or six years ago, the Communist government decided to sell five-acre parcels of land to private individuals. They were hoping to entice small farmers to increase the food supply for area residents. Papa was able to buy five acres, prepare the land, and plant fruit trees. It was a lot of work added to his regular workload. After two years, he was able to buy another five acres. When the trees began to produce fruit he began to make a profit. He kept the money in a fruit jar in our kitchen. As the savings grew, I asked him one day what he was going to do with it. He laughed and said that someday, something very special would come along and the money would be ready. Several years passed, and then one day, I was scheduled to meet with my high school counselor to discuss classes that I would need to enter the university. While I was there, I saw a poster on the wall that read, 'AFS: American Field Service. Come to the United States for one full year and live with a host family. The only expenses will be for plane fare. Your host family will pay for your food and housing.'

"My heart jumped up into my throat! As a little girl, I had often dreamed that one day I would go to America, and here was an opportunity. However, the counselor said that plane fare would be 800 American dollars, which, for me, would be impossible to obtain. We finished our talk, and I took along a pamphlet and completed the day. That night at dinner, Papa asked his usual question, 'Ingrid, what did you learn in school today?'

"I responded, 'Same old, same old, Papa; but there was something unusual. I met with my counselor to plan my classes for next year, and he showed me this.' I pulled out the pamphlet and shyly slid it over to him. He looked at it briefly. 'I know it would be impossible for me to go, but I thought it was a wonderful idea that Americans would welcome strangers into their homes.' Papa glanced over at Mama, put the pamphlet down, and finished his dinner. The event passed, and the next day was back to normal. However, one week later, at dinner Papa said, 'Ingrid, America is very far away from here. If you were to go, how could I be certain that you would be safe?'

"I couldn't believe my eyes or ears. I was speechless for a second.

"'Oh, Papa, Papa, I would be safe,' I said. 'You and Mama have taught me to take care of myself. I am sure that if I could go, my new family would take good care of me too.'

"'Well,' he said, 'your mama and I would be very worried about you. Maybe it would be better if you stayed home.'

"'Well,' I said, 'it doesn't matter anyway. We cannot possibly afford for me to go. That is a big amount of money.'

"'Ingrid,' Papa said, 'do you remember when I told you that the fruit money would be used for something very special?'

"My heart was in my throat again.

"'Yes, yes, Papa,' I said, 'I remember!'

"He said, 'Well, do you think that this is something special that you would like to do?'

"'I do,' I said. 'It has always been my childhood dream, but I knew we could never afford it.'

"He said, 'Well, your mother and I are not too happy to let you go, but you can ask your counselor to inquire about the process.'

"I leapt out of my chair and hugged my papa with tears running down my face. And now, I am here. I have been to Yosemite, which is one of the most beautiful places in the world. I am down here at the bottom of the Grand Canyon, which is one of the most mysterious places in the world. So, when I go home, how can I ever repay my papa for what he has done?"

It was my turn to be speechless.

We hiked up several switchbacks while I tried to gather some sort of reply. Finally, I began, "Ingrid, I have found the beauty, wonder, and mystery of this place to be too much. It is too deep, too wide, too long, too quiet, and sometimes too spooky. The canyon generates a lot of different emotions, but one of them is not arrogance. Of the millions and millions of visitors, I can't imagine that even one could have left here with the feeling that they 'conquered' the Grand Canyon. Walking down along the bottom, especially, can offer a feeling of such utter insignificance, that it can be an extremely humbling experience."

After two or three switchbacks I began, "I have noticed that one of the qualities of truly great men is their sense of humility. Albert

Einstein and Isaac Newton both mentioned that their success was due to the men whose shoulders they were able to stand on. Your father has given you a gift that is greater than the Grand Canyon. He can die a happy man knowing that he lifted his little girl up on his shoulders and allowed her to see visions over the horizon that he would never see. You had the courage to come to America, and your father had the courage to let you go. I am guessing that your father's deepest hope is that some day you will hold your little girl up on your shoulders, to let her see things that you will never see. But equally important, he has helped you discover that you will encounter many Grand Canyons in your life, and this one will help you understand them."

I continued, "Several years ago, Dr. Scott Peck wrote a book, *The Road Less Traveled*, in which he stated that much of the sorrow and suffering in the United States is caused by our inability, or unwillingness, to delay gratification. It is a very old story, illustrated by the story of the Garden of Eden. Adam and Eve were not able to delay gratification. And maybe that's the point of life. If everyone were perfect, what then? More than one writer has noted that many of the saints began as sinners. We all can't be Mother Theresa, but when someone like your father makes sacrifices for his daughter, it's a beautiful thing."

By that time, tears were trickling down both of our faces. We hiked a few more switchbacks in silence. I wondered if I sounded too preachy. Suddenly, she started to laugh uproariously.

"Oh my God," she said, "Little Ingrid from tiny Yugoslavia has been swallowed by the whale. It is changing me and no one will believe this story when I get back home."

She would be right. Over the years I shared trips with over 50 foreign students. All, or nearly all, of them experienced painful reentries into their respective cultures. The piper had to be paid, and the reentry fee was a hefty dose of humility. They had to deal with families and friends who said:

> You think you are so smart, using your American accent. (They didn't know they had one.)

You are too emotional. (They called it coming alive.)
You are so enthusiastic; it must be fake. (They had
    much to be thankful for and excited about.)
And most painful of all: you are acting like an Ameri-
    can (as in ugly).

Only their closest, loving family members and friends could understand and celebrate the loving bonds that they shared with classmates, friends, and their host families. As for their teachers, they were often jealously indifferent or even antagonistic about the student's new sense of liberated thinking. Students were supposed to listen and not opine. Any discussions of truth, beauty, and goodness should be avoided until they reached 30 years of age or more.

On our walk down the South Kaibab Trail, we stopped at one of several thousand points of interest. There are 21 major layers of rock, with countless (?) sublayers. At this location, we could see a layer that was 400 feet thick, 350 million years old, that lasted 50 million years. Our geology field guide identified a quarter inch distinctive grey band and noted that the layer represented 10,000 years of geologic history. Armed with this and a thousand other ideas, I hoped that all the foreign students would survive their reentry in fine shape.

Labels, designations, and comparisons can be as misleading as much as helpful, but the three trips often proved to be thematic. Yosemite was, by far, the most physically demanding. Perhaps persuaded by the gentle Pacific Ocean, the Mendocino trip proved to be an "intensive carelike unit" experience for young spirits.

And "the canyon," proved to be the most baffling, beguiling, enigmatic, and, therefore, mentally challenging of the three. A common parting comment offered by foreign students as they prepared to go home was, "Before I die, I must somehow get back to the Grand Canyon for one final visit."

I hope they make it.

"To see from an inverted angle, however, is not a gift allotted merely to human imagination. I have come to suspect that within their degree, it is sensed by animals, though perhaps as rarely as among men. The time has to be right; one has to be, by chance or intention, upon the border of two worlds. And sometimes these borders may shift or interpenetrate and one sees the miraculous."

The Immense Journey, Loren Eiseley

16: A Religious Experience

ONE OF THE greatest mysteries on earth is the complexity and meaning of animal behavior. As Western Europeans spread across the Americas, they scoffed at the relationships the native people maintained with animals. Many tribes were not only totally dependent on animals for food, clothing, shelter, and tools, they were woven into the sociocultural and religious fabric. The nearly total relocation of people from farms into cities and towns has greatly diminished our kinship with animals. Eiseley and others (Jane Goodall especially) have shown that animals know far more than white people ever guessed or expected. Trips into the wilderness often reacquaint walkers with animals.

For classes that did the Half Dome hike in one day, it would be the most physically demanding experience that some would ever undergo. For the students that reached the top, there was usually a mountaintop celebration. They had to work hard all day, endure sweat, pain, and sometimes blisters. They may or may not have had an epiphany moment, but they felt good about working together and seeing scenery that was spectacular.

The first hint that the canyon trip was not going to be like Yosemite occurred during our first walk out to the rim. This experience was going to be literally and figuratively upside down. They would start at the top, well rested, and only carrying day packs. Instead of the view getting wider and more expansive, it got narrower and more restrictive. There would be no group-effort bonding experience. The esprit de corps enjoyed on Half Dome would dissipate into small groups or individual hikers.

During the walk into the canyon the next day, we descended down, down, and more down, into a seemingly bottomless abyss. We reached the Tonto Platform, walked to an overlook, and saw another 1,800 feet of down. The approach to the canyon by air belied the fact that the Kaibab Plateau was nearly 7,000 feet elevation. Hikers unaware of this would surely think they were hiking into the center of the earth. The gravity positive trail and lack of heavy backpack freed minds to sink into the canyon. When we arrived at Phantom Ranch, the mood was not euphoric but subdued, even a bit solemn. Some expressed a claustrophobic feeling; others felt spooked. Along the trail they saw ruins of the Anasazi, who may have lived there 6,000 years ago. The fact that scientists had invoked pre-Christian terms, including the Hindu trinity of Brahma, Vishnu, and Shiva, to name the formations added an exotic sense of antiquity.

The students had slept on the granite top of Half Dome, and now would sleep amidst Zoroaster granite and Vishnu Schist. We learned that the formation of the Schist, like all creations, was shrouded in mystery, this one involving heat, pressure, and time. Minerals like garnet, muscovite, staurolite, and hornblende appear to be arranged, crystal by crystal, in a process that one geologist described as "a miracle that defies scientific description."

If the hike was unlike Yosemite, the food and sleeping arrangements would be even more so. Unlike sleeping "on a rock" atop Half Dome, students luxuriated in dorm rooms with clean linen, towels, and hot showers. Instead of burnt green-pea soup and Top Ramen, they enjoyed a dinner of hearty beef stew, green salad, canned fruit, and oven-fresh corn bread. Milk, coffee, and either chocolate or vanilla sheet cake were served as dessert. Instead of a breakfast of lumpy instant oatmeal, gorp, and tea, a classic ranch breakfast of scrambled eggs, bacon, pancakes, canned fruit, orange juice, and coffee or hot tea was offered. Lunch included a choice of ham and cheese sandwich, peanut butter and jelly sandwich, fresh apple or orange, granola bar, etc.

On day three of the trip, the students were usually "turned loose" to explore on their own. If Muir was right about one day in the canyon being worth cartloads of books, then lectures or discussions that I had to offer would likely be forgotten after "the test."

They were advised to hike carefully and not put their hands or feet where they could not see them. Rattlesnakes were rarely seen, but had evolved with a distinctive pink color so to blend in with the canyon. Some made the challenging 15-mile round-trip to Ribbon Falls; others hiked up toward the Cottonwood camp area. Evenings were spent sharing stories, prose, and quotes from Eiseley and others, as well as journal jottings and reflections from student adventures.

Day four meant that it was time to make the 10-mile hike, up to the rim and our lodge. We gathered after breakfast for last-minute instructions. I encouraged them to take their time and enjoy the trek out. They would likely never return, so they should make the best of it. I knew that they had to go there to know there, but I encouraged them to saunter as much as possible. Some would power out as quickly as possible, and then wonder why. Some would worry that if they dallied too long they would not make it out. All would have to hike it once in order to hike it more prudently the next time. I requested that they check out with me so I would know that everyone was accounted for, and assured them that I would bring up the rear and be available to anyone who needed assistance. Singles, pairs, and small groups checked out, and I was aware that a final group of four or five guys hadn't departed. When they approached and asked if I were ready to go, I was surprised.

Because Christie had opted to stay up at the rim, I looked forward to enjoying a last cup of coffee and a solitary walk on one of the most fantastic trails on planet Earth. Most high school boys tend to be macho hikers, and so I was confused as to why this group wanted to hang back with the "Old Man." I decided not to probe, thinking that maybe they were worried that I might "croak off" and that they would be needed to go for help.

As we walked along the tamed Colorado River, we acknowledged the courage, tenacity, and wisdom of the legendary John Wesley Powell. His curiosity drove him to lead a three-month expedition down a river that natives called "the river of no return." Similar to the "flat-earth" sailors that Columbus led, the Arizona natives were convinced that the river flowed into a bottomless and inescapable abyss. Powell and most of his crew survived, and he wrote the first of what would become a library of scientific books on the Grand Canyon. We noted several stationary waves that were a docile three or four feet high, and remembered how he and his men faced waves easily 10 times as high. Exhausted, cold, wet, and eating moldy rations, the anxiety level of Powell's team grew. Each day they awoke, wondering if this would be the day that the infernal river-monster would swallow them alive. Three of his men were overcome by fear and the brutal demands of the ordeal and opted to hike out in search of safety. They were never seen or heard from again. They were a sobering reminder of the dangers of exploration, including educational adventures, into uncharted curricula.

The guys exhibited a sincere interest in their surroundings and asked questions that I could not always answer. There was so much to learn there. They were aware that I had previously led 10 classes to the canyon and were eager to learn what they had experienced. As we left the river, however, and headed up the wall of the inner gorge, the demand for breathing reduced our ability to converse freely. Questions, comments, and observations had to wait for the rests we took at the head of switchbacks. About one mile up from the river, the trail opened up and revealed the rim of the inner gorge, 1,000 feet above us. Chris spotted two or three antlike people dressed in brightly colored coats. They were standing on the rim of the inner gorge.

He asked, "Where is that?"

"They are standing at the Plateau Point overlook," I replied.

He pressed, "Does our trail go there?"

"No", I responded. "That trail branches off of our trail and backtracks out to the point."

He continued, "Can we go there? It looks cool."

"No," I answered. "It's one-and-a-half miles out to the point from Indian Gardens, which makes it a three-mile round-trip. I don't think we should risk the time and energy; we have a schedule to keep."

As I spoke, I realized how ridiculous that it must have sounded; however, I was responsible for the whole group and not just a single hiker. We regained our breath and proceeded up the trail.

About a half mile up, the trail opened again. Chris continued, "Mr. Young, that point looks really intriguing. I really want to go out there."

I began to feel irritated and ignored him. The trail banter, questions, and conversation carried us easily into Indian Gardens. We were there a half hour ahead of my goal, and I should have expected what would happen next. Chris walked 100 yards out to the trailhead marker which read, "Plateau Point, 1.5 miles."

He walked back and said, "Mr. Young, do you remember when you said we will probably never get back here again? I can make it out there, spend 15 minutes, and be back in less than an hour. You and the guys can go ahead, and I will easily catch up to you."

The other guys joined in, "Hey, we want to go too; we can all catch up."

I offered the feeble argument that if something happened to any one of them, I would be responsible. As I was talking, however, I remembered a similar "rogue" male student, 10 years earlier, who wanted to take a side trip, coming down the Half Dome trail. He knew that John Muir had said that we should all be baptized in Yosemite's waterfalls, and that is exactly what he wanted to do. He actually wanted to stand under Nevada Falls. I had mumbled something then about a schedule, and then relented. The side trip not only proved to be a watery success, but led to 15 more years of beautiful baptisms. We were always there in the autumn, and the river was at its lowest; otherwise, we would have not been able to approach. Even so, swimming under Nevada Falls was exhilarating. Looking back now, it was a risky thing to do, but many of Muir's adventures were risky.

"OK! I'm in," I said to Chris, "but if you guys have to carry me up the last mile of the trail, don't say I didn't warn you."

They cheered, and we headed for Plateau Point.

As we approached the rim, the chatter subsided and there was an air of anticipation. We could feel the silence of the inner gorge before we arrived. Standing on the rim, looking down 1,800 feet to the Colorado was stunning and made me shudder to think that we nearly missed the chance. The mood was quiet, reflective, as we munched on our lunches. After what seemed to be a reasonable time, we packed our day packs and readied for the return walk.

Suddenly, someone shouted, "Hey, check this out!"

Two ravens were flying about 500 feet above us and 500 feet out over the inner gorge. They were flying in a tight formation with their wing beats perfectly synchronized. They were coming from the southeast and heading to the northwest. There are many ravens in the Grand Canyon, and so their presence was not surprising. What they were about to do, however, was anything but common.

About a quarter mile beyond us, they suddenly locked their wings in the gliding mode. They banked to the left, made a swooping U-turn, and headed in our direction. I had never considered that birds could calculate, but their glide angle was such that they would be at our eye-level when they passed by. They were about 50 feet out in front of us, flying over the inner gorge. At the exact moment that they passed, they did a perfectly synchronized snap-roll, while making their familiar clicking sound. In a flash, they righted themselves and soared about 100 yards before they caught a thermal draft coming up from the lower canyon. With only minor wing beats, they gracefully ascended to their previous altitude, exited the thermal, and resumed their flight to the northwest.

We were the only people present, and none of us moved. After a respectful pause, we shouldered our packs and gathered at the trail-head sign. The guys formed a loose circle, which is what we would normally do. This, however, was not a normal, but a wilderness, moment. The ravens left us with many questions and zero answers. As a science teacher, students relied heavily on me for answers to their thousands of questions. I had been trained to fill any quiet moments with endless explanations. Fortunately, in this case, I had nothing to say and realized it. Any utterance would have spoiled an extraordinary moment. I nodded to the trail, and our little band trudged along back to Indian Gardens.

About 100 yards out, one of the guys broke the silence. It would have been biblically correct if it had been "Thomas," but memory tells me it was Chris. He was in the lead and turned his head back over his shoulder and said, "I think I have just had a religious experience."

Early in Loren Eiseley's career, he was assigned to collect animal specimens for scientific study. He captured the male half of a mated pair of sparrow hawks. The next morning, however, he had a change of heart and released the bird. Exploding skyward, the hawk quickly joined his mate that had waited all night for him on the cliff above. They frantically called to each other in a rapturous reunion of spiraling wings. The event drove Eiseley to his spirit knees. Like the famous bumblebee, the birds were exhibiting behavior that was considered scientifically impossible. I felt the same way after the two ravens circled back to offer their cryptic message to us.

The following year, Sasha, an exchange student from Croatia, opted to hike out of the canyon with me. As we emerged out of the Devil's Corkscrew, he, like Chris the previous year, kept glancing up at the Plateau Point overlook. Neither one of us mentioned it. When we arrived at Indian Gardens, however, he asked if we could make the three-mile round-trip out to the point. I was already tired and, certain that the ravens would not offer us an encore, nearly said that we should continue pressing upward. Instead, I said, "Well, they didn't have to haul me out last year. What the heck; let's go for it." As we headed out to the point, clouds began to roll in. I had little concern, knowing that the annual rainfall on the Tonto Platform was less than four inches. We arrived at the 1,800-foot cliff and enjoyed its breath-stopping view.

After John Muir was temporarily blinded, he went for a walk and described beauty so powerful that it hurt. I had long been intrigued by that line. Standing on the cliff, I suddenly had an intense abdominal ache which subsided when I closed my eyes. Then Sasha did something very strange. He raised both arms to the heavens and yelled out over the inner gorge, "I vant to see a storm." I had no idea of what he had in mind, but cautiously edged several feet away from him. Almost immediately, the wind began to blow fiercely. Within minutes, we could see sheets of rain showering the upper canyon walls. As we began to trudge back to Indian Gardens, a few large raindrops made pockmarks on the dusty trail. And then it happened! The light became very strange and slightly spooky. Words like *otherworldly* and *eerie* were woefully inadequate. The fact was there were no earthly words available to describe what we were experiencing.

Three hours later when we reached the South Rim, the first thing Christie said was, "Did you see the rainbow?" Sasha and I looked at each other and simultaneously answered no. She laughed and said, "I am not surprised. You two looked like little ants marching out to the point, but just as you approached the inner gorge, the clouds moved in. It snowed lightly up here, but it didn't look like it was reaching down to your level. Then, after a few minutes, the clouds cleared partially and a rainbow appeared. I couldn't see you guys, but it looked like one end of it was directly over where you were." The memory of Chris's voice echoed up from 3,000 feet below, and one year earlier, "I think I just had a religious experience."

"Angels of Life and Death alike
are His;
Without His leave they pass no
threshold o'er;
Who, then, would wish or dare,
believing this,
Against His messengers to shut
the door?"

The Two Angels, Longfellow

17: Angels on the Trail

TEACHING FULL TIME, being the father of four, and planning three extended field trips each year required a good amount of schedule juggling. One of the many necessary tasks was finding time for staying in good physical condition. Although the trip to the Grand Canyon was not as physically demanding as the backpacking trip to Yosemite, the hike up the Bright Angel Trail was nearly 10 miles long with a 4,500-foot vertical climb.

One year, my schedule was particularly hectic and there was little time for conditioning. I tried to assure myself that I would be all right and tended to tasks with a higher priority. The third day of the canyon trip involved several nonchallenging short walks on the canyon floor, which offered little indication of my physical state. On the fourth day, after a hearty breakfast, we gathered together for a final briefing for "The Hike." Then, students and chaperones were turned loose. Typically, I assumed the "sweep" position in order to assist any of the students in need of help.

The thought that *I* may need help never crossed my mind until the first few switchbacks up "The Devil's Corkscrew" section of the Bright Angel Trail. I had covered nearly three miles, was breathing hard, and my legs lacked their normal strength.

The canyon generates myriads of emotions, a common one being of utter personal insignificance. The immensity of time and space was so great that I realized that, like a blip disappearing from a radar screen, the canyon could swallow me with the net effect being zero. This thought sent shivers down my spine and turned my legs to rubber. It was February, and I knew that the ranger station at Indian Gardens was closed. I could return the three miles to Phantom Ranch but would have to wait until the next day for a mule ride out, destroying our tightly tuned itinerary. Helicopter rescues were only used in dire emergencies. The horrible thought of the embarrassment of being rescued contributed to what was a little dark moment of my soul. I decided to press onward and upward and either make it out or die trying. At least, that way, I would be spared from humiliation.

I regard Loren Eiseley as the most influential naturalist of the twentieth century. In his amazing book *The Immense Journey*, he invites readers to share "the prowlings of one mind which has sought to explore, to understand, and to enjoy the miracles of this world, both in and out of science." I didn't know it, but I was about to experience an Eiseley miracle.

About three switchbacks up from my meltdown spot, I chanced upon two army GIs. They were in their midtwenties and looked to be in great shape. They were wearing "camo" fatigue Desert Storm tee shirts and joked and laughed as they hiked. This was strange because the dinners at Phantom Ranch are served in two groups. The mule passengers are served at one seating, and the hikers are served at another. The GIs were not at dinner the previous night, nor had I seen them around the ranch. It never occurred to me to ask them where they came from. I am certain that there was an explanation as to their appearance; however, in the canyon, the borders of physical, mental, and spiritual blend so completely that they are difficult to discern.

I had coached track in a previous assignment and was familiar with training techniques for the many events. Long-distance runners were encouraged to focus on the runner ahead and "rope him in." This meant to concentrate on his back and imagine that you were drawing energy from him to help you catch up. Some of our best runners swore that it worked and used it for every race. I was not a runner, and so I had not tested the technique but desperate times call for desperate actions. I quietly fell into line and imagined a rope from me to the waist of the second hiker. Within minutes, my legs felt relaxed and stronger. I thought it must be a dream but was in no mood to question. After a few switchbacks, my "ropee" said:

"Hey, little buddy, you can pass if you like."

I said, "Oh, no, if it's OK with you, I am doing just fine back here."

He responded, "Hell, it's fine with us if ya don't mind eatin' our dust." (Laughter) "Well," I said, "you might not think so if you knew what I was doing."

"Well, so what are ya doing back there?" he asked.

I briefly explained the roping technique and expected more laughter.

"Well, I'll be danged," he said. "Don't feel like I'm draggin' nothin', so go for it."

I was content to listen to their playful banter, and the switchbacks seemed to glide by. I couldn't take in what was happening but kept focused on my mysterious source of energy.

We rested several times, and then eased into Indian Gardens. We had covered about half of the mileage, but we still had nearly 3,000 feet of vertical to climb. The GIs wanted to stop for lunch, but I was feeling strong enough to press on alone. I shook both of their hands and thanked them for the lift that they provided. They both laughed and waved good-bye.

About a mile up the trail I encountered Caroline and Patty. Patty was crying, and they were both showing signs of stress and despair.

"Will we ever get out of this hole?" Patty asked.

I assured them that they were doing fine, and besides, reinforcements were on the way, and I was sure they would like them. They looked confused but were too tired to inquire. It was, of course, only a wish or hope, but perhaps a little drama might take their minds off of their aching bodies. We agreed to continue at their pace, and I would gladly follow. I sincerely meant it, especially knowing that I was probably not going to need to be rescued. We continued to ascend two switchbacks and rest, in a slow but steady ascent. At the three-mile mark, from the top, the two GIs came from behind and joined us. Their faces lit up with huge smiles, and one said, "Hey, it's little buddy. Are we glad to see you! You know when you told us about your rope, we thought you were smokin' something, but we didn't say nothin' against it. But after you left, we both noticed that the trail was harder and our legs were weaker. You had your story right-way-wrong. You was pushin' us, rather than us pullin' you."

We all laughed except for the girls, who looked totally confused.

After a rest, one of the GIs said, "What if we lead and y'all can follow and set the pace? If y'all need to get out your rope, so be it, as it could likely help us."

One of them stepped over to the girls and politely said, "Why don't you let us take those packs and give those pretty shoulders a rest?" The glow on their faces was pure radiance. They practically jumped up and seemed eager to get going. After all, they were 18 years old and the chance to hike with two good-looking, muscular GIs may never happen again. The guys led thoughtfully, glancing back at each switchback and adjusting their pace to suit the girls.

Even though we were ascending the steepest section of trail, the guys teased, bantered, and joked with them, offering them a full measure of Southern comfort. After a relatively short 2.5 hours, we were surprised to arrive at the upper canyon rim. The GIs graciously handed over the day packs, gave each of the girls a warm hug, and shook my hand.

One said, "Y'all should know that this was the best hike of my life, and I'll never forget it."

I agreed, and as they left, my legs turned to rubber. I wondered if I would be able to walk the quarter mile back to our motel.

"So, what about this rope of yours?" the girls blurted out simultaneously.

"I'm too tired," I said. "I'll tell you about it some other time."

Unfettered spirits can likely travel anywhere, anytime, negating the need for hiking. Perhaps that is why Christie does not have to hike there to know there. Nevertheless, the mystical power of the Grand Canyon lured her into opting to trek down to Phantom Ranch five of the 15 trips. The first adventure was only slightly less traumatic than the birth of our firstborn. A subsequent visit to the doctor revealed a prolapsed heart valve which sapped her stamina. Therefore, I was delightfully surprised when she expressed interest in hiking a second time. During one of her ascents, however, she encountered another severe bout with adversity. She began to struggle gamely a little above Indian Gardens. Not unlike our Lamaze experience, we arrived at the point when she needed me to be somewhere else. My left brain understood that she wanted to struggle privately. My right brain worried that if she suddenly needed me, I would not be there for her. Reluctantly, I headed up the trail, after assuring her that I would maintain regular visual contact. Shortly after I departed, I was relieved to see another hiker had joined her. I wondered what a stranger could possibly offer that I couldn't, but strangely, felt that she was going to be fine. I relaxed and remembered an article about a premarital counselor who advised engaged couples to gauge their compatibility by riding a tandem bicycle and paddling a two-person canoe. I thought that hiking the Grand Canyon could be added to the list. Then the words of a song I wrote, describing our first trek out together, came back to haunt me:

> We heard the coyotes across the way
> Her blood ran cold and I heard her say,
> If I ever make it out of this devil's tomb
> If I never come back, it'll be too soon

But she did come back, and with the same courage and determination that guided her through her second pregnancy.

Three hours later, I reached the rim and waited for her. Thirty minutes later, she and her companion traversed the final switchback and arrived. I hurried to greet her with a congratulatory hug. She was exhausted, but otherwise, all right. After she caught her breath, she said, "I'd like to introduce you to my hiking partner. I couldn't have made it without him." We turned to thank him, and he had vanished. We both did a double take, up and down the trail; he had simply disappeared.

Even though we were standing on a snowy trail, in a chilly breeze, I was warmed by an inner glow that resulted from a cornucopia of spiritual gifts, endowed by Loren Eiseley. This particular gift encouraged me to look for, and celebrate, the miracles of the world, both within and outside the realm of science. I felt blessed beyond imagination to have him as my mentor.

Years later, I discovered that it was impossible to comprehend the immensity of his influence on my life and work. He not only inspired and guided 15 trips to the Grand Canyon, he constantly reminded me of the importance of contemplating spirituality in nature. If John Muir's favorite word was "glorious," Eiseley's favorite word must have been "mystery." The words marry well, and describe nature in general, and the Grand Canyon in particular: Glorious

Mystery. I heartily agree with the many who have suggested that Eiseley was truly the twentieth-century heir-apparent to Henry David Thoreau. Furthermore, *The Immense Journey* should not only be required reading for beginning college biology students, but all professors, priests, and pastors. If this were to happen, perhaps students could learn in an environment with less bickering, vitriol, and recrimination.

It is little wonder that those hiking from the Colorado River up to the canyon rim often use Jonahesque phrases to describe being egested from a process that leaves them wonderfully bewildered. In the book *The Velveteen Rabbit*, the rabbit wondered, "What is real?"— thus prompting a debate over real vs. imaginary and symbolic. A walk into the Grand Canyon erases the confining lines of those words and harkens back to native cultures who are puzzled as to why we had drawn them in the first place.

"The wonders of the Grand Canyon can not be adequately represented in symbols of speech, nor speech itself. The resources of the graphic art are taxed beyond their powers in attempting to portray its features. Language and illustration combined must fail."

John Wesley Powell

18: Thomas

HENRY THOREAU WOULD not be a fan of modern recreational hiking. Any walk in the woods, he believed, should be deliberate, tranquil, even meditative. He preferred the word "saunter," which he claimed derived from the French *a'la sainte terre*: "to the holy land." Thoreau also would not likely have connected with modern teenagers. Even so, after walking eight miles down into the Grand Canyon, another 15 miles round-trip from Phantom Ranch to Ribbon Falls, and hiking the 10 miles up the Bright Angel Trail to the rim, students and especially the chaperones were ready for a saunter. Our itinerary called for a leisurely 1.5 mile stroll from Bright Angel Lodge to the Yavapai Point Visitor Center. The trail hugs the canyon rim and offers panoramic views of two billion years of history. There are probably as many theories about the formation of the canyon as there are viewers. If beauty is in the eye of the beholder, perhaps creation is as well.

A Native American legend states that the Great Spirit created the Earth perfectly smooth, but found that to be boring, so he used his fingernail to make a little scratch. A cowboy legend suggests that the first wrangler that chanced upon the canyon rim said, "Something happened here."

In his epic poem "The Grand Canyon: Daybreak," Henry Van Dyke offered this reflection:

"Then is thy gorge a canyon of despair,
A prison for the soul of man, a grave
Of all his dearest daring hopes! The world
Wherein we live and move is meaningless,
No spirit here to answer to our own!
The stars without a guide: The chance-born Earth
Adrift in space, no captain on the ship."

And so our little gimpy band headed east, which meant that the canyon loomed at our left. They walked alone or in small groups, like owls with left-turn-only heads. During or between conversations, their heads kept turning to the left in an effort to decipher the gaping mystery. Thomas was walking alone, ahead of Christie and me, and he seemed to be agitated by what he was seeing. He would take a long look, shake his head in disbelief, and resume his walk. Two of our girl students approached him from behind, right after one of his cobweb-clearing attempts.

One of them asked, "What's happening, Tom?"

He replied, "I just don't get it!"

She asked, "You just don't get what?"

He replied, "This place has my brain in a bind."

She replied, "Aw, come on, Tom, can't you see that EEE-ROW-SHUN made this place?"

The girls burst out laughing, locked arms, and skipped forward. Tom looked at us a little sheepishly and said, "Ha-ha, that's pretty funny; erosion did it." I smiled and shrugged. Tom was struggling to find words to help define and communicate what he was seeing. There is a common saying among canyon visitors that the only thing God left out of the Grand Canyon was the words necessary to describe it, which may be tantalizingly similar to the creation of man. As we sauntered, my mind drifted back to a teachers' workshop that I was required to attend.

I had attended seemingly hundreds of them, and they were usually a waste of time. When the presenter in this case opened his session with the simple declarative statement, "Words have no meaning," I thought we had reached a new nadir of inanity. He paused long enough to let us absorb the impact. We can think at 600 words per minute, which gave me time to do a quick reality check. I had recently completed a master's degree in biology, which culminated in eight years of college classes. Added to my 12 years of elementary and high school, that gave me a total of 20 years of learning words that suddenly had no meaning. Nevertheless, seeing that he had hooked his audience, he continued. "People have meaning; deep, profound, meaning; however, there are no words that can adequately explain this meaning." I don't know whether the speaker was a Buddhist or not, but it dawned on me that he had presented us with a Zen-like koan that seemed to be enigmatic if not oxymoronic.

He continued, "Cultures have necessarily invented words, symbols, idioms, myths, and legends in an attempt to transcend the gap between words and the meaning of life, yet the gap remains." He gave several illustrations and concluded his talk. What I thought was going to be a farce turned out to be enlightening.

"Of course," I thought. "This is precisely what Muir and Eiseley had described."

I almost burst out laughing because of the plaque I had mounted on my classroom wall:

"I know that you understand that you think
You heard what I said,
I don't think that you understand that what you heard
Is not what I meant."

Anonymous

He opened a floodgate of ideas that had been brewing within me for a long time. Isn't this what Buckminster Fuller meant when he said, "I seem to be a verb not a noun"? Working with foreign exchange students provided many opportunities to prove that idioms often refused translation; they were too deeply embedded in the subliminal ethos of the culture. Then three examples came to mind where words fail: laughter, tears, and dirty words. By laughter, I am not referring to superficial giggling but body-rocking belly laughter that releases endorphins. By tears, I am not referring to transitory drops induced by nostalgia, but the horrifying, heartbreaking sobs accompanied with the death of a child, parent, mate, or friend. And lastly, non-Western European visitors to the United States are often amused that our dirty words are usually anatomical parts, products, or processes that have nothing to do with what the users are trying to communicate. As a biology teacher, I used to urge students to call each other an irregular verb or igneous rock, rather than a biological term.

I was reminded of the first time I was asked to describe the biology of an orgasm. (By a boy, of course) I blushed, laughed, and shrugged my shoulders. I explained that, however explicit, words could not describe the synthesis of the physical, mental, and spirituality of the event.

Darwin fathered 10 children, so he obviously knew what was up, when it was up. Surely, he must have known that having an erection and achieving an orgasm could not have resulted from random chance and competition. This meant that there were at least two lethal flaws in his theory of human evolution: one involving his brain and the other involving his penis. The battle between a man's brain and his penis rages on today. On the other hand, picturing God encoding DNA instructions necessary to create the equipment to achieve "The Big O" was a little awkward, albeit humorous.

As an aside, as I was writing this, my five-year-old granddaughter smiled and said, "Paw, I saw two lady bugs on top of each other, and Mom said they were making babies. People don't do that, do they?"

I blushed, laughed, and said, "You should talk with your mom about that."

Of course, we as teachers use words; however, every letter is symbolic and often words fail to communicate difficult concepts. The great American wordsmith, John Steinbeck, illuminated the paradoxical potential of words when he penned in *Cannery Row*:

> "The Word is a symbol and a delight which sucks up men and scenes, trees, plants, factories, and Pekinese. Then the Thing becomes the Word and back to Thing again, but warped and woven into a fantastic pattern."

I recalled an English teacher saying, "Use a word three times in a sentence and you own it." Maybe this is not completely true. If not, we may be forced to exist in a quasi Tower-of-Babel environment, where we assume that we know what words mean, but often we do not.

I once had a student say, "Mr. Young, you don't understand what I don't understand."

Marriage counselors often suggest that males and females may talk the same language, but are often on such different frequencies, that communication is difficult, sometimes impossible. I read a study where several hundred couples that claimed to have a dynamic marriage were asked to rank the 10 most important factors of their successful relationship. The same number of divorced couples was asked to identify deal-breaking flaws. Both groups identified communication as the key reason for their success or failure.

My mind wandered back to a Bible study class I attended years earlier. It was suggested that the early Israelites understood this concept by refusing to name their holiest of holies: their concept of a supreme being. They feared that their limited knowledge would be perceived as disrespectful or even sacrilegious. Even worse, they feared devaluing Yhwh by naming "Him." They also feared that it would give the

Hebrews the blasphemous misperception that they somehow knew, understood, or even "owned" the ultimate mystery. Maybe the early Jews had a Hebrew teacher who taught, "Use a word three times in a sentence and you will own it."

The Greeks coined the word, *scientia*, "to know," and ever since, scientists have assigned names to many of nature's verbs and nouns, and then assumed that they understood the phenomenon. Light is a classic example of this mental miscarriage. Certainly much is known about light; however, scientists are at a loss to actually define what light is.

Many science teachers proclaim that religion is invalid knowledge based on illogical and un-provable tenets. They fail to balance the equation by stating that every branch of science begins with similar, illogical, and un-provable assumptions. Einstein fully understood this when he wrote:

"The most beautiful thing we can experience is the mysterious. It is the source of all true art and science."

He could have completed the triad by adding religion.

The students were not alone. My head kept turning to the left and the gaping chasm was challenging me to go back to "the beginning," and absolute paradox. Either we materialized out of nothingness, or according to the Gospel of St. John: "In the beginning was the Word." In either case, according to Eiseley, we have been destined "to search and bicker and disagree. The eternal form eludes us" (*The Immense Journey*).

Paraphrasing Robert Frost:

"We dance around the rim and suppose; The secret sits in The Canyon and knows."

Tom was experiencing a wilderness moment. He was in a state of bewilderment, and it would be his privilege or obligation to find his own way out. Words would be of little use.

Note: Tom was one of the first ex-students that I contacted for feedback. My concern for him was justified. We talked after he read his story, and he agreed with the authenticity and the use of his name, but then he blushed slightly and said, "It does make me look a little dorky." I protested. "Tom! You were just being real. I am guessing that 100 million people have visited the Grand Canyon and not a single one of them has walked away without a bind in his brain. After John Powell spent three months navigating the Colorado River through the Grand Canyon in 1869, he emerged and said it best:

"The wonders of the Grand Canyon can not be adequately represented in symbols of speech, nor speech itself."

Tom was in very good company. When John Muir wrote (1870), "I have a low opinion of books," he was not denigrating the value of literature; he was properly illuminating the fact that as physical and mental creations, books were incapable of describing the wordless world of Mother Nature's spirituality. In her book *Their Eyes Were Watching God*, Zora Hurston wrote (1937), "You gotta go there to know there." While this may be mainly true, evidently three months of intimately exploring the depths of the Grand Canyon did not enable John Powell to "know there." Loren Eiseley would have been proud to know that Tom had discovered that the mystery still exists; and so was I.

I see Tom occasionally around town, and when I do, both of our faces light up with joy. His eyes sparkle and dance, and we can both enjoy an echo from the canyon:

"Aw, come on, Tom, can't you see that EEE-ROW-SHUN made this place?"

"We oscillate between wishing we were unreflective animals and wishing we were disembodied spirits, for in either case we should not be problematic to ourselves. The Carnival solution of this ambiguity is to laugh ..." W. H. Auden

The Star Thrower, Loren Eiseley

carnival, n: an organized program of entertainment.

Merriam-Webster Dictionary

19: Carnival

AS 95 PERCENT of the American population left the land and moved into cities and towns, they left behind folk music, folk dancing, hoedowns, and barn dances. Agrarian organizations like the Grangers, as well as fraternal organizations, declined or became obsolete. They have been replaced by movies, television, computers, video games, and sporting events.

For thousands of years, tribal cultures have recognized the spiritual and social value of a carnival. They performed rituals and ceremonies by singing, dancing, and using paint, feathers, masks, hides, etc. The carnival spirit is nearly absent in our society, with the possible exception of Halloween and the Mardi Gras celebration of New Orleans. Many Americans would be surprised to learn that the two are rooted in Christian spirituality. Halloween occurs the evening before the commemoration of the departed which occurs on All Souls' Day. The term *Mardi Gras* (Fat Tuesday) derives from the custom of feasting before the Lenten period of fasting, spiritual reflection, and personal reevaluation, which all precede Easter. Unfortunately, the near-total absence of spirituality has resulted in a celebration that emphasizes drugs, alcohol, and sex.

As mentioned earlier, most of the pivotally creative ideas for Biodesign were not my own. In fact, I typically resisted or rejected them at first exposure. One of the classic examples of this involves a class that I was required to take in order to complete a master's degree program in teaching biology. The class was a survey of all the latest audio-visual techniques that were designed to enhance teaching. These were precomputer days, but I would discover the precursor to power-point presentations. One of the required projects involved producing a modern "slide show." I had to select a biological subject or theme; shoot several hundred color slides; arrange them into two carousel projectors; record an integrated stereo soundtrack which included silent cues; attach a patch to a programmer which fed into a dissolve unit, all of which controlled the sound and twin projectors. The class and projects required a tremendous amount of time and energy for a measly two units of credit. The results, however, would open a huge door to the world of carnival and profoundly enhance the program.

Two years later, on the first Biodesign trip, I took my 35mm SLR camera along and shot 200 color slides chronicling our activities. The completed program gave the illusion of animated still shots of students being reborn at Yosemite. The kids loved seeing themselves interact with each other and nature. One of the photographers in the class said, "That was awesome. Can I do the program for the next trip?" It was the last slide I took. For the next 23 years, students willingly assumed the formidable task and created 61 programs by selecting the best of approximately 50,000 slides. It was not unusual for them to start out with over 1,000 slides and thousands of tapes or CDs and end with a 30-minute, 200-slide program. Some of the photos were worthy of *National Wildlife* or *Audubon* magazine. The slides were shown on an eight foot wide by ten foot high screen which yielded a glorious exclamation of youthful physical, mental, and spiritual adventures. San Francisco's Grace Cathedral features magnificent stained glass windows depicting many of the saints. Christie and I often felt that each slide projected a larger-than-life illumination of living saints.

On one of the return trips from the Grand Canyon, we had a two-hour layover at the Las Vegas airport. The students were turned loose to get lunch and explore the shops, but not the casinos! After our return, when the slide-show team began their project, they discovered two slides of girls clad in very teeny bikinis. Evidently the girls wandered into a women's boutique and decided to slip into samples of "Vegas" swimwear. The students were eager to include the photos in their slide show; I was not! In the end, however, I had to concede that they inserted them at critically comical moments, and I acquiesced.

While the papers were being presented in class, students were invited to select the ones that would best represent the trip to their parents and friends. The papers along with the slide show and refreshments comprised our Parent's Night carnival. When the evening arrived, I was anxious when the slide show began. This had never been done before, and it was risky as well as risqué. During the third song, the first racy slide appeared. The audience gasped briefly, and then hooted and roared. They were probably expecting the second slide which nearly brought the house down. The two slides provided a perfect comic balance for the more dramatic, thought-provoking scenes. When the program ended, the audience sat in an eerie total silence. It was not unlike being in church when a stirring sermon was delivered and you wanted to applaud and shout AMEN, but decided not to. After a thoughtful moment, the audience erupted. The two girls must have felt like Hollywood stars.

After the slide show, one of the dads approached me with watery eyes and said, "I have never seen a bunch of such healthier looking kids." I smiled and assured him that John Muir would have heartily agreed.

One of the highlights of the three trips was a canoe trip several miles up Big River in Mendocino. While paddling along the quiet river, we were often able to see river otters, harbor seals, sea lions, egrets, ospreys, and a variety of ducks and seagulls. It was as if we were traveling back in biological as well as human history.

As most of the students had not used a canoe, it was also an opportunity for them to quickly learn to paddle or swim. The boathouse was situated where the river empties into the Pacific Ocean, and so the water was brackish and a chilled 55 degrees. I gave each class a crash course in canoeing, quickly covering the basics, which included a mandatory life-jacket requirement. I mentioned that the person in the stern was the pilot and controlled the vessel. He/she should communicate to the bow blade whether he needed help on the left or the right side. I also mentioned the delicate situation that the heaviest in each of the three-person groups should be in the middle or rear. The guys didn't care but none of the girls wanted the distinction of being the heaviest. After the instructions, the chaperones and I helped the kids board and launch. They generally adapted quickly and were quite successful; however, there were some exceptions.

During the instructions one year, three of the guys were chattering rudely and not paying attention. When I asked them to be quiet, one of them said, "This is boring, and besides, we already know how to canoe." Nevertheless, they complied. I finished the lesson, and we headed for the pier. The three guys bolted for the dock and grabbed the first available canoe. Two of them were average size and one tipped the scale at over 200 pounds. They had decided to put the largest in the middle, and the two smaller boys carefully boarded the bow and stern of their craft. After they were settled, the larger one clumsily stepped off of the dock and planted his foot firmly, 18 inches wide of the keel-line. Instantly, all three of them were catapulted into the chilly brine. The class erupted with laughter, perhaps more out of sympathy rather than malice. I didn't respond, knowing better than all of them how it felt to be hoisted by my own petard.

Another exception involved three chaperones. One weighed 250 lbs; one weighed 175 lbs; and one weighed 150 lbs. I had launched earlier and was headed upriver, not concerned about them. A short while later, however, I heard bellowing across the water. "How the hell do you steer this goddamned thing?" My crew burst out laughing, and we decided to circle around and investigate. When we arrived, we saw something straight out of *The Three Stooges*. John (250) was in the bow with the gunwales dangerously close to water level. Bob (175) was in the middle with a look of total exasperation. Mark (150) was in the stern which was slightly above the water level. Mark was an experienced canoe-man; however, the wind, current, tide, and improper weight distribution made their canoe unstable and nearly impossible to maneuver. No matter how hard Mark paddled, it was as though they had an anchor attached to their bow. They were about to go to blows except that they could not move without capsizing. The scene provoked hilarious laughter, which was not helpful.

We approached, and I suggested that if they wanted to get anywhere, John was going to have to move to the stern and Mark to the bow. There was a sandy beach nearby, and they were able to flail their way over to it and change positions. Their situation improved immediately, and they were able to rejoin the group.

On another trip, I started out with two girls; Lucy, an exchange student from New Zealand, and Rachel. As we boarded, I noticed that Rachel was slightly miffed about being directed to the bow position. She indicated that she had canoeing experience and wanted the stern position. I suggested that it was important for me to direct the group to where we were going and that she could take the stern on the return trip. The first leg progressed smoothly, and we all arrived safely at our rendezvous location. After our lessons, we headed back downriver. Rachel was pleased to be in the stern. I should have remembered that the return trip was often more challenging; this day was the worst. The river was flowing west. A flood tide was surging in toward us; the wind was stiff and blew at 45 degrees across our bow, creating dangerous cross-current waves. We were caught in the middle of a very little but "perfect storm." I proudly watched the other teams quickly assess the situation and make adjustments.

Rachel and I were working beautifully together and her skills were apparent. That is, until we met a little rogue wave. It was only about one foot high. Unfortunately, it occurred just as she had tacked to the right to gain more space from the shore. I would have done the same thing. We both read the wave and tried desperately to compensate. Our attempt was futile, however, and the wave gently lifted us into the first half of an Eskimo roll. We would not be bobbing up to face another wave. As we began to roll, Lucy screamed, "I can't swim!"

In a flash, we were all in the icy water. I surfaced and waited for her to bob up. She emerged gasping and spitting out the salty water. I took two quick strokes and grabbed her life jacket and assured her that she would be fine. Fortunately, there was a small island nearby. Lucy clung to the canoe, and Rachel and I towed the swamped vessel to the sandy shore and dragged it onto land. I was exhausted and shivering badly, but then something very strange happened. I began to laugh uncontrollably, like I had never laughed before. The laughter came from deep inside my being, and I didn't know why. Then I remembered Auden, "The carnival solution of this ambiguity is to laugh."

Maybe I was reconnecting with the many times we stood under the icy Nevada Falls in Yosemite. Maybe I was reminded of the many times students eagerly took the optional 15-mile round-trip trek for the privilege of standing beneath Ribbon Falls at the bottom of the Grand Canyon. Or maybe it was simply a cathartic pressure release that protagonists periodically experience to avoid blowing up. Whatever the cause, Rachel and Lucy regarded me with great curiosity, if not alarm. They were cold and wet and saw nothing funny about it, and so I struggled to regain my composure. We emptied the canoe, relaunched, and proceeded without further difficulty, even though the wind was brisk and our bodies were cold. As we entered the warm boathouse, looking like drowned rats, one of our more spiritually sensitive girls approached me with a towel, bright smile, and said, "You look like you have a secret." She was correct. I was cold and shivery, but my soul had been cleansed by the miracle of carnival.

I was saddened by the fact that in a nation blessed with glorious natural resources, we teach children the importance of bathing their bodies without mentioning the same need for their minds and spirits. It later occurred to me that it was a shame that in the Christian faith people are only baptized once. It seemed clear to me that people are spiritually starving and should be baptized many times. Not only that, they don't need anyone else to help them. I have been baptized by Mother Nature, for Lord only knows how many scores of times, and it is always rejuvenating and often hilarious … carnival.

I don't know if teachers are more ethical than other workers. I do know that they are prone to bend copyright laws to provide students with a timely poem, quote, or insightful paragraph. This must have been in my mind during the final evening of the first trip to the Grand Canyon. The evening seemed disjointed, anticlimactic, and lacking some sort of closing ceremony that would wrap up all the loose ends.

Several years earlier, I attended a four-day Christian men's retreat, which focused on spiritual renewal. The afternoon of the third day, the 40 participants were gathered together and instructed to join a drama, music, or art workshop, and use the medium to translate and reflect the lessons and experiences of the three days. We would be given two hours to complete the assignment, and the finished product would be presented to all staff and participants that evening. I was skeptical and doubted that 13 men could complete much, if anything worthwhile, in two hours. I was hugely mistaken. The workshop presentations were a roaring success. The retreat was spiritually enlightening, but what was equally important was the depth of creativity that was revealed in every participant. Being the skilled idea-thief that I was, I wondered if the plan would work with a bunch of high school students.

On the last afternoon of the second canyon trip, the students were instructed to join one of three workshops: art, music, or drama. We had planned ahead and brought a small suitcase filled with art supplies. The drama and music groups would have to fend for themselves. Chaperones were assigned to run errands for props and keep kids focused, if necessary. There were some anxious moments when Christie and I thought we had made an error in judgment. For the second time I would be proven wrong. A kiva is a ceremonial room or chamber that native tribes used for communal and religious celebrations. The Thunderbird Hotel, directly on the canyon rim, had "The Kiva Room," which was available for group meetings. The room could not have been a more perfect setting for us, and the evening was a wonderful success. Perhaps, more important, the students created a template that other classes seemed to mysteriously build on and improve.

The evening performances were nothing short of spectacular. The students were like baby ducks, released in a pond of water for the first time. They seemed to instinctively return to deep wells of creativity and spontaneity. They used comedy, pathos, satire, farce, and a highly skilled ability to interpret and integrate teacher, chaperones, classmates, and, of course, the canyon. Original melodies and lyrics were composed, or traditional tunes with new and canyon-specific lyrics were used. One class used a dozen lunch bags to create 12 puppets that performed a show. Each puppet represented a person with ideas, poetry, facts, and information pertinent to our studies. The presentations soared high with laughter and plunged as deep as the canyon, illustrating Gibran's adage that joy and sorrow flowed from the same cup. The artwork often succeeded in the illusive task of capturing the spirit of the canyon, at times with pieces that would make Grandma Moses proud. Each class would only get to see one set of workshops. Christie and I had the pleasure of seeing 14, and the ideas were always fresh, new, and exciting. On most, if not all, carnival nights, I was overwhelmed by the synchronicity of events that brought us to a land of enchantment and mystery. I felt proud that we were participating in a ceremony that most Native American tribal members would have understood and appreciated.

Early in the evolution of the canyon experience, Christie and I decided to take an active role in promoting personal and class appreciation. During the first circle, she handed out little folded cards, each with a brightly colored rainbow. They also contained the poem from Allen, "… he thinks in secret and it comes to pass, environment is but his looking glass."

The cards were handed out randomly; however, she had previously marked each one with a small m or f. Inside each card was the name of a secret pal. We had discovered that it was more fun when the kids selected members of the opposite sex. Students and chaperones were invited to simply do what they could to help their secret pal have a great trip. She also jokingly announced that, "There are no coincidences, so the name you draw is the person you are supposed to draw."

Students are amazingly creative, and they found many ways to secretly enhance their pal's experience. Countless acts of kindness resulted. Secret notes were passed, "magical pebbles," candy bars, and shoulder rubs were offered by messengers. On several occasions, chaperones got caught up in the process and wondered who their secret pal was. Some finally concluded that all the kids were treating them with such kindness and respect that they all must be their secret pal. The canyon trip did not require the brute strength that the Yosemite trip required, and the more relaxed hikes provided many opportunities for them to appreciate each other.

During the carnival celebration, secret pals were revealed. Again, student creativity blossomed. Poems, odes, cards, small art projects, or small symbolic gifts were offered to thank the pal for being part of the experience. As was common in the class, the roles of giver and receiver were blurred and they became one and the same.

It was not uncommon for some of the matchups to be mysteriously poignant. Events, revelations, and discoveries occurred between the two pals that simply could not be explained. When this happened, students were surprised, curious, or delighted by the mystery. One of these special moments occurred the year one of the girls had invited her dad along to be a chaperone. When the pals were revealed, they discovered that they had drawn each other's name. I looked at Christie and asked silently, "Did you plan that?" She smiled knowingly and shook her head in denial and shrugged. It was a very special moment, yet only one of hundreds that she and would be gifted with.

On one of the trips, one of the father/chaperones addressed the carnival circle and said, "The Grand Canyon has offered you kids a gift that is nothing short of miraculous. You have a responsibility to go out into the world and tell people what you have seen." Twenty years later, I accepted his challenge and started *Out For A Walk*. The carnival night proved to be the perfect way to help us let go of the canyon and fly home on spirit-filled wings.

We had just reached our cruising altitude on our return flight from Las Vegas, and the captain came on the intercom and said, "We would like to welcome the St. Helena High School biology class returning from the Grand Canyon. We hope you had a great trip." Passengers had little trouble spotting the group of cheering, grinning teens. The head flight attendant welcomed us and thanked us for choosing United Airlines. Then she mentioned that upon our arrival the captain would end his 35-year career. The cabin erupted with applause. Immediately, Suzie jumped up and retrieved the small suitcase/art box from an overhead bin. The case contained the unused supplies from our carnival night. She announced that it would be "fun" if everyone made a congratulatory card or design to present to the retiring pilot. Although they were travel-weary, they eagerly spent the next 45 minutes in rapt creativity. The flight attendants took notice and marveled at what they were seeing. As each design was completed, Suzie pasted the work onto an eight-foot piece of butcher paper. As we began to descend, she carefully rolled the project into a scroll.

After landing, the students patiently waited to deplane. The pilot stood at the front exit and shook hands and thanked each of the passengers. The flight attendants huddled behind him and kept glancing back at us with thinly veiled excitement. When all the others had left, Suzie led our happy little band to the front of the plane. She gave the captain a warm hug, thanked him for the personal attention, and said we had a little present for his retirement. For someone who had to be in control of thousands of details, the pilot was thoroughly bewildered. One of the flight attendants stepped forward and thoughtfully said, "Jim, let me help you out a little." She undid the tape, handed one end of the scroll to the captain, and then unrolled the scroll to the delight of the students. It helped, but the man continued to shake his head in disbelief. He finally mumbled, "This is the neatest retirement gift that any pilot could receive. I can't wait to read all of your messages."

Things often happened so quickly in class and on the trips that I could not absorb them thoroughly. Worse yet, there were times when I simply regarded their creative, spontaneous acts of kindness as routine; usually they were not. In this case, they created something for a total stranger and someone who they would likely never see again. The students were not only able to grasp the meaning of the spirit of carnival; they were able to apply it in a loving way. Gibran described this kind of giving as man's highest calling, and it represented one aspect of the high degree of humanity that Biodesign students aspired to.

"And there are those who give and know
not pain in giving, nor do they seek joy,
nor give with mindfulness of virtue:
They give as in yonder valley the myrtle
breathes its fragrance into space.
Through the hands of such as these God
speaks, and from behind their eyes He
smiles upon the earth."

Gibran

20: Sasha

THE 24 YEARS of field trips to the Mendocino coast of northern California yielded a cornucopia of biological discoveries. The village of Mendocino is at the epicenter of a 15-mile radius of extraordinary biological diversity. Arguably, it has more plant and animal species than existed in the Garden of Eden. Our studies were rich and diverse and included visits to the redwood forest, pygmy forest, intertidal community, sand dunes, a fresh-water fen, marine cave, and a canoe trip up Big River. In addition, we visited a master potter and a bird carver who carved birds that were used by presidents Reagan and Clinton as gifts for visiting dignitaries from around the world. If "one day in the wilderness is worth cartloads of books," then each destination would have provided enough experiential information to easily fill a book. When we slogged through the fen, some thought that leeches or other parasites would slither into their pants and suck their blood. When we climbed the sand dune, they understood why coastal Indians called it "Nipomo," the wanderer. They noticed that it was impossible for life to take hold, and some compared it to trying to build relationships on sand. One of them had read an article that suggested that some astronomers predict that there are more stars in the universe than grains of sand on planet Earth. William Blake's poem suddenly seemed more appropriate:

> "To see the world in a grain of sand
> And heaven in a wildflower
> Hold infinity in the palm of your hand
> And eternity in an hour"

When they hiked down Fern Canyon, they could imagine giant dinosaurs munching ferns or feel the earth tremble as a terrifying Tyrannosaurus Rex approached, looking for a baby Brontosaurus for lunch. When they walked on the beaches, they noticed the paucity of life and snickered at the one-time theory that a fish with superpectoral fins triumphantly flipped its way up the beach to become man. Conversely, on their canoe trip up Big River, they saw mudflats with overhanging trees and could envision the evolving mudskippers that Eiseley described in *The Immense Journey*.

But one of the most interesting stops was at the intertidal ecosystem. Here, they learned about lunar phases of conjunction and opposition, creating high-high, high-low, low-high, and low-low tides. I usually mentioned that marine invertebrates often use the moon to synchronize spawning activity. In fact, there are times when the surf is milky-white due to cosmic numbers of male sperm cells. The girls usually thought the idea was disgusting. On more than one occasion, a girl said, "I'm never going swimming in the ocean again." In an area that involved high-tide flooding, low-tide desiccation, and the pounding of crashing waves, they found forms of life more abundant and diverse than any other ecosystem. Upwelling, they found, was the cause of the abundance, and one student wrote, "I tromped out into the tide pools and tiptoed back."

Many admired a kelp named postelsia (sea palm) for selecting the most exposed rocks to anchor to. They learned that a "super-glue" grip and a flexible stipe enabled it to withstand the fiercest pounding waves. Some saw it as metaphorical.

The natural beauty and charm of the north coast attracted me and led to a master's degree focusing on the pygmy forest. However, if anyone had suggested that there would be a spiritual connection to the pygmy forest, I would have scoffed. The Biodesign seeds had not been planted, and I was a left-brain-dominated biology teacher. As far as I was concerned, the first classes to visit Mendocino were strictly two-dimensional, physical and mental. Mendocino would change that, and me. The metamorphosis was largely student-directed. Whether they were responding to distant memories of saline amniotic fluid or further back to their oceanic origins, I did not know. I do know that the kids picked up on it before I did, and described spirit stirrings.

Each year, the spiritual element grew, but one year took a major leap, and, as in all things spiritual, it was not of my doing. Susan, a friend of Christie's and mine, knew a potter that she thought would have a lot in common with me. I ignored her suggestion and doubted that a potter would have any relevance to our program. As usual, my first reaction was wrong.

The following year, her husband Tom accompanied the Mendocino trip as a parent/chaperone. We completed our studies, including a visit to a sand dune north of Fort Bragg. It was Saturday, and the kids were allowed a free afternoon. Some of the students wanted to go into the village of Mendocino and visit the numerous artisan shops and galleries. Others wanted to go back to the dune and play in the sand. Tom was adamant in his desire to visit Sasha the potter and check out his studio. A carload of students opted to go along with him. When all three groups returned to camp prior to dinner, there was a highly animated discussion. The potter visitors were electric with their enthusiasm and described a man with magical hands that simply brought clay alive. These kids had learned to trust each other, and the sad faces of the other campers (including me) revealed that we knew that we had missed something special. I made a mental note: Next year, if you are welcome, add "the potter" to the trip.

I am convinced that no small part of the magic experienced by the class of '79 was generated by their visit with Sasha. When they arrived, they were warmly greeted and immediately escorted to a tour of the pygmy forest. His love of the land and nature was clearly evident. Each species was known by name and almost seemed to be his friend. He explained how the underlying soil conditions, known as the pod sol, caused the stunting process. Trees were from six inches to six feet tall and 150 years old. A state park bordered his property, and he led the students into the redwood forest. He described trees that were 350 feet tall and 20 feet in diameter that lived only a few feet from the pygmy trees. The soil under the redwoods was deep and rich and could absorb up to 300 inches of rainfall annually without eroding. By comparison, even though I held a master's degree, my previous lectures were dry, lifeless academic exercises.

For the next 20 years, I gladly welcomed his offer to lead kids into the land of pygmies and giants and entrance them with his wisdom. But, that was just the beginning. When the tour was over, he led the class through his outdoor showroom. The pieces ranged from large garden planters to vases, ewers, dinnerware, and artful designs. When someone asked if the weather damaged the art, he said that it actually improved it and added to its value. From the "showroom," they were led to a semicircle made of old logs, with his wheel positioned in the center.

What happened next can only be described as transformative. The previous students were right. Immediately, the clay began to move and convulse under his careful hands. As the wheel and the clay turned, his mind turned as he shared stories, metaphors, parables, and poetic wisdom, which were gained by his 30 years of working with clay. He suggested that humans were made of the same stuff as his clay, but had the advantage of the most mysterious element known: the spark of life. He described the two fundamental skills that potters must attempt to master.

"The grip," he said, "is extremely important and determines the eventual shape of the piece; however, knowing how to let go is equally important. The potter must learn to let go with unspeakable tenderness. If he does not, he will leave a bruise on the clay." He demonstrated by letting go abruptly and two lumps of clay wobbled eccentrically on the piece.

"Human relationships are like that," he went on. "If people don't let go gently, they can leave bruises that can last for years."

The students were glued to every word. Sasha's hands and clay had a mesmerizing, almost hypnotic, effect. But equally important were his dancing, sparkling eyes. This was truly a man who loved what he was doing.

During one of many of Sasha's poignant demonstrations, he fashioned a cream pitcher. He paid meticulous attention to the pouring spout, saying that "pottery should be artistically pleasing, but also functionally correct. If the angle of the lip of the spout is not perfect, the last drop of cream will drip onto the table linen and not 'sniff' back into the vessel. Thus, by calling attention to itself, it can disrupt an otherwise beautiful meal. One of the great human gifts is to be able to serve others quietly, even anonymously, without calling attention to ourselves."

I immediately thought of Christie and the thousands of meals she had prepared, the endless loads of laundry she had done, the countless beds she had changed, and the many times she got up in the night to comfort and clean up a vomiting child.

During a quiet moment, a mom began to cry and said, "You kids can't fully appreciate what he is doing. I've been using a wheel for 20 years, and what I am seeing is incredible, if not impossible."

One of the students asked him what he thought was the most

pressing issue in our society. It appeared as a scripted moment. Acting as if he knew the question were coming, he responded, "Situation ethics. Sociocultural, family, and religious traditions are being eroded and replaced with the doctrine of 'If it feels good, do it.' It's a spiritual disease, but the farther people drift, the less they will be aware of that."

I had never heard the term, but some of the students had.

He went on to say, "Living is quite an intimate process. We are all breathing the same air and interact socially, which involves a great gift. We have the potential to appreciate or improve the value of each other."

My mind drifted away to the countless circles and papers where students had invited me into the intimate regions of their minds to share hopes, dreams, and aspirations. It took several visits to Sasha for me to realize that this is exactly what the students were doing: appreciating each other, and including me in the process. It was an awesome privilege.

During the 19 years of demonstrating and discussing pottery, only one vessel failed in his hands. He was working quickly, and the piece suddenly collapsed. I saw a flash of surprise, anger, and tad of embarrassment, but he recovered quickly. He gathered the clay, patted it into a ball, slammed it onto the wheel, and in moments, the clay was formed into a new shape. Sasha had probably thrown over 50,000 vessels, and unwillingly, perhaps serendipitously, he may have offered students the gift of seeing that even masters make mistakes.

Like the pygmy tour, the pottery demonstrations were always new and fresh. The stories, vessels, and metaphors varied. There was, however, one example that he preferred to end with, for reasons that will become obvious. He started with his normal process of throwing what would be a medium-sized pot. He carefully shaped it into a perfectly round ball with an opening at the top. Then he stopped the wheel to retrieve a flower that he had previously picked. We always visited in the spring, and often the native rhododendrons were in bloom. They have a very large, showy, pink flower that attracts many tourists each year. He placed the flower inside the ball, turned the wheel on, and sealed it closed. He probably did not need to explain, but he did.

He said, "Everyone has something beautiful inside of him, or her, that is unique in the entire universe. There may be times when society, family members, or even friends may mistreat you, but they can not harm that inner beauty that is yours."

Then he switched off the wheel to allow the students a few quiet moments to absorb.

Sometimes in the fall when Christie was preparing the student journals, she included thoughts from our favorite authors. Some years included this idea from J. Woolman:

> "There is a principle which is pure, and placed
> In the human mind, which in different places
> and ages has had different names. It is, however,
> pure and proceeds from God. It is deep and inward,
> confined to no forms of religion, nor excluded from any,
> where the heart stands in perfect sincerity."

The campfires that followed Sasha's presentations were usually alive with reflections of his artistry and wisdom. The "situation ethics" idea got a lot of attention. One year as students were sharing, a young man began to cry. His parents had divorced when he was two years old. His father moved to a nearby town and remarried. He was now 18 years old and lamented that he had not heard a word from his dad.

"Not even a single birthday card," he said.

Typically, on the last night at Mendocino, we held a "birthday" celebration for all of us. One of our recurring themes was, "Every day is a 'birth' day for the creative mind." There was a wonderful old meeting hall that smelled of thousand-year-old cedar and allowed the preparation of what would be the last dinner we would share as a class. Interestingly, the guys often volunteered to do the cooking honors and did a great job.

No birthday would be complete without gifts, even if only token. Each class member and chaperone received a hand-crafted pottery mug from Sasha, with the year and class logo imprinted in the clay. I have a complete set of 19 mugs on a cup rack on my office wall, which is among my most cherished possessions.

"My soul preached to me and showed me
That I am neither more than a pygmy,
Nor less than a giant …
But now I have learned that I was as both are
And made from the same elements. My origin
Is their origin, my conscience is their conscience …
My pilgrimage is their pilgrimage …"

Kahlil Gibran

21: The Land of Pygmies and Giants

NO WONDERLAND WOULD be complete without pygmies and giants, and Mendocino did not disappoint. It may be the only place on
our planet that features pygmies and giants in both plant and animal
kingdoms. There is still at least one remaining sequoia sempervirens
that towers over 350 feet tall, has a diameter of over 24 feet, and is
over 2,000 years old. The record number of board feet harvested from
a single redwood tree was nearly 500,000, or enough to build over 20
modest homes. Although the present trees bordering the pygmy are
only 150 feet tall, they stand in sharp contrast to the nearby pygmy
cypresses that can be adult at six inches tall, less than an inch in diameter, and are rarely more than 150 years old. The redwoods have
either marched up to the pygmy and stopped or visa versa. Seeing the

drastic difference in plant variation often triggered a flashback to an Eiseley soliloquy about a wisteria pod that exploded one night, strewing shiny seeds all over his living room:

> "A plant, a fixed, rooted thing, immobilized in a single spot, had devised a way of propelling its offspring across open space. Immediately there passed before my eyes the million airy troopers of the milkweed pod and the clutching hooks of the sandburs. Seeds on the coyote's tail, seeds on the hunter's coat, thistledown mounting on the wind—all were somehow triumphing over life's limitations."
>
> *The Immense Journey,* Loren Eiseley

A short distance from Russian Gulch State Park, our favorite campground, there was a grassy meadow covering the headland. We saw many tunnel openings of field mice, which average three inches in length and weigh two ounces. Looking west, out to sea, we imagined seeing a breaching Blue whale and sometimes I read:

> "A Blue whale can grow to 110 feet long; about the length of three tour buses.
> An adult can weigh nearly 150 tons; about as much as ten tour buses or
> as many as 3,000 people.
> Its tongue can be ten feet thick, or heavier than an elephant.
> Its heart can be the size of a small automobile.
> Males can have seven-gallon-sized testicles.
> It can ingest four tons of food per day.
> It can have as many living cells within its body
> as there are people in the world.
> A calf can be 20 feet long and consume 50 gallons of milk each day."

The students had studied the evolution of the seed-bearing plants and learned that the gymnosperms began replacing the fern forests about 300 million years ago. The flowering plants, not unlike "Matthew's whales," arrived quite recently, in geological terms. In both cases, they were able to see that plants and animals had undergone tremendous change. This supported Darwin and Mendel's work that proved that independent assortment led to natural variation; which led to biodiversity, which is a key factor in evolution. It was not surprising that the thoughts along these lines harkened back to our discussion about human evolution.

Eiseley discussed the possible origin and several possible pathways of human growth and migration. He did not, however, include the Batwa and Masai tribes of Africa, which we added later, and became a magical connection to Mendocino. The average height of Batwa males is less than five feet. The Masai tribesmen, living several hundred miles away, average over six feet. Some of the redwood trees are over 2,500 years old, and the Batwa tribes may date back 60,000 years. The redwood trees cannot live in "pygmy" soil, and pygmy trees cannot grow in the "redwood" soil. Similarly, both African tribes have adapted so keenly to their habitat that swapping cultures would likely result in the ruination of both. If being tall is a selective advantage for living on the plains, and being short is a selective advantage for living in the forest, neither tribe would have enough time to genetically adapt. The law of natural variation has contributed to the survival of each tribe. Although this may be stunning, with pygmies and giants, it is not unique. The genetics of every living thing on the planet has to match its habitat, or it dies.

Henry Thoreau is often regarded a literary giant because of observations and reflections engendered while living at Walden Pond. It is intriguing, however, that it is rarely noted that his noble attempt to reverse cultural evolution and become biologically self-reliant was a failure. He is not alone. It is probable that fewer than 5 percent of the 300 million Americans living today could survive without the current industrial/agriculture infrastructure.

Native Alaskans living near the Arctic Circle have a layer of high-density brown fat to insulate them from the frigid climate. Bedouin nomads in the Middle East have no brown fat and very little white fat. Switching both cultures would likely be lethal. There are examples of this in every species, race, and even some ethnic groups. Black people rarely develop skin cancer but are susceptible to sickle-cell anemia. White people rarely develop sickle-cell anemia, but are more susceptible to skin cancer. Ethnic groups like the Masai and Batwa have adapted to their specific habitat. At the species level, this means that there is no such thing as biological equality, only variety. Just as every snowflake is unique; every human is unique. Even identical twins are not identical, because they began influencing each other in the womb. All of this led back to my days coaching track, which produced two lasting experiences. One created the joyful surprise that happened in the Grand Canyon, and the other provided me with years of grief.

In the late 1960s, the 440-yard relay team that I was coaching qualified for the California state track meet. We traveled to Los Angeles for the competition and qualified for the semifinal race. Twelve teams entered, we finished eleventh, with one team being disqualified. We had the dubious honor of being the fastest "all-white" team in the state. Our guys were not bitter or envious, but proud of what they had accomplished. They even joked about being "smoked," and regarded their competitors with great respect. They felt that black sprinters were in a different league than white athletes. This would later be supported by the fact that the last white sprinter to represent the United States Olympic Track Team was 50 years ago, which is when black athletes were first recruited to compete at the college level. Since then, over 90 percent of the Olympic medals in track and field events have been won by black athletes, even though they represent only 13 percent of the United States population.

Based on my biological work, this all seemed quite logical; however, it was neither logical nor tolerable for others. Whenever stories and examples like this were used, I received grief from colleagues, administrators, even family and friends, who thought that

I was a racist, bigot, or an insensitive, white, male chauvinist. This was disturbing and confusing, and so I began to explore the origin of the conflicting viewpoints. Whenever I chanted my mantra, "there's no such thing as biological equality," I could expect to get flack from one of three sources.

The first group was defending the honor of two American political giants, and it involved five simple words. Thomas Jefferson used them in the Declaration of Independence, and Abraham Lincoln used them is his Gettysburg Address: "All Men Are Created Equal." If Uncle Thomas and Honest Abe said this, it must be so. So where does a lowly biology teacher get off by saying something different? I tried to explain that these men were speaking in a political context, which I vigorously supported; however, the biological model was quite the opposite.

The next group was the secular progressives who stated that it was intellectually corrupt to suggest that gender, race, and ethnicity were not entirely equal. This was neither new nor surprising. In the '60s, "progressive" kindergarten teachers were determined to rid society of male-imposed stereotypes. It was the "unisex" age, and little boys were required to play with dolls, and little girls were required to play with trucks. When many of these (mostly female) teachers had little boys of their own, they laughed at their own folly. Evidently, little boys came prewired to play with trucks and little girls with dolls.

Today, progressives will watch National Basketball Association basketball teams which, in many cases, are 90 percent black, and tell you in forceful terms that blacks do not have special talents. What is biologically disturbing about this is that black athletes cannot celebrate their gifted talent lest they be labeled as racist. When one of professional basketball's greatest white players said, "White men can't jump," he was branded as a racist, but not by basketball players. His black teammates laughed. When one of professional golf's greatest female golfers commented that the best women golfers were not equal to the best men, many feminists were furious with her.

It is common knowledge to most marriage counselors that the

truly dynamic marriages are those that identify and celebrate male and female differences as well as their commonality. Modern research shows that male and female brains are far more different in structure and function than was previously known. After reviewing Dr. Louann Brizendine's two books, *The Male Brain* and *The Female Brain*, it appears that males and females are very different animals. When two closely related species mate, a phenomenon known as hybrid vigor occurs. When male and female humans mate, there is a similar shuffling of genes which enhances diversity. Males have a Y chromosome that actually makes them a different animal than females. Or if you prefer, females have two X chromosomes, making them different than males. They are not biological equals.

My critics obviously did not know or understand that without biodiversity, the human race, and all of life, would have died out millions of years ago. Without diversity, we would have never known Einstein, Da Vinci, or you, or me. Following the origin of the universe, the origin of life, the origin of the human brain, skeptics of biodiversity became the fourth group of people that I perceived as rejecting the very process that brought them to the level where they could contemplate the process. O'Henry would love the irony.

But the third group would prove to be the most delicate, challenging, and confusing. The Christian fundamentalist students often respectfully disagreed with my premise, because they thought that they were made in the image of God. If God were perfect and all loving, he would certainly not make people unequal. I found this argument compelling, haunting, and paradoxical. When this discussion came up, I would usually say that people far more intelligent than I have suggested that God can carry on 5,000,000,000 conversations simultaneously. If this is so, and I am only one voice, how much do you think I understand about creation?

I would usually say that unless I am dreaming, we are having a discussion that seems to suggest that we have consciousness and free will. If this is true, then it will be your privilege and responsibility to figure these mysteries out. It was not my intention to recruit for any religion, nor did I want to discourage or interfere with any student's personal experience. As a father of four beautiful kids, I knew that it was impossible to treat them equally; yet, I did everything I could to treat them fairly. Their individual personalities, pecking order, and thousands of uncontrollable variables made this the second-greatest challenge of my life; every husband will know what the first was. It was also the greatest challenge to me as a biology teacher.

Personally or professionally, I had no problem if the best black athletes could run faster and jump higher than the best white athletes. I thought brown fat in Native Alaskans was ingenious. They have survived thousands of years while others died out. Would I expect a Batwa athlete to compete on a professional basketball team for the sake of political correctness? Should I request that the ACLU sue NOW for gender discrimination because I could not get pregnant? Should white sprinters sue the AAU for athletic discrimination every time they lose a race to a black athlete? Just like switching the Batwa and the Masai tribes would kill them, biological equality would make us all clones and modern man would die out very quickly. I would gently ask them why we didn't celebrate who we are and the gifts we have, rather than complain about who we are not and our often, self-imposed limitations.

As a biology teacher, I welcomed the chance to acknowledge Dr. Martin Luther King's birthday. It was a wonderful opportunity to celebrate the courage, wisdom, and color that he added to our society. The sorrow of his death was felt worldwide and remains today. Not only his life, but his work and legacy were prematurely shortened. I don't know what he would think today; however, I hope that we are approaching the day when children can walk hand in hand and joyfully celebrate their biological gifts of race, gender, and ethnicity. It would be biologically, if not politically, correct. When I shared this thought with students, they agreed. As for mystery, who could have guessed that a field trip to Mendocino and a chance encounter with pygmies and giants could have helped launch a 24-year magical odyssey, either back to the Garden of Eden or a wild goose chase?

"Nature is a sea of forms …
A leaf,
A sunbeam,
A landscape,
The ocean,
What is common to them all
Is beauty."

Emerson

22: Newton in the Tide Pools

ALTHOUGH EACH MENDOCINO trip had a similar itinerary, each was a unique adventure. The millions of environmental and human variables made it impossible to guess, let alone predict, the outcome. Each trip was like a five-day treasure hunt with students wandering into Mother Nature and wondering what she had in store for them. They were like a pack of curious puppies, running around sniffing the landscape, seeking information that they could record in their journals, minds, or souls. A question, observation, or reflection could direct or redirect the course of the adventure.

This was the case one year when I casually made a remark that triggered a discussion about one of the most mysterious, yet subtle, forces of nature. We are surrounded by it daily, could not live without it, and yet, we rarely give it any thought. In over 30 years of visiting the north coast, I had never seen the water totally placid. Whether the surf was gentle or raging, its noise was considered an inseparable component. On one of the trips, Mother Nature had a surprise for us. As the class hiked out to the tide pools for their explorations, the Pacific Ocean truly lived up to its name. It was absolutely placid. It would have been a yachtsman's nightmare. The quiet was so complete that an eerie pall was cast over the area. Even the birds seemed to be spooked and refused to fly.

One of the kids remarked, "This is really creepy. They say it's always calm before a storm. Should we be worried about a tsunami or something?"

I assured her that park rangers would have notified us if that were so, but I found myself looking out to sea more often than usual. Two years earlier, we had to evacuate our camp area for three hours due to a tsunami alert. It gave us pause to think because our campsite was located a mere 50 yards from the beach and only five feet above the highest high-tide mark.

We completed our observations and were hiking up the headland trail when I remembered that a friend of mine said that in a body of water as small as one acre, at eye-level, you could see the curvature of the Earth.

I mentioned that to the four or five guys I was hiking with, and they said, "Let's go have a look." I grumbled something about having to get back to camp before I turned around to join them. When we got down to the water, we all knelt, raised butts in the air, and got a single eye as close to sea level as possible. What happened next was comical. There was a collective, "Oh my God!"

One of them blurted out, "That's the most beautiful curve on planet Earth!"

Another one said, "Well, maybe the second-most beautiful."

We all laughed and didn't need to be reminded that they were 17-year-old males.

Earlier, we had grabbed a quick bowl of cereal in order to catch the low tide. The plan was for the breakfast and lunch crews to combine and prepare a brunch that would sustain the group until dinner time. When we arrived back at camp, the combined crew was busily preparing the meal. The guys were intrigued with what they had seen and wanted to continue the discussion.

One of them said, "This is what I don't get. We are not that smart, and we don't live close to the ocean, but certainly someone must have known that the Earth was round before Columbus."

I responded, "They did, at least in theory, but they had the same problem that we still have today. There is ample evidence that for thousands of years indigenous tribes assumed that the earth was round, and nearly 2,000 years ago, Eratosthenes, the Greek philosopher, developed the first-known mathematical model to prove it. Sailors noticed boats traveling away from them, dipped below the horizon, while boats sailing toward them appeared from below the horizon. This phenomenon was even witnessed from shore. Many didn't think that the Earth was flat, but they did think that if they traveled too far down the arc, they would either fall off or not be able to sail back 'uphill' and be lost at sea."

I admitted my bias by suggesting that I had long felt that Columbus got far more credit than he deserved. He did not discover North America. By 1492, nearly 1,000 tribes had evolved and spread from the Arctic Circle to Mexico, and many had been living there for over 10,000 years. He was courageous enough to push the limits of knowledge, but the risk was neither entirely foolish, nor uncalculated. He must have reasoned that as long as they had water to sail on, they would be all right. In order for him to fall off, the water would have to have fallen off as well and drained the sea. By then, there were mathematicians that calculated that the Earth was round and would possibly enable a quicker route to the Spice Islands. He did prove empirically what Newton would prove mathematically 200 years later; gravity was responsible for holding his boats and seawater in place.

"So let's do a simple Newtonian experiment," I said.

I stepped over to the cupboard and grabbed four cups, filled them with water, and handed one to each student. "Three of you are going on a very quick trip around the Earth," I said, "so hold your cups against your chest so that no water spills." I pointed to David and said, "Alpha Newton, report your current position, attitude, and water level."

David responded smartly. "Current position is home base, attitude is vertical, and water level is full."

I continued and pointed to Vince and said, "Beta Newton, transport yourself immediately 90 degrees due west and report your position, attitude, and water level."

Vince followed David's cue and barked out, "Current position is 90 degrees due west, attitude is 90 degrees or perpendicular to home base, water level remains full."

I pointed to Stephen and said, "Gamma Newton, transport to 180 degrees due west and report your position, attitude, and water level."

Stephen responded quickly, "Position is180 degrees due west, attitude is totally inverted from home base, and water level remains full."

Kurt was either impatient or overly eager and grinned widely and said, "Delta Newton reporting; my position is 270 degrees due west, attitude is 90 degrees or perpendicular to home base, and water level remains full."

One of them said, "This is causing a warp in my brain."

I laughed and said, "A common side effect of probing mysteries is a healthy brain cramp. Newton once said, 'I have explained how gravity behaved, not what it is.' We still don't know what the 'power' in the power of gravity is. How can a force be gentle enough to not crush us and strong enough to keep our feet on the ceiling of the Earth? Einstein admitted that his famous formula described some of the relationships of matter/energy, but it did not explain where it came from or how electrons could orbit a nucleus 'forever.' Furthermore, I have been told that to believe in The Big Bang Theory, we have to allow for space to be warped. I have no idea of how space, which is nothing, can be warped.

I think there is something other than space that is warped, and so, you are in good company." We all enjoyed a hearty laugh.

While preparing this manuscript, I started to share the "cup" story with Heather's dad, Tom, a retired game warden. He abruptly interrupted me by shouting, "Stop! I don't want to go there. I know that people in Australia are not walking around upside down any more than we are walking upside down, so what are we supposed to think? It keeps me awake at night if I think about it, so I just don't." He didn't think it was a bit funny and was perturbed that I brought the subject up.

Since its origin, the economy of Mendocino has been driven by the timber and fishing industries. For over 100 years, the stands of Douglas fir and redwoods were logged to build San Francisco and the Greater Bay Area. By the 1980s, most of the original forests had been logged and the lumber industry was in a steep decline. The fishing industry was also suffering due to overfishing and habitat degradation, largely caused by poor logging practices. A few cattle, sheep, and dairy farms were widely scattered through the county but were not a major economic factor. Tourism flourished and became the main source of revenue generation. Vineyards would be greatly expanded in the 1990s, but meanwhile, there was an exotic crop that was secretly, or not so secretly, being cultivated. It had many names including Whacky Tobacky and Mendocino Gold. The students were well aware of this crop, and even suggested, during the planning stages, that in order to get a "full feel" of the land, we should visit a pot farm. I assumed that they were not referring to Sasha's place.

The brunch crew was mostly girls and during our brainstorm session, I had the distinct feeling that some of them thought that we had lagged behind the group and sampled some of the local botanical bounty.

Robert Frost suggested that poetry often begins in delight and ends in wisdom. Later, while sitting on a rock contemplating the ocean and our lively discussion, I penned a poem that started on a whim and ended with delight.

Newton's Holy Grail

While sitting one day, deep in thought
Beneath green branches finely wrought,
An apple chanced to bonk him on the bean;
Immediately across his mind,
Danced visions of the science kind,
Revealing things that man had never seen;
With tenacity and telescope,
He stretched the science envelope
And probed the cosmic mystery of time;
Optical, mathematical,
His God was problematical,
Creating things that
Truly were sublime.

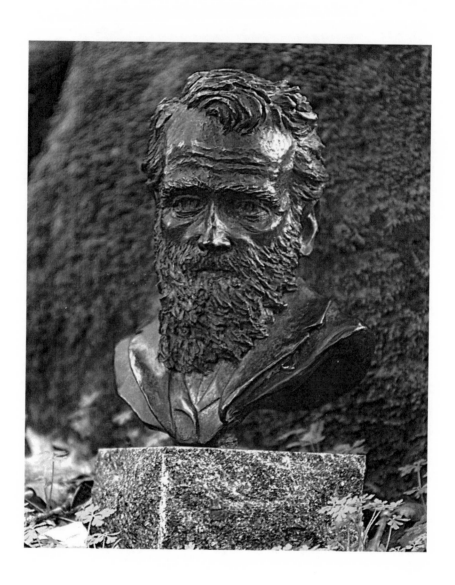

"Tis the gift to be simple, tis the gift to be free,
Tis the gift to come down where we ought to be,
And when we find ourselves in the place just right,
Twill be in the valley of love and delight."

Elder Joseph Brackett

23: Simple Gifts

MAMMARY GLANDS ARE not only essential for human survival, they are richly symbolic of the precious mental and spiritual nourishment that flows from mother to offspring. Perhaps this is related to one of the deepest human callings, which is to appreciate (improve the value of) our fellow man. This ancient phenomenon is evinced by bestowing physical, mental, and spiritual gifts to family or tribal members. More often than not, the lines that defined giving and receiving between Biodesign students, chaperones, and the teacher mystically morphed into circles whereby we all were "appreciated."

Peter:

We had just turned right off of U.S. 101 onto State Highway 1, heading for the village of Mendocino, when a voice bellowed from the backseat, "I give up! I give up, I tell you!"

I looked over at Christie, and she returned my quizzical inquiry.

He continued, "You Californians have it all. You have mountain ranges with peaks of 14,000 feet. You have the tallest, widest, oldest trees on Earth. You have the rugged north coast and the warm beaches of the south. You have the high and low deserts as well as Death Valley. You have nearly 250 reserves, wildlife sanctuaries and parks, including Redwood, Yosemite, and Sequoia/King's Canyon National Parks. And now, you are taking me to a pygmy forest. When I shop at Safeway, I feel like I am shopping at the Garden of Eden Grocery Store. In the UK, we have 13 parks, Ben Nevis is only 4,000 feet, and we can drive to its top. Now do you see why I have given up?"

Peter had worked himself into a lather, and Christie and I were dumbfounded. Neither one of us was familiar with much of what he was referring to. Peter was a proud Londoner who was on his second extended trip to California. He had visited many of the places that he had referenced and wanted to see a grove of virgin redwood trees, so I volunteered to be his driver. He described his solitary walk among the giant trees as one of the most sacred walks in his life. To think that they were nearly all destroyed was a sobering thought.

When John Muir founded the Sierra Club, one of the first tasks was to try to save the redwoods. His critics labeled him an ignorant tramp or sheepherder with no knowledge of the forests. Only a fool, they said, would suggest that all the redwoods could be harvested. Muir died in 1914, and the forests were being heavily logged. After World War II, a meaner, leaner, lighter chainsaw was developed, and the logging became frenetic. Only 3 percent of the original redwood forest is left, and nearly all of that is protected in parks or preserves.

Many years earlier, Christie and I spent a month with Peter in England. We marveled at the history, architecture, and deep traditions of the country. Walking through Westminster Abbey, alone, was like walking through a graveyard of Who's Who of many of the world's greatest people.

We traveled to Scotland, where we visited the birthplace of John Muir. His home includes a tiny museum which is visited by more tourists than native Scots. When we returned to London, however, a bit of tourist tension arose. Peter knew that I was a biology teacher and was eager for me to see the rugged Scottish highlands. I wasn't aware of it at the time, but the biodiversity of California had spoiled me. I found the highlands monotonous and reminiscent of our chaparral forest, which was reasonable because they are both dominated by members of the heath family. About the only value I saw in the chaparral was for deer hunting, which I had long ago given up. Peter knew me well enough to sense that I was pretending to wax eloquent in describing scenery that I found lacking, and his British pride was punctured.

I had forgotten about the little tiff until his outburst from the backseat. He was overwhelmed by the flora of a state that was not only fantastically diverse but included over 700 endemic species. That night, lying in bed in our Mendocino motel, listening to the lonely moan of the foghorn, I heard Peter's voice say, "You've got it all!" I didn't know whether to feel proud, joyful, or embarrassed.

Peter's friendship was not only a gift, he unknowingly revealed how blessed the Biodesign class was. We were allowed to ascend a granite stairway and stand at the doorway of the universe. We were able to descend into the fathomless abyss of time, and life, and change. We were able to walk through a modern Garden of Eden and contemplate life on the edge of Newton's vast ocean of truth. These events stretched our minds higher, deeper, and wider, and all happened simply because we were at the right place at the right time. It was a very strange, yet very wonderful, celebration of synchronicity.

Rob:

In the fall of '84, a father of one of the Biodesign students looked over the shoulder of his son at some of the required reading material. He decided to read *The Wilderness World of John Muir*. He was not only captivated by Muir's biological descriptions, but also his stories, wisdom, and message. Rob is a dentist by profession, but also a highly talented sculptor and painter. For reasons known only to him, as he read, he began to sculpt a clay bust of Muir. The final rendition featured a youngish Muir with piercing eyes and a windswept beard. He took the bust to a foundry and had four copies cast in bronze. Each finished bust was mounted on a chunk of black sierra granite and looked absolutely stunning.

I was aware of none of this until June of '85 when Rob and the class presented me with one of the copies as a gift. Muir sits on my desk and supervises every word I write. I must have read his words a thousand times: "These hollow words rattle in my teeth and refuse to communicate the beauty of the mountains ..." Not in my wildest dreams would I have guessed that I would follow in his footsteps so closely, that I would attempt the equally impossible task of trying to describe some of glory that he and Yosemite had inspired within me.

Two years later, Rob's daughter enrolled in the class, and he accompanied us to the Grand Canyon. Both he and Kirsten were properly baffled by the journey back 1.8 billion years in time. After she graduated, she and her dad made a pilgrimage to the east coast of Scotland. They presented the second bust to the people tending the tiny museum in Dunbar, and it was warmly received. After nearly 150 years of wandering around the world, John Muir was returned to his place of birth. Few, if any, of the local visitors or tourists would be able to comprehend the magnitude of his contribution to humanity. This self-described tramp wandered west to Yosemite, climbed its mountains, and came down with thoughts and visions that have moved the world. There are currently nearly 400 United States national parks, monuments, and reserves that are managed by the National Park System that he inspired. States also have answered his call and the total number of state parks is nearly 4,000. His message spread globally and has been a beacon for other countries to follow. The term *ecotourism* would not be coined until 100 years after he envisioned it. Muir's life and legacy annually influence millions of scientists, naturalists, teachers, students, campers, hikers, and tourists. He has been dead nearly 100 years, and yet, his message is more urgent today than when he was alive.

> "No synonym for God is so perfect as beauty.
> Whether as seen carving the lines of the mountains
> with glaciers, or gathering matter into stars,
> or planning the movements of water, or gardening—
> still all beauty."

Paul:

Only the families of teachers can understand the depth of fatigue that teachers often sustain. Classrooms are highly demanding, high-adrenaline battle zones that sap teacher energy. It is for this reason that I was part of a very small group of Scrooges who were not excited about the creation of *Sesame Street*. As my kids watched the ultracreative program, I ached for the kindergarten teachers who would no doubt be hearing the three most dreadful words teachers can hear: "This is boring." Shortly after *Sesame Street* began, I saw somewhere that the Children's Television Network was paying $100,000 per episode in production costs. I imagined thousands of teachers struggling to match the lighting, props, and costumes while emulating Ernie, Bert, and Big Bird.

I have long suspected that Eden isn't really a place but a spiritual state where rock stars and monks can blissfully coexist. The Grand Canyon offered thousands of these sacred places, and Native Americans know many of them well. They were totally antithetic to the noise, stress, and demands of the classroom. When conditions were right, there could be several on the Bright Angel Trail above the sound of the Colorado River and below the rim of the inner gorge. When I found one, I would stop and absorb the silence. A boot that I had not heard squeak suddenly sounded like a loud stair squeak. A squeaky clevis pin on my backpack sounded like a rusty gate opening. The blood rushing through my ears became audible and a little spooky. This happened when no air moved, no insect buzzed, no bird chirped; it was the silence of death. Ironically, as in many close encounters with death, life often takes on a deeper, richer meaning. I was humbled to think that Helen Keller and perhaps millions of others would spend their entire lives in tomblike silence. I would usually wonder what a week of utter silence would feel like before an inner bell would ring and remind me of the students ahead on the trail and the schedule we had to keep.

On such an occasion, I began to press on up the trail. Several switchbacks ahead, I encountered Paul, who had discovered his own silent vacuum. I stopped abruptly, hoping that neither boot nor backpack would squeak and disturb his reverie. It occurred to me that I was only seeing his body; his mind and spirit were somewhere on errands of their own. I waited quietly until he was back together and we could both proceed. While I waited, I remembered the riddle, "If a tree falls in the forest"; there is no sound without an arresting ear. However, the converse is also true. If there is no wave energy vibrating tympanic membranes, there is also no sound.

Perhaps our spirits met because, after a brief interlude, he turned and greeted me warmly with a smile. Without discussing it, we began a natural peripatetic exercise. I quickly discovered that Paul was bright and witty; I was methodic and pragmatic. He was sociopolitically liberal; I was more conservative. He was highly literate; I read mostly science stuff. Above the rim, this may not have been a good match; in the canyon, it didn't matter. In fact, what happened was a mystical union of what the Greeks called *philos*. It was an instant case of brotherly love that is, sadly, often lacking in siblings. By some cosmic convergence, two men were given the rare opportunity to walk and talk in holy communion and share their hopes, dreams, and visions of the world.

Quoting C. S. Lewis, Paul suggested that hiking down into the Grand Canyon was not unlike going through the door in the wardrobe of *The Lion, the Witch, and the Wardrobe*. I laughed and indicated that *The Chronicles of Narnia* were about my intellectual limit. Paul laughed. I mentioned that I enjoyed the *Screwtape Letters*, but had trouble sorting out who was God and who was the devil. As for his heavier works, like *The Great Divorce* and *Mere Christianity*, they were beyond my reach. Then I remembered one exception and connected it to Henry Thoreau, who wrote:

"Man can not afford to be a naturalist,
to look at Nature directly, but only
with the side of his eye. He must
look through and beyond her."

I recalled being deeply moved by Lewis's small but powerful book, *A Grief Observed*. Lewis thought that he would be a lifetime, confirmed bachelor before he met Joy. In her, he discovered a true soul mate, and they were married. The marriage lasted a brief three years and her death, understandably devastating, shook him badly. He was, however, a thinker and proceeded to process the elements of the tragedy. I mentioned to Paul that I didn't recall that Lewis stated a quantity, but he left me with the impression that Joy's death helped him realize that 98 percent of what he thought was important was really only fluff. The remaining 2 percent, which constitutes the pure essence of life, which was openly before him every day, he had ignored as worthless. I don't recall if Paul had read the book or not. It didn't matter.

His eyes widened, and he nodded in agreement. He continued, "I think he was right, but bringing these kids to the Grand Canyon certainly has to change those odds."

"Funny you should mention that," I said, "because each new year, I usually mentioned Lewis's premise to incoming students. They too would get wide-eyed and say, 'Mr. Young, will you show us that 2 percent?'"

I would laugh and tell them that, of course, I couldn't, but if Muir, Thoreau, and Eiseley were right, odds were good that they would discover some of it in Yosemite, the Grand Canyon, or Mendocino.

Magic on the Bright Angel Trail, like rainbows, was never predictable, and therefore, was always an exciting surprise. Somehow, five hours of what normally would have been difficult hiking passed with little effort. Paul and I frequently noted and were awed by the ever-expanding canyon views that enhanced our camaraderie. Appropriately, we lost track of time.

When Christie didn't make the trek to Phantom Ranch, she remained on the rim and took care of reassigning rooms and other logistical details. She would position herself at the trailhead at 1 p.m. in order to greet tired hikers and give them their new room assignments. The ever-devoted mate, she had to patiently wait, often in freezing weather, the three extra hours it took for me to bring up the rear.

As Paul and I reached the rim, she smiled and said, "You two look like you are having way too much fun for this stage of the hike."

Paul and I looked at each other and burst into laughter. Every hike out of the canyon was special. This one, however, seemed a little more so. He didn't particularly look like an angel; however, Paul contributed to what was truly a once-in-a-lifetime experience.

One of nature's most outlandish displays of mystery is demonstrated billions of time each year and goes mostly unnoticed and never fully understood. It involves the "common" caterpillar. Whether it spins a cocoon or secrets a chrysalis, what happens next is pure mystery. Essentially, the pupa dissolves itself into a sort of cellular/molecular soup. Molecule by molecule, cell by cell, all internal and external systems are reconfigured. A score of legs are reduced to six. Leaf-crunching mandibles are morphed into a tubular proboscis that will suck nectar. The lethargic "worm" is transformed into a feather-light gossamer that literally floats on the air.

Louis Pasteur noted that, "Chance favors the prepared mind." If this is so, the prepared mind that emerges from the Grand Canyon has a greater chance of experiencing a butterfly-like transformation.

Chip:

On a warm spring day after school hours, I was in the classroom grading exams. The door was open to allow for better air circulation. I heard the familiar whine of an electric-powered wheelchair approaching from the hallway. In a flash, a pang of panic surged through me. I instantly knew who it was and what he wanted. The chair motored into the room with its broadly smiling occupant.

Chip was a junior who was completing my beginning biology course. He was very bright, very curious, and was coping with a genetic form of muscular dystrophy. He had lost all of his appendage motor skills, except the ability to move his right hand and forearm. He was fiercely independent and managed to get through each day by manipulating a small joy stick with his thumb and index finger. Mike Snowden, the woodshop teacher, fashioned an adaptive table which allowed Chip to do his laboratory work, which included hours of looking into a microscope. Other students graciously helped him prepare the many necessary slides. He did a remarkable job, but that was not why he was visiting.

Chip spoke very economically, avoiding unnecessary words, and so he went straight to the point.

"Mr. Young," he said, "I would like to enroll in next year's Biodesign class."

I knew the statement was forthcoming, but there was no way to prepare for it. I was suddenly unable do or think anything. Chip thoughtfully read the panic in my face and allowed me the time to recover my senses. When I did, my heart was racing, and my mouth felt like it was filled with cotton. After a very anxious moment, I got my brain and mouth to respond. "Chip," I muttered, "you have seen one or more of the slide shows that chronicled the trips. I am guessing that 90 percent of the trip experience occurs on the hiking trails. I have no idea of how to solve that challenge."

I could not have known ahead of time, but I was about to undergo one of the greatest learning moments that I would ever experience.

Chip smiled warmly up at me and said,

> So you think I can't handle disappointment. I am physically challenged, but I am not dumb or naïve. Of course, I realize that the trips focus on the hikes, which

I will not be able to do. However, I have learned that 10 percent of something is 10 times greater than nothing. And who knows, maybe 10 percent for me will equal 90 percent for someone who can walk. Furthermore, I have done some research and found out that there are over 30 miles of wheelchair-accessible trails that Noah [his nurse/aide] and I could take. There are nightly campfires at Curry Village and daily guided walks and ranger/naturalist talks. Who knows (he laughed), I might learn more than you guys. I could participate in the first circle you are certain to have, attend the first campfire ceremony, and sleep in a tent.

Mr. Young, I promise I won't be a burden to you, and I am certainly not looking for sympathy. It's just that my doctor's prognosis is that I will probably not live much beyond 22 years. Watching the slide shows and listening to your stories made my heart jump for joy. I knew I was taking a big risk by coming here to ask for permission. However, I figured the worst that you could do was say no, and I could handle that.

Earlier classes taught me how to cry. Actually, they created many deeply touching moments that left me no other option. I was so utterly overwhelmed by Chip's courage, honesty, and wisdom that I nearly wept. I felt embarrassed, pathetically weak, and shameful. However, I sensed that if I fell apart, he would be embarrassed. It was a major battle between my left and right brain, but, I was somehow able to maintain some degree of composure.

Finally, I said, "Chip, I had to quit the high school baseball team because I could not hit a curveball. You threw a curve at me, and although it frightened me, you have given me a clue as how to handle it. You obviously have done your homework, and your plan is brilliant. I am certain the class will welcome you with open arms."

Chip graciously thanked me, hung a U-turn in his chair, and motored out of the room. As he left, I thought, "Of course, he knows more about C. S. Lewis's 2 percent than I do."

Chip had no way of knowing that the following year, sitting in a Yosemite meadow on a glorious autumn day, I would share part of an interview with Emmett Kelly, arguably the world's greatest clown.

> "What's the hardest thing in the world to be? I can tell
> you in one word: yourself.
> Especially if what you are is different from the crowd.
> But I'll guarantee this: If you can find the courage to
> be yourself, to be the person God intended you to be,
> you are going to come out all right."

I glanced over at Chip and saw the countenance of a young man that simply defied description. I could only hope that in his spirit world, for one ecstatic moment, he was freed from the gravitational bondage of his wheelchair. Adhering to his plan, he and Noah motored numerous miles of trails and attended ranger talks and evening campfire talks at Curry Village. The trip was even greater than he predicted. He and Noah cheered us off on our hike and welcomed us back to camp. He participated in three campfire meetings and the critically important, first and last circles.

The Grand Canyon trip had not evolved Chip's year, but he took a lightweight wheelchair along on the Mendocino trip. Noah and Chip's classmates pushed and carried him on a five-mile hike. They took him to the tide pools, beach, redwood forest, and Sasha the potter's studio.

The students had established a goal of excellence for their posttrip papers. Chip understood this, perhaps better than any student before or after him. His reflections of celebrating life, nature, and the importance of camaraderie were crystal clear and amazed us. Even so, he stunned us when he invoked John Muir:

On no subject are our ideas more warped and piti-
able than on death. Instead of sympathy, the friendly
union of life and death so apparent in Nature, we
are taught that death is an accident, a deplorable
punishment for the oldest sin, the archenemy of life,
etc. Town children, especially, are steeped in this
death-orthodoxy, for the natural beauties of death
are seldom seen or taught in towns ... But let the
children walk with Nature, let them see the beautiful blendings and communions of death and life,
their joyous inseparable unity, as taught in woods
and meadows, plains and mountains and streams
of our blessed star, and they will learn that death
is stingless indeed, and as beautiful as life, and the
grave has no victory, for it never fights. All is divine
harmony.

He continued, "I signed up for the class because I thought it
would be fun; I had no idea that it would help prepare me to face the
end of my life. Such great feelings of happiness, goodness, and love
have filled my heart and warmed my soul. John Denver's song, *Love
Is Everywhere*, was right on. Love was everywhere; in our classroom
circles; at Yosemite; at Mendocino. It was there in the cheers, tears,
laughter, hugs, songs, and metaphors. I saw it, heard it, touched it,
and felt it. You guys have not only helped me prepare for dying, you
have encouraged me to make every living minute count."

He thanked the class for including him and mentioned that along
the way, he gathered the strength and courage to enroll at the University of California at Berkeley.

The circle was emotionally drained, yet erupted with thunderous
applause as they gave him the only standing ovation in the history of
the class. Understandably, no one wanted to follow his presentation,
and so we quietly reviewed and tried to absorb some of his wonderful lines.

After Chip graduated, he moved to Berkeley and into an inde-pendent-living complex which offered assistance in mornings and evenings. He motored his chair up and down the hilly sidewalks of the campus to attend classes. Several times his chair slipped off of disability nonconforming curbs and dumped him. He was greatly ap-preciative to passersby who were both thoughtful and strong enough to right his chair and get him safely repositioned.

Chip's doctors were right. We read in the local paper that Chip died at the age of 22. A week or so later, when the phone rang, Christie yelled, "It's probably for you and if Chip's mom wants you to speak at the funeral, don't you dare tell her no!" It was an odd thing; for someone who made a living by talking in front of people, I was very uncomfortable speaking before nonstudent groups. Even so, it was a huge honor to share some of Chip's qualities, lessons, and reflections. The funeral was followed by a luncheon at the ranch where he lived. Many of his friends from "Cal" were driven 60 miles north to St. Helena. Many of them were in various states of decline, yet all possessed an amazingly optimistic attitude. Their conversa-tions were terse, pinpoint accurate, and revealed a Lewis-like sense of clarity, as if saying, "I may not have much more time, so let's focus on the 2 percent."

Lofty thoughts on top of Half Dome and deep thoughts in the Grand Canyon were as natural as breathing. Emerson was correct, and frequently, student minds and the extraordinary scenery were engaged in a fantastic dance. Sensations of euphoria were common, and even if they were transitory, they often led to the feeling that all was right with the universe, and they really would "all live happily ever after."

Coming down off of the mountain or up from the canyon, how-ever, meant that they had to reenter civilization with all of the physi-cal, mental, and spiritual diseases that Thoreau abhorred and warned about. The students were not alone in getting caught up in a state of natural wonder and awe; however, each would "crash" as he/she returned home. Did John Muir truly believe his words that if children walked with nature, "death would have no sting"? Did he not weep bitterly when his beloved Louie Wanda died before he did? Would he not have wept if one of his cherished daughters had predeceased him? Loren Eiseley discovered many joys and wonders of the natural world; he also warned about potential terrors that haunted human beings.

Along with the extraordinary gifts that we received, there were moments, even days or weeks, of nearly unbearable sorrow. Although Crystal Gayle's lyrics became a mantra, there were times when it was impossible to smile.

During the 24-year history of the class, five students sadly died in their early twenties. In every case, when the news arrived, unlike Job, I joined C. S. Lewis and waged a personal war against God. Terms like "the God of love," and, "What would Jesus do?" became irksome, even nauseating. I guessed at what Jesus "would" have done, and it was certainly not anything I could do. These kids were on the brink of heading into careers, marriage, family-life—their entire future and the assurance that they would live to 75 years were all prematurely lost. I joined the ranks of hardened nonbelievers and decided that no loving father would let his son or daughter die prematurely, so how could God allow this? At each of their funerals, I felt helpless, weak, and that my smug attitude that "there are no coincidences, and everything happens as it should" seemed cruel and pathetically inadequate. Like C. S. Lewis, I was driven to my knees in confusion and despair.

When each of the kids died, Christie and I felt devastated. I thought that talking (perhaps bragging) about no coincidences may have been a terrible mistake. On the other hand, each of their deaths shook me out of the spiritual fog of taking life for granted. Each of them was an irreplaceably precious gift. Their deaths did not make any sense. However, on a cosmic calendar, we will live here briefly, and I am guessing that we will discover later why Chip, Chrissy, Jessica, Stephen, and Jenny were all called home early.

Tim:

"It costs so little, I wonder why
We give it so little thought;
A smile, kind words, a glance, a touch—
What magic by them is wrought."

Anonymous

Simple gifts are often so common that we can miss them or take them for granted. Children are God's little messengers and arrive with an abundance of spirit, which parents, teachers, and society, unintentionally teach out of them. Sitting in a classroom for nearly six hours a day, even if interesting, often dampens enthusiasm (Greek origin meaning "filled with spirit"). Even so, spirituality is omnipresent and can be as subtle as a wink or as profound as sharing the pain of the death of a loved one.

I have long suspected that females have an inside track to spirituality. Recent studies of how they integrate their left and right cerebral hemispheres may hold the key. Females are often far better at identifying and interpreting love, compassion, joy, and sorrow, all of which influence our spiritual health. I am convinced that without Christie, I would have ended my life as a homeless drunk. The challenge, especially for males, is to identify and communicate spiritual experiences, which can be as difficult as chasing a rainbow or flying blind.

The problem lies partly in the fact that the word *spirit*, not unlike the word *God*, defies the restraining bondage that words demand. If loving and being loved is our greatest expression of spirituality, it is not surprising that symbols such as flowers, hearts, smiley faces, wedding rings, halos, and stars abound. However, just as words often have mysterious origins, signs and symbols often are also mysterious. I never cease to be intrigued by the people who developed the signs for sign language. Often their symbols are better than the words hearing-people use. Such is the case for the sign for the word *spirit*. I had to enlist the help of a signing expert to help me describe the sign, which seems ironic:

> Flex the left forearm into a 90-degree angle with palm up.
>
> Partially squeeze thumb and fingers into an open flower form.
>
> Touch the right hand index fingertip to thumb-tip forming a circle.
>
> Reach out with the right hand, dip thumb and finger-tip into the flower.
>
> Raise the right hand vertically, about 16 inches, in a wavy motion.

The symbol, of course, lacks words, but conjures up a message of rising smoke or a genie or spirit being released from a lamp or a flower. While many spirit signs and symbols evoke a verbal response, often the ones with the deepest meaning involve sublinguistic communication. Early in the class history, on top of Half Dome, Teresa, who had worked with deaf children, taught the class the universal sign for "I love you." The right hand is raised with the thumb, index, and little fingers extended, and the middle and ring fingers folded down. It could be easily flashed across a room, down a hallway, or out on the quad, and the kids used it frequently. Nearly every following class used the symbol freely. It was not used without consequences, however. Some thought we were flashing the sign of the devil. Several parents observed students using the symbol and wanted me fired.

There is a place on Bright Angel Trail, halfway between Indian Gardens and the South Rim, where a huge sandstone cliff forms a natural amphitheater. Hikers yelling, "Hello," enjoy a crystal clear "Hello" echo in response. In spirit terms, however, when the "hello" is offered, there is often a deafening silence.

This is in no small part the wonder of being human. Husbands and wives, families and friends, pastors and doctors, authors, poets, and nature can and must substitute for God and answer the call. It is also the joyful part of being a teacher with students who care, perhaps love, enough to answer that call.

We were in our last Biodesign circle prior to graduation. The students were presenting their final papers. Most of them have blurred over time; some remain timeless. Tim completed his paper with:

> Mr. Young, as you are well aware, I have been one of the most nonverbal students this year. I am naturally shy and was rarely able to properly communicate what I was thinking or feeling. I want you to know, however, that I have been quietly making mandorlas with you all year and that I am eager to go out into the world and see how many stumbling blocks I can remake into stepping-stones.

> My spirit soared.

"Is it not by his high superfluousness we know
Our God? For to equal a need
Is natural, animal, mineral: but to fling
Rainbows over the rain
And beauty above the moon, and secret rainbows
On the domes of deep sea-shells …"

Selected Poems, Robinson Jeffers

24: Synchronicity and God

I NEVER THOUGHT much about what God looked like; however, Michelangelo's rendition on the Sistine Chapel did not reflect a sense of humor. Even so, it dawned on me that in the classroom, on field trips, and in my personal life, I had encountered events that were illogical, often whimsical, and always unexplainable. I later discovered that Carl Jung had coined the term *synchronicity* to describe such events. It occurred to me that with all the woes of the world, surely God had more important things to do than to play tricks on people. Yet, I was left with events that left no other reasonable conclusion. My only regret was that I did not record most of them but instead, dismissed them as amusing but not important. Apparently, they happen all the time. However, like Newton's force of gravity, we don't understand them and simply take them for granted. For many years, I trivialized them with a shrug and question, "What are the odds?"

While researching the life of John Muir, I found a reference to a court battle that he was involved with regarding saving a wilderness area. One of his opponents testified that Muir had no particular talent and was merely at the right place at the right time. My first response was one of incredulity. On further review, however, I realized that in his ignorance, Muir's opponent was saying something profound. After all, had every cell that had ever lived on the planet not lived at the right place at the right time? Was every human, living or dead, not the result of a once-in-a-universe zygote, created by an "o-i-a-u" sperm and a "o-i-a-u" ovum? And finally, was the Earth, Solar System, Milky Way galaxy and the universe not existing at the right place and the right time? Was this not the ultimate of all synchronicities? My mind drifted back to the mythical mountaintop, only this time, the secular scientists were chanting, "We are not in the right place at the right time."

While visiting Yosemite, the Grand Canyon, and Mendocino, there was an obvious tendency to appreciate the latest views that were being offered and diminish the death, destruction, and upheaval that was necessary to create the respective masterpieces.

John Muir survived an avalanche ride and an earthquake that caused a rock slide that crushed 200 foot tall trees into matchsticks. He thought each was a grand adventure, heightened by the fact that he could have died. Perhaps this is the spirit of the African people who often deal with trials, trauma, and even death with a sense of equanimity or even magnanimity. I was unaware of this until I discovered Isak Denison's book *Out of Africa*, in which she described the phenomenon with the phrase, "God is playing with us." The African attitude that all trials or unknowable events are a sign that God was playing with them reflects courage, humility, and the wisdom that even death is part of life. Anthropologists generally agree that Africa is the birthplace of humanity; perhaps African people retain an ancient, intuitive awareness of the original game of divine hide-and-seek.

Many local elementary students were watching the space shuttle, Challenger, on its fateful return to Earth. They were shocked speechless as they tried to process the horror of the event. One of the teachers quickly turned off the television, handed out paper, and asked the students to write a short essay describing what they were feeling. A fourth-grade Mexican boy wrote one of the most profound lines that a human can write. "I am at war with God."

To understand the deep importance of religion to the Mexican culture is to understand that this young man was doing the unthinkable: challenging God, and perhaps risking a bolt-of-lightning response. He was, however, verbalizing a sentiment of what I suspect was, or will be, a feeling that every human, even those with the dimmest sense of spirituality, will utter at least once. Many of the billions of people who have been killed, maimed, or adversely affected by floods, fires, famine, earthquakes, hurricanes, tsunamis, avalanches, tornadoes, and the brutality of war must have wondered why. The Hindu religion deals with this tension with its triad of Brahma (the creator), Vishnu (the preserver), and Shiva (the destroyer). Some accounts suggest that Shiva enjoys raising hell in his (or her) destructive actions.

For those who believe in the symbolic, if not literal, interpretation of Genesis, God must have included humor as an integral facet of personhood. Some of our class discussions plumbed the depths of our humanity, while others erupted into laughter and hilarity. There was no way to know which way the wind would blow. Putting all these pieces together, I arrived at the antithesis of the Mexican boy's feeling and wondered if God had a sense of humor and enjoyed playing, perhaps toying, with us. To me, this was as problematic as declaring war on God.

Eric:

Eric's family moved to our area when he was in the fourth grade. They rented a house out in the country where Eric and his sister enjoyed exploring the nearby fields and woods. On one of their outings,

Eric spotted a bead that was half-buried in the dirt. Upon examination, it was actually only half of a bead. He took it home, washed off the dirt, and saw that it was brightly colored ceramic. Like all nine-year-old boys, he put the bead in the collectables drawer of his dresser. Several years later, his family moved into town and rented a townhouse, which included pool privileges in the community pool. During the summertime, Eric and his sister spent hours tossing coins into the pool and seeing who could retrieve the most. On one of his dives, he dove down and spotted a brightly colored bead at the bottom. Actually, it was only a half of bead. Before he reached the bottom, his heart began to pound. The half bead was retrieved, and he erupted from the pool like a trained dolphin at Sea World. Darting by his puzzled sister, he ran down the street, into the house, and tore upstairs, knowing that he would have to deal with his mother and the wet footprints later. When he yanked the dresser drawer open, his hands were trembling with fear and excitement. Pressing the two halves together produced a perfect match. The long-lost bead halves were reunited. Eric was baffled by the mystery. So was the class after he shared his story.

Laurie:

One of my funniest synchronicities involved a goddaughter and former student. Our favorite location to camp in Mendocino was Russian Gulch State Park. The group camp area was 50 yards from the beach and isolated from other campers. The tide pools were close-by, as was a prominent headland, which provided an excellent site for viewing sunsets. High school kids can be worldly, pseudosophisticated, even aloof, but all of our students forgot their pride and rejoiced in watching a "killer" sunset. "One touch of Nature and all men are kin" (Shakespeare).

The itineraries would vary, but a constant was to catch the sunset when possible before we snuggled around the campfire for the evening class. It was while were on the bluff one spring evening, waiting for the sun to set, that a most bizarre event occurred. I was sitting with my back up against a shore pine, mesmerized by the setting sun and ancient rhythm of the waves, when a human face appeared six inches away from mine. It startled me, but when I sensed no danger, I commenced to try to figure out whose face it was. It was as if I had contacted some remote Web site and the computer kept blinking, "still searching." When I finally figured out the face, it became a twilight-zone-moment. The face did not belong here but in the past. It seemed as if we were trapped in some kind of time warp. She knew I was struggling and giggled with delight. She finally backed off, sat down beside me, gave me an arm hug and acted as though nothing unusual had happened.

After Laurie graduated from my class, her parents moved away. She married and though we attended her wedding, we lost contact with her. Several years later, she and her husband decided to celebrate their anniversary in Mendocino. One evening, they were riding around and she wanted to show her husband where she had studied years ago. Her memory of the park name and location was sketchy, and they drove up and down the highway several times without locating the entrance.

Her husband was losing patience when she said, "Turn in here. Maybe this is it."

They turned off the highway and saw the park entry. Driving down the hill, they soon spotted our tent village. She remembered thinking, "Oh-my-gosh, oh-my-gosh, could they really be here?" When her assumption morphed into reality, she said, "I got so excited I almost wet my pants."

They parked quickly, and she grabbed her husband's arm, and they headed up the trail. She said that when she saw our group, she couldn't process what was happening and decided to pass her confusion along to me. She reintroduced me to her husband, and we all had a good laugh. I had no idea of how the class would react, but it proved to be interesting. The interlopers were not unwelcome, but they were not quite welcome either. The whole event seemed to be confusing them, and I could totally relate.

Rainbow Time:

When our children were little, a family friend gave us a large prism that created rainbows. Every sunny morning, the prism would do its magic in our dining room at a slightly different time and slightly different angle. It became a custom for the first family member to notice the event to announce, "It's rainbow time." One of our children's books of poetry included the poem from William Wordsworth:

> "My heart leaps up when I behold
> A rainbow in the sky:
> So it was when my life began;
> So it is now I am a man;
> So be it when I shall grow old,
> Or let me die!
> The child is father to the man;
> And I wish my days to be
> Bound each to each by natural piety."

When we started the Biodesign experiment, I had an army-surplus, four-drawer filing cabinet with one empty drawer. Twenty-four years later, the drawer was filled with hundreds of articles, quotes, and ideas, including many student contributions. This story is really their story.

When we started gathering designs from nature, the rainbow assumed a prominent position. It was colorful, magical, mysterious, ephemeral, and totally unpredictable. I got caught up in the spirit of the moment and cut a 30-inch rainbow out of plywood, painted it ROYGBIV, and hung it over the entrance to the biology lab. Students enjoyed entering and leaving the room under the colorful arch.

Sometime in the late '70s, we experienced rainbows on three or four consecutive field trips. It led to a prideful attitude on my part, evidenced by the fact that I announced to one incoming class that based on the recent history, we could expect to see a rainbow on the Yosemite trip. I soon forgot the prediction, but some students did not.

The Yosemite trip progressed nicely until the third day, when one of the students reminded me that we had not seen a rainbow. I suggested that it was still early. On the fourth day, a few more joined the doubters and enjoyed playfully heckling me. I stalled for time, dreading that I had boasted about something that I had no control over. The humbling thing about teaching is that when you make a mistake, there is no place to hide. The fifth and last full day at Yosemite arrived. The circle was held in the morning, followed by lunch, and then the students had a free afternoon. Previously, students had gone into Yosemite Village to shop or visit the Ansel Adams photo studio or the mountaineering shop. Sometimes they hiked or rode the shuttle buses to see more of the valley.

After lunch, this class elected to go out into the nearby meadow and play a game that was a blend of rugby and human destruction-derby. I watched for a few minutes, but when girls began launching their bodies into the scrum, I left. I had much to do, cleaning and storing all of the kitchen equipment in preparation for a morning departure. As I worked, I noticed the increasing cloud cover, but smiled confidently. We were not on the Dome or on the trail so it was of little concern. About 40 minutes later, however, I heard a bloodcurdling yell from the meadow.

Denise screamed, "Mr. Young, come quick!"

I pictured a broken arm or leg or maybe worse. Hurriedly, I dried my hands and raced up the trail toward the meadow. Denise met me halfway, grabbed my arm, and dragged me along. When we reached the meadow, no one was huddling over an injured student; instead, all were standing and staring skyward in total silence.

One of the most beautiful rainbows that I had ever seen arched across the sky, with Half Dome perfectly positioned below the arc. I joined the silence and was stunned and embarrassed at the same time. After a few minutes, one of the hecklers edged over and whispered, "OK, how'd you know?"

I shook my head in denial and said, "I didn't, and I won't make that mistake again."

It was not a "Noah-on-the-Ark" moment; however, an English teacher once said that there were no very unique experiences. Either the experience was unique, or it was not. I concluded that the same was true for miracles. Three hours earlier, in the final circle, the students unwrapped souvenir plaques that Christie and I had prepared for them. They were painted by a previous student and showed two Indian children standing in the snow, wearing little buffalo robes and moccasins. A brightly colored rainbow arched above them and ended on each of their shoulders. The inscription read:

> "May your moccasins make
> Happy tracks in many snows
> And the rainbow always
> Touch your shoulder."

The rainbow faded, and the students drifted quietly away, alone or in small groups. Whether cathartic or not, the humbling process followed by the spirit-gift left me physically lighter. I floated back to my KP duties feeling absolutely pampered.

"All things bright and beautiful,
All creatures great and small,
All things wise and wonderful,
The Lord God made them all."

Cecil Frances Alexander

25: Lessons from the Ark

ALTHOUGH ONTOGENY MAY recapitulate phylogeny, it tells us very little about what animals or plants know. An amoeba glides by under a microscope in a ghostlike body, lacking definitive form. Mysteriously, it oozes left or oozes right, sensing a food particle which it then ingests. After digestion, it simply leaves the waste behind. It reacts to warm and cold, light and darkness, toxic and healthy environments. Its ciliated relatives, paramecia, are capable of locating each other, coupling, and swapping reproductive material in a glorious act of having sex. Unicellular algae are often flagellated and swim freely. Strands of spirogyra are capable of locating each other and reproducing sexually. When students saw this under their microscope, their response was often, "Wow! Plants figured out how to have sex! How cool is that?" One rock group even named their band Spirogyra. A storm breaks a limb from a tree; the tree "senses" the damage, heals the wound, and eventually fills in the open space and restores its symmetry.

The quintessential question is, what do these forms of life know? An amusing clue may come from Walt Disney. Disney is credited with bringing cartoons to life, giving them animation which can be defined as filling them with spirit. Is it possible that the same Spirit that created the universe as we know it instilled spirit into every living cell? It is even more mind-boggling when we realize that the hundred trillion cells of our bodies are variations of our microscopic ancestors. Ciliated epithelial cells sweep the dust and grime from our airways. Phagocytes ooze their amoeba-like bodies throughout our bodies searching for dangerous, even life-threatening diseases, often sacrificing their lives in order to save us from attack. But it does not stop there. There is something that all the lesser creatures know that is carried with us today. It is the brotherhood of life, and as Eiseley mentioned, there is most likely something more beautiful than us waiting in the wings.

So Adam raised his middle finger to God and ate the apple. According to St. Paul, we are all prone to a similar weakness. Man emerged from the darkness of instinctive behavior, and the triad of values, consciousness, and free will was born. Like all words, however, these are man-made, anthropocentric, and can be elitist. There are vast areas of animal knowledge and behavior that are waiting to be explored. The worlds of instinct and learned behavior, from protozoa to primate, have barely been examined, and much of it was done, not to discover what animals knew, but how they could benefit man. It took the feminine brain of Jane Goodall to change that when she began to study chimpanzees, simply to discover what they knew. Unfortunately, with every new wave of technological discovery, there has been a corresponding growth of man's egoism, arrogance, and sense of entitlement at the expense of other forms of life, including his fellow human beings.

The Raven

I have long admired the storytelling skills of the aboriginal tribes. They lacked television and radio and often sat around campfires at night and told stories that were both instructive and entertaining. Many tribes possessed a rich sense of humor which likely evolved thousands of years before the Greeks formalized the dramatic styles of comedy and tragedy. They frequently used animals in their myths and legends to illuminate human frailties. Without a written record, it is impossible to verify the time of origin; however, there is little doubt that myths, like the following one, greatly predate the better known story of Icarus and Daedalus and St. Gomer's clang bird. This version came from a northern tribe that regarded the raven as a harbinger as well as a trickster.

A raven chose a mate, nested, and hatched two chicks. When it was time to teach them how to fly, the father noticed that one of them had one wing that was shorter than the other. Regardless of how hard the young raven tried to fly straight, he ended up flying in circles. The father warned him that his condition was potentially dangerous. Nevertheless, the young bird kept trying to fly higher and faster. One day he flew higher than he had ever flown and decided to go into a dive to feel the exhilaration. As he plummeted toward the earth, he flew in an ever-decreasing spiral at an ever-increasing speed. As he pulled up to avoid crashing, he flew up his own butthole.

Alaskan folklore

Grampa Harry's Chickens

How could I have guessed that one of my first known observations of animal behavior would occur when I was six or seven years old? My parents went away for an anniversary weekend and left me with my grandparents. My grandfather was retired and had constructed three large chicken sheds in order to sell eggs and supplement his small pension.

Early Saturday morning, I got up, eagerly dressed, and got ready to help him feed the chickens and gather the eggs. The sheds were 100 feet long, 12 feet wide, and the sides were covered with 4 x 8 foot sheets of plywood, nailed sideways along the eaves. This left the bottom open for ventilation. There were two rows of elevated cages with an aisle down the middle that ran the length of the shed. A water-drip line supplied each cage, as did a food trough that also ran the entire length. The floor of each cage was wire to allow the waste to drop through, and slanted at seven degrees to allow the eggs to gently roll away from the danger of the hen crushing them. There were approximately 100 birds per shed. It was efficiently, albeit not humanely, constructed. When we got to the first shed, Grandpa held up his hand and said to wait outside. I was crushed and ran into the house to share my sorrow with Gramma. She took my hand and marched me out to the shed. When Grandpa emerged from shed #1, Gramma said that he should take me with him. He glared at her, grabbed my hand roughly, and guided me to shed #2. He opened the door and slowly pushed me in. The chickens nearest to the door immediately began squawking and flapping their wings wildly. Their panic spread and in moments, the entire shed was in a state of pandemonium. Feathers and dust filled the air, and the noise was deafening. I wheeled around and hurried out the door.

Grandpa looked at Gramma and growled, "Our egg production will be off by 50 percent tomorrow."

Although humans did not evolve along the line that chickens did, we still share some basic instincts of fear of the unknown. Over the years, I have observed people, including me, react in the same way. New ideas are often scary or foreign and difficult to understand, much less accept. The Biodesign experiment generated a lot of flapping-chicken responses with noise, dust, and ruffled feathers.

Sasha's Ducks

For nearly 20 years Sasha shared his wisdom and skills with the class. This is one of his stories.

A local farmer had a pair of migratory mallard ducks build a nest on his farm. About halfway through the incubation period, the man noticed a pile of feathers that indicated that one or both parents met an untimely end. He didn't want the eggs to spoil, and so he gathered them in a towel and drove them to a neighboring farm. His neighbor had chickens, and the farmer was hoping that one of the hens would adopt the eggs and complete the incubation process. He was in luck as there was an old mother hen who welcomed the chance to raise another clutch of eggs. After the ducklings hatched, she proudly led them around the barnyard, enabling them to find grubs, worms, and bugs. On one of their outings, however, the hen led the ducklings down to a small irrigation pond. Responding to an instinctive urge, the ducklings made a beeline for the water. They immediately waddled in and began ducking and bobbing in the water. The mother hen flew into a state of frenzy and raced back and forth, frantically trying to get the ducklings to come to the safety of the bank. After meeting some unknown instinctive need, the ducklings emerged from the water, waddled up to the hen, and they all returned to the barnyard.

With a wink and nod, the mule skinner at the Grand Canyon reminded me that variety is indeed a tonic for life. Like his trips into the Grand Canyon, every Biodesign trip was unique. There was, however, a vast difference between a bucolic mule ride into a canyon and walking six days with 30 teens. The beautiful views and subsequent revelations were coupled with potential danger, even peril. My brood-hen mentality was sometimes triggered as I watched students triumph or flounder in their newly discovered wilderness.

Cathy's Dogs

Cathy transferred to our school district from a neighboring district. She was bold, confident, and responded to my style of teaching. She had met Christie on one of Christie's visits to my classroom and decided to start visiting our home. Sometimes she would need a ride to her home which was 20 miles away. On one of the trips, we arrived at her home as her two dogs were returning from an afternoon run in the nearby woods. She lived on a ranchette, which included a horse paddock with an electrified fence in the front acre. The dogs had learned to scrunch down and crawl under the wire, thus avoiding the electric zap. This time, they made it safely under the far fence. However, when the lead dog was under the near fence, he saw Cathy and instantly began wagging his tail. When he got zapped, he wheeled on his haunches and bit his companion on the nose.

A week or so later, I was telling that story to a class when Cathy walked into the classroom. Just as if the whole scene were scripted, she said that there was a sequel to the story. On another day, the female dog had a sore foot and was unable to run. When Cathy returned one afternoon, the male was returning from his run and repeated the scene. He made it under the far fence and halfway under the near fence and began to wag his tail. When he got zapped, he wheeled and tried to bite the female but found nothing there. The dog looked around, spotted the female sleeping on a nearby deck, ran over, and bit her on the nose.

Over the years, I shared Cathy's story, and students often learned to use it. If someone was retaliating unfairly because of bruised feelings, someone else would likely say, "Cathy's Dog," and the class would erupt into laughter.

These stories were not randomly selected but chosen because I was intimately involved with each one. I flew in circles and up my own butt many times. The *Very Bad Idea* event was a mistake because it contradicted everything that we were trying to do in terms of building trust and confidence while discussing difficult topics. It also foolishly attempted to use bad behavior to model good. I was lucky the students were willing to move on and not be afraid that I would do something hurtful again, simply to prove a point.

On the second trip to Yosemite, I foolishly miscalculated the difficulty of the hike and led students on an 18-mile trek over the famous El Capitan. The last four miles were hiked in darkness. The following day "we" all had blisters, some of which were bleeding. I could have been jailed for student abuse. Ironically, I recently met one of the hikers, and she assured me that the hike was one of the most important events of her life. She said, "After that hike, I knew that I could accomplish anything that I set my sights on."

Boasting about rainbows was naïve at best and foolish at worst. I told each class that it was a good thing that man could never control spiritual events, for it was certain that if we could, we would abuse them. I cited a study conducted on mice and the use of cocaine. Laboratory mice can quickly learn to drink and feed themselves in their cages. A button or target can be installed, and each time a mouse presses it with his nose, food is released. When the food was removed from the feeder, mice would normally try eight to ten times before losing interest. When a mouse was issued cocaine, after pressing the food button, he pressed the button hundreds of times until his nose was bloodied. Researchers mercifully put the animal in a safer cage. It was humbling to realize that I came very close to repeating that experiment at Yosemite. I didn't know who was in charge of making rainbows, but if it were an aberration of nature, it was a very strange aberration. I certainly didn't deserve it, and for me, it was a warning, perhaps a heavenly one. I never predicted a rainbow again.

Perhaps the best metaphor of all is the brood hen and the ducklings. The only thing I remember from my wedding day, aside from getting married, was Christie's choral instructor passing through the receiving line.

He said, "I hear that you want to be a teacher. Just remember that the first thing that you will always want to teach is the last thing that you learned."

I never fully understood the concept until I was knee-deep in Biodesign. There were many gaps between the students and me. The generation and teacher/student gaps were the obvious ones, but there were many others. My goals were lofty; they were just beginning. I repeatedly had to remind myself that I had the advantage of each previous trip and class to build on, while they had to start from scratch each September.

The students were overwhelmingly good. However, early in the program, I realized that there were forces "out there," and internal ones, that threatened each trip. When this happened, I would run back and forth and flap my wings wildly. Despite having signed a contract, promising to avoid the use of drugs and alcohol, a few students smuggled pot along and puffed in secret. They selfishly ignored the fact that if the school board found out, the class would likely have been canceled. Before I met Sasha, I was naïvely unaware of the concept of situation ethics and the threat it would pose to each trip and the entire program.

Many of the duckling discoveries were amazing and contributed greatly to the class. Adding the spiritual component, getting "baptized" under Nevada Falls, adding extra days, adding the Grand Canyon trip, and meeting Sasha were only a few; there were countless others.

Cathy's dog story was so simple, so classic, and so pervasive, that it would be easy to give up all hope for mankind. Hostilities between families, tribes, races, ethnic groups, religions, and nationalities are ubiquitous. Some of them have lasted for thousands of years. Sometimes after a rough day or week at school, I would return home in the evening and bite Christie on the nose. She lovingly diagnosed the symptoms of battle fatigue.

The raven myth from the northern tribes is hauntingly foreboding. Like Dr. Albert Schweitzer (later), the raven people knew that they would not get answers to life's greatest questions. They accepted the dilemma with humor and humility.

As we become more detached from nature and our spirituality

declines, there is an inverse increase in ignorance and arrogance that conspire to suggest that all mysteries have been solved and all relevant questions have been answered. For native tribes, it would have been quite ordinary to see Peregrine falcons mating in the air or two ravens combine enough trickery and revelation to fill cartloads of books. Our two "canyon" ravens reduced Newton's ocean by one small drop and inspired one young man to cautiously raise his index finger and touch the untouchable mystery.

I can envision indigenous people snuggled around a thousand different tribal campfires, with a chief or elder saying, "The paleface without traditional values is in great danger of flying up his own butthole," followed by peals of laughter.

"Humor must be one of the chief attributes of God.
Plants and animals that are distinctly humorous
in form and characteristics are God's jokes."

Mark Twain

"The universe was swinging in some fantastic
fashion around to present its face, and the face
was so small that the universe itself was laughing."

The Star Thrower, Loren Eiseley

26: Soul Medicine

IT IS POSSIBLE that humor is one of the greatest of the spiritual gifts. As far as we know, man is the only animal who laughs with humor, delight, or joy. When people laugh so hard they cry, or face a situation where they don't know whether to laugh or cry, it is a good bet they are experiencing a deep sense of spirituality. In his book *Hunting the Divine Fox*, Robert Capon suggests, "theology therefore is fun. The inveterate temptation to make something earnest out of it must be steadfastly resisted." He posed the same daunting/haunting question that Jennifer did: what would happen if people laughed more and hated less?

Many of the most sacred moments in Biodesign occurred through laughter. Their laughter was of the highest order, showing no sign of being grubby, pornographic, cruel, or mean-spirited. They laughed easily and often, especially at the many intimately embarrassing moments incurred while studying, traveling, and camping together. Their laughter was contagious and healing.

On one of the visits to the pool beneath Yosemite's Nevada Falls, the guys were the first to jump in. The icy-cold water produced yelps and gasps. One of the guys asked a buddy, "Are you squinching?" Whether they had heard the term or not, all the guys immediately understood and burst into laughter. The girls looked on with puzzled expressions. One of them finally asked, "What is squinching?" This produced more laughter, and finally, one of the guys said, "You should ask Mr. Young."

I remembered a conversation with a French teacher-colleague of mine who spent a summer in France. When I asked about the highlight of her trip, she said, "I was standing in the Louvre, admiring Michelangelo's statue of David, and I suddenly burst into rapturous laughter. It occurred to me that after God created Adam, he said, 'Oops, I almost forgot! You will need two of these and one of these.' The people around me must have thought I was a nut." I shared the story and said she might be right.

The event provided a natural opportunity to describe, but not explain, one of nature's many bizarre mysteries. Embryonic testicles originate in males in the same area that ovaries originate in females. During gestation, they are programmed to migrate down and out of the lower abdomen. In cases where this does not happen, the organs will not function properly. Apparently, the normal body temperature of 98.6 degrees is too warm. The problem was solved by moving them out of the body, allowing them to cool slightly. They can, however, become overly cold, and when this happens, males squinch. The scrotum shrinks and draws the testicles close to, or even up into, the lower abdomen. It was too much information for some of the girls, but most joined the guys in laughter.

On another Yosemite trip, the autumn weather was unusually warm and the descent from Half Dome produced many sweaty hikers. When we reached the pool beneath Nevada Falls, almost as if someone gave the command, all the kids spontaneously stripped to their underwear and jumped into the cold water. I was shocked and not quite sure what to do. I mostly looked up at the scenery and tried to avoid looking at them. It was a purely platonic event, but I was well outside my comfort zone. It occurred to me later that for some mysterious reason they traveled back as close to the Garden of Eden as they could, and I was thankful that they kept their fig leaves on. Nevertheless, I was relieved when they put their clothes back on. I have never been clear on the concept of infant baptism, but John Muir's description of Nevada Falls having the mystical power to foster born-again experiences was perfectly clear. For those students who stood under the 600-foot column of pounding water, a lot more than their bodies was being cleansed. Any revelations were natural, personal, and were not exclusive to any brand of religion. Even so, I worried about what my principal, the school board, and my critics might say. "Have you heard the latest? He baptized a whole class under a waterfall, and they were only wearing their underwear!" Miraculously, the event was never criticized.

Shortly before one of the Yosemite trips, a distraught mother called our home. "I am very sorry to bother you," she said, "but I am worried sick and can't sleep. Our son will kill me if he finds out I called you, but, Mr. Young, John frequently walks in his sleep. I keep dreaming that he walked off the edge of Half Dome and fell 4,500 feet."

I laughed and corrected her by saying that he would likely only fall about 3,000 feet to the talus slope below. Then I quickly thanked her for calling and providing valuable information. "Furthermore," I said, "I always carry a widget bag with spare parts, which includes a small coil of wire. I will wire John into his tent at night and let him out in the morning. If he is going to sleepwalk, he is going to have to do it from inside with two or three tent-mates."

"Thank you, thank you," she said. "Maybe I'll get some sleep tonight."

At bedtime, on Half Dome, I quietly mentioned to John that a little bird told me that he liked to saunter in the dark and that I needed to take precautions. "I was afraid she would rat on me," he said sheepishly.

"John," I said, "if it were your son or daughter, would you have made the call?"

"Yeah," he said, "it's just a little embarrassing."

At 5:30 the next morning, I was awakened when John yelled, "Mr. Young, let me out. I gotta go pee." There was heavy frost on the ground, and so I wasn't sure of whether it was the cold air or the thought of John wandering off the edge of the Dome that sent a cold shiver up my spine. Of course, the story sparked hilarity, and John became famous. He also knew that his mom loved him enough to make the tough call.

The teenage version of Sperry's triad of values, consciousness, and free will includes an insatiable capacity for laughter. Currently, there is no biologically utilitarian definition that explains laughter. While there may be some preliminary inklings of laughter in other animals, anthropologists generally agree that man laughed, cried, and sang before he could speak. In typical cyclical logic, scientists say that laughter releases endorphins, which are good for us, which is why we laugh. This is not unlike the Brownie camp song that Christie sang as a child: "We're here because we're here because we're here ..."

It is intriguing that laughter is associated with enthusiasm, high-spiritedness, hilarity, even rejoicing. The opposite of it is gloom, doom, despair, and depression. Perhaps laughter is a God thing, which would explain why scientists are unable to quantify, define, or explain it. On one occasion, I semifacetiously suggested that I thought it would have been helpful if Jesus had told a funny story or two. Some of them laughed, some agreed, some thought I was being irreverent.

The reality for me, however, was that the time and energy demands, especially on the trips, were such that laughter became a luxury. Plato and C. S. Lewis were right. We were engaged in a spiritual battle and laughter would usually have to be deferred to moments of triumph and celebration. The students who were spiritually aware sensed this and offered support. Without them, every trip, and, thus, the program, would have failed.

I had little knowledge of Aboriginal totems, myths, and legends. I was, however, aware of a Psalm, which describes teenagers as "fearfully and wonderfully made." It was a perfect definition for the students. They **were** fearful and wonderful members of our modern-day ark. They had the power to destroy me and the Biodesign program; they also had the power to build each other up and form something beautiful. They were creative, spontaneous, and adventurous, which was evidenced by the fact that they enrolled in the class. They were intensely curious about their physical, mental, and spiritual growth and development, which included their emerging sexual identity. They made observations and asked questions that many adults were too shy, afraid, or embarrassed to ask.

One of the greatest biological mysteries, and certainly one of the single-most important sources of joy and sorrow, involves human sexuality. We shouldn't have needed John Gray's, *Men Are From Mars, And Women Are From Venus*, but he cleared some of the fog that can cloud identities and, thus, relationships. It is fascinating to wonder at what point of human evolution the first man and woman became aware that they were formed differently. It is a ritual that is completed secretly, or not so secretly, millions of times each year when little boys or little girls say, "I'll show you mine if you show me yours." It marks the period of development when children are discovering that males and females have different plumbing, and will later discover, different wiring. These discoveries will provide great drama, consternation, and often-underrated humor.

As a lad, John Muir was unmercifully beaten by his father until he memorized the entire Old Testament, and half of the New Testament. It was, therefore, a stunning revelation to find himself immersed in the beauty, wonder, and water of Yosemite. He was baptized by Mother Nature and experienced a spiritual rebirth of the greatest magnitude. This rebirth caused him, along with James Allen, to reject the cruelty and harshness that they found in the Old Testament. This surely must have included the line from Psalm 51, that reads;

"Behold, I was brought forth in iniquity, and in sin my mother conceived me."

Muir and Allen must have wondered how a process that was so natural and so essential could be considered sinful. It would be the same as if breathing air were sinful. I have wondered how sadly ironic it is that Puritans, and strict biblical literalists, have had to "sin" in order to procreate. There are, of course, ubiquitous abuses, perversions, even atrocities, that reflect sexual cruelty as a horrific aspect of humanity; nevertheless, who can deny that one of the most beautifully sublime, and some suggest, divine, human experiences occurs when a man and woman join in hopes of creating another living mystery? Most males (and a growing number of females) function well without the caveat. However, when time and place are right, even most testosterone-rich males will stand humbled, awed, or in tears when they hold their own baby for the first time. The moment is not lightly called, "The Miracle of Birth." Is this a God thing or a Darwin thing, or perhaps a little of both?

Tragically, modern science tacitly teaches young people that they are "accidents." Some religions teach that they were conceived in "sin." With the equally destructive identity crises that both views offer, it is little wonder that we have a massive problem with alcohol and substance abuse. The students that stood on top of Half Dome and could nearly touch the stars were high in the most beautiful sense of the term. Males celebrated, and described, newly discovered masculinity. Females celebrated and described a deeper kinship with Mother Earth. Many of them experienced the exhilaration of feeling that they were indeed fearfully and wonderfully created. It really didn't matter how that happened.

Meanwhile, between the seminal moments and before we die, we must deal with the daily joys, sorrows, and challenges of our sexual identity. This, according to W. H. Auden, will require and result in much laughter.

Galileo warned us that, although the Bible was a rich source of wisdom, inspiration, and guidance, its many metaphors were often obscure and difficult to decipher. He was correct, however. The students handled many difficult and potentially volatile situations with levity, humor, and grace.

While discussing the debate over creation versus evolution, Jeff asked, "How could Adam and Eve have grandchildren without, well, you know?"

Kerry responded, "It's a metaphor, Jeff. Moses was using symbolic language."

Jeff responded, "That's my problem. I don't understand the metaphor. It seems to me that either mankind evolved as a group, or God created more than two people, or else the first family acted in a way that we consider disgusting."

"Thanks a lot, Jeff," Kerry said. "Now I am confused."

At the start of class one day, Patrick announced that he had watched a PBS program on elephants. He informed us that when they mate, all the other females raise their trunks and trumpet loudly. He wondered if I knew why. I responded that I did not but guessed that they were either cheering or protesting. The boys voted for cheering, the girls thought they were disgusting.

Carrie snipped, "If that's how those animals behave, it would have been a wonder if Noah and his wife got any sleep."

Rodeo clowns can literally save a bull rider's life by distracting an angry bull away from the fallen rider; the same was true with the class. While planning a trip menu, one class had a small but very vocal group of girls who were devout vegetarians. They announced that they thought eating the flesh of dead animals was disgusting. One of the boys responded, "At least when I eat a hamburger, it's dead. When you girls eat carrots and celery, the cells are still alive. How do you think they feel?" The guys laughed. The girls were surprised, but not swayed. A meatless menu was planned.

One of my favorite posters that I hung periodically proclaimed: "Let love and laughter form the plow that prepares the soil for seeds of love to grow in." Even though I grew up on a farm, the students were often better at this than I was.

While walking in the Mendocino woods, the students came upon a pickup truck with a camper. The back bumper featured a sticker that boldly stated, "Don't come a-knockin' if this truck's a-rockin'." The boys began to cheer, and the girls said the boys were disgusting. I discovered that the best word that defined the teenage humor gender gap was "disgusting."

Once we were discussing the importance of Mendel's laws of segregation and independent assortment in evolution. I reminded them that a good example was the fact that every corn kernel resulted from a sperm that swam down a silk thread and fertilized an ovum. Gina blurted out, "Mr. Young, ever since you told us that in our sophomore year, I haven't been able to eat corn; it's disgusting." I reminded her that apples were simply enlarged ovaries, and she frowned at me and said, "I'm sorry, but you are disgusting. How would you feel if I told you that apples were simply enlarged testicles?" Pandemonium ruled. She had hoisted me, and the whole class knew it. After class, she gave me a hug; we both laughed.

While discussing the role of genetics and instinct regarding animal sexual behavior, I suggested that the urge to mate in both males and females was often nearly as powerful as the desire for food, air, and water, but for different reasons. Females are usually driven by a deep-seated need to procreate, which is essential for species survival. Males, on the other hand, are more concerned with doing the honors of helping females achieve their goal, as well as expanding their own gene pool. I cited the African lion as an example. Aside from occasionally defending his pride, the male lion sleeps up to 20 hours a day, and rises long enough to eat and have sex with one of many females. The guys thought that was an excellent role model. The girls booed loudly.

I pointed out that in both lions and humans this behavior is driven by a phenomenon we call instinct. To illustrate the point, I asked, "How many of you guys had to have your mom or dad teach you how to have an erection?" The girls giggled nervously; the guys looked shocked, but quickly broke into laughter. No hands were raised.

Rachel raised her hand and said, "My mom is in charge of the imaging laboratory at the hospital, and she performs sonograms. She has a picture of a six-month male fetus playing with his hard little 'you know what.'" The guys roared with laughter. Suddenly, Brian exploded up, while still attached to his desk. "That's it!" he shouted. "*That's* the answer! It's not our fault! Guys are hardwired to have hard—" He stopped at the hyphen, paused, and then said, "to be turned on." All eyes were focused on Brian, and he blushed bright red before he sheepishly returned himself and the desk to the sitting position.

That did it. The whole class was launched into a cosmic level of sustained belly laughter. We laughed so hard we cried. We literally lost control of being human. Or, perhaps, we may have seen a glimpse of what it's like to be truly human. After they settled down, I commended Brian for his enlightened thinking. Furthermore, I asked if he knew that the ancient Sanskrit term for *penis* translated into "wand of light." More peals of laughter. The guys thought that was an awesome metaphor. You don't have to guess how the girls responded. I referred to *The Great Evolution Mystery*, by Gordon Taylor, and noted that he suggested that Darwin's theory could not explain organs of extreme perfection. Did the guys think the male sex organ qualified? They beamed before bursting into more laughter. The girls acquiesced and joined them. The students created a comic moment that professional comedians could work for their entire careers and not achieve.

After class, I wondered if every woman who carried a baby boy walked around with her son comfortably submerged in his seawater-like amniotic fluid, happily playing with his little "you-know-what." Little wonder they laughed until their sides hurt.

Surprises occurred almost daily and were usually welcome. Sometimes, however, I reacted with mild shock or in a gun-shy manner. When I asked the males of another class about parental penile instruction, James raised his hand. He properly read the shock on my face and laughingly said, "No, my parents didn't; however, last year I had my appendix removed. On the way to the hospital, I remembered someone saying that they would shave my lower abdomen. I prayed that the nurse would be an ugly old man. I knew that I was, uh, err, easily excited, and I was afraid of what might happen. My prayer was not answered. My prep-nurse was a gorgeous, 20-year-old student. Within a minute, my fear became a nightmare that I wanted to end— but I was horrified as to what that end might be. She noticed my panic, calmly took a pencil from her lab coat, and gave me a sharp twack. I was shocked by how quickly my anxiety, ego, and erection were deflated." The guys grimaced and groaned sympathetically.

One of the girls exclaimed, "That was mean!"

James quickly took the high road and said, "No, it was not mean. In fact, she squeezed my hand and said, 'You were acting in a normal, even predictable, manner that was neither sinful nor dirty.' Then she laughed and said, 'Besides, I'll be the first one to report back to class that the procedure works. We had to practice on bananas, but the real thing is a lot more exciting; oops, sorry, I should have said interesting.'"

Interestingly, the class did not laugh. They seemed to be genuinely intrigued with the mysterious process that brought us all there to that place, at that moment.

The students enjoyed learning about the plant, animal, and human symbols that we use to enhance and celebrate our holidays. Black cats, pumpkins, turkeys, Pilgrims, Indian corn, fir trees, Yule logs, hearts, flowers, and Easter eggs were some of them. One year prior to Thanksgiving, I read an article that described the turkeys that the Pilgrims ate. The males weighed about 12 pounds, the females about seven; the meat was tough and nearly all dark. Modern turkey farmers, however, responding to economic pressure and the more popular white meat, have bred large birds that develop quickly and are mostly white meat. In fact, the article went on: Modern breeding males weighed nearly 90 pounds and females weighed over 60 pounds. The article ended by saying that due to the massive males, natural breeding had become obsolete. One creative farmer fabricated saddles for the females, but they slid off or got in the way. Typically, a male student asked, "So how do they do it?" I responded that I had no clue. Jenny shyly raised her hand and said, "I belong to 4H and am working on a poultry project this year. I have a book that explains the process; I will bring it in if you like." I agreed that she should.

The following day, I was busy gathering notes and materials for the day's lesson. I had forgotten about the previous turkey conversation until several boys arrived, earlier than normal. One of them said, "Today should be really interesting." The rest of the class arrived. Jenny was the last to arrive and casually dropped the poultry book off on my teaching table. I gathered all of my stuff, including her book, and found an open seat in the circle. After preliminary notes, I opened the book to the marked page. The book iterated the news article, but continued on. Immediately, I realized that I should have read the passage before class. I don't know if it would have saved me, but I sensed that I was heading for troubled times.

Christie can multitask and even think two conversations simultaneously; I usually can not. However, while I was reading, I was preparing my argument that would surely be needed for our principal. "After all," I would say, "this was a book approved by the local 4H chapter." Did he not know that the organization was over 100 years old and provided wonderful "coed" experiences for rural teens? Did he not know that the logo stood for Head, Heart, Hands, and Health? And then I thought of Christie. She would absolutely kill me. She was a city girl, and I was raised on a farm. The first year we were married, she taught second grade in a small rural elementary school in Calistoga, California. She came home one evening in a state of minor shock. During "show-and-tell," Mary shared that their calf got stuck while being born and her dad had to tie a rope around it and pull it out with their Jeep; everyone was fine, except Christie. It was not unusual news for the students. I found the story delightful. Christie was not sure she wanted to continue teaching in a "country school."

I continued reading. "Many modern turkey farmers have built state-of-the-art breeding rooms where birds are brought in. The birds and farmworkers have learned to work together. The male birds are manually aroused, brought to the ejaculation stage, and the semen is collected in sterile vials for later use. The birds seem to understand the process and are willing to cooperate. When it is the female's turn, the process is completed." I was doing my very best to maintain a stolid professional composure. I would have been OK if, just before I finished, I hadn't peeked over the book and around the circle. The guys' eyes were as big as saucers. The girls were shaking their heads with looks that could kill. I glanced over at Jenny who was the only picture of composure in the circle. They were all seniors and had college applications and job résumés on their minds. Aaron caught the humor in my eyes and blurted out, "The guy could put down on his résumé that he was an expert in avian artificial insemination."

Eric, the class clown, snorted, and said, "Or keep it simple and say that he was a turkey jerker." If I had had a bleeper I would probably have bleeped Eric out, which would have been silly. He was using an idiom that they all knew, even though the girls rarely, if ever, used it. It didn't matter. They had innocently wandered into a sociobiologically taboo territory which contained potentially dangerous gender and age gaps.

Of all the possible emotional responses available to them, the guys instinctively and instantly chose hilarity. They erupted into uproarious laughter. The girls dismissed propriety and joined in the carnival spirit. Suddenly, the class was spinning wildly out of control. I thought that as long as I was going to be fired, I might as well go down laughing. Then I thought, "Thank God for clowns." Aaron and Eric had surely saved me from instant spiritual death from visual, voodoo darts.

Interestingly, one topic that came up nearly every year but was not discussed, and definitely not laughable, was that of their own conception. The subject involved "tmi" (too much information) or was considered disgusting. Evidently, they must have still believed in part of Psalm 51.

The only exception involved a girl named Cessna. When she entered the Biodesign class, I commented about how unusual her name was. She laughed and casually explained that her parents loved to fly. Their plane was equipped with an autopilot which allowed them the opportunity to redefine the familiar airline slogan, "Flying United." "I was conceived at 5,000 feet in a Cessna aircraft," she said, "so that's how I got my name." The story seemed to be as coolly logical to her as it would have been to peregrine falcons explaining how they have been conceived for the last 10 million years.

Using them as a model, perhaps it is not surprising that few adults dare to consider the sexuality of God. Are we supposed to believe that He (like some people believe we are) is the result of spontaneous generation? As for God's wife, I think that she must be absolutely truthful, absolutely beautiful, and absolutely good. I would never have arrived at this had I not discovered Christie.

Growing up in a Judeo-Christian environment, I was perplexed by what I perceived as the Hindu preoccupation of using phallic symbols in their religious art. I later understood that as an ancient religion, they perceived that the entire history of humanity depended on the mystical power of the male sex organ. They could not have known that for 60 million years mammals depended on the same organ for species survival. I am not trivializing the equally important sociosexual role that females have played in human biological history; after all, the terms *Mother Nature* and *Mother Earth* are appropriate descriptors. During class discussions, however, motherhood was considered sacrosanct and not something to laugh at. Teens in general, and boys especially, were curious about their emerging gender identity and enjoyed strutting, preening, and bragging whenever they could. It is a very old ritual that the Hindus and our Founding Fathers agreed on; after all, the Washington Monument is a 555 foot tall symbol of George's "Wand of Light."

The class of '97 must have agreed. We were camped at Yosemite's

Illiloutte Creek the night before we climbed Half Dome. Some of students were sitting around the fire ring quietly celebrating the process of being re-created. I had just dozed off when the entire group stood up and screamed, "Penis!" into the wilderness. Millions of ancestral years had gone into that primal scream, and surely God and the angels were laughing.

Galileo was correct, and the students knew it. Biblical metaphors and great truths were often difficult to decipher. Unfortunately, the debate between creation and evolution, generally devoid of humor, has devalued the importance of human spirituality and left many of our teens lost in a soulless wilderness of materialism. This world includes memorizing all the parts of a fetal pig; a world that I may have been lost to were it not for Lettie, Matthew, Aaron, Erich, and hundreds of spirit-starved students.

Note:

After Cessna read her story, I asked if she would prefer that I not use her name or use a fictitious name. She laughed and said, "I think you will have to use my name or the story won't make sense."

It was my turn to laugh. "Well, not exactly," I said. "I had a girl student named Piper and her name would work." There was a hilarious moment when we both relished the irony. In an age of massive ersatz originality, I had the feeling that Cessna truly enjoyed the distinction of belonging to a very small (?) group of people who were conceived in a rarified atmosphere.

"Much of your pain is self-chosen.
It is the bitter potion by which the physician
within you heals your sick self.
Therefore trust the physician, and drink
his remedy in silence and tranquility.
For his hand, though heavy and hard,
is guided by the tender hand of the Unseen,
And the cup he brings, though it burns your lips,
has been fashioned of the clay which the Potter
has moistened with his own sacred tears."

The Prophet, Kahlil Gibran

27: The Importance of Pain

WHERE I HAD previously worked, our high school baseball team was undefeated and had the best pitcher in the league. Our cross-town rivals were also undefeated and had the best batter in the league. As fate mandated, they met at season's end to determine the league championship. The game was played at home, which was important for two reasons. There was a hometown advantage, and if we were ahead, we would not have to bat in the ninth inning.

The game was hard-fought and arrived at the ninth inning with our team ahead, one to zero. There were two outs, the bases were loaded, and it was the best hitter's turn to bat. He worked the count to three balls and two strikes, which meant that one pitch could determine the league championship.

The pitcher reared back and threw the hardest pitch he could throw. The batter expected as much and drove a rifle-shot back to the mound. The ball hit the pitcher in the chest, knocking him to the ground. Both sets of fans gasped in disbelief, and then something amazing happened:

The pitcher got up on his hands and knees;
Picked up the ball and threw the runner out at first;
Looked over at his fans;
And rubbed his chest with his palm and said, "Ummmm, good!"

Christie does not like the story. Perhaps it's a male thing, but to me, the story illustrates that a high school athlete was well aware of the reality that if he was going to enjoy the glory of the game, he was going to have to endure some pain.

One of the first triads to be introduced each fall involved stress, pain, and growth. It was not a new concept; however, visualizing the design seemed to help. Students were told that getting the whole class up to the top of Half Dome would likely be painful. There was a price to be paid for the view and privilege of sleeping closer to the stars. They were reminded that that the trip was not a requirement. Half Dome frequently provided an excellent introduction to the idea that stress and pain were often perquisites to mental and spiritual growth. Pain, like laughter, usually means that something unusual is happening that probably deserves our attention.

One of Ansel Adams's most famous photographs is a full moon over Half Dome. Several classes were lucky to have seen full moons rising, setting, or at their zenith at Yosemite or the Grand Canyon. These were always rare, but beautiful and much-appreciated events. Therefore, there was no way of guessing that a moon could jeopardize the Biodesign program.

Chinese fire drills were popular at the time and occurred when cars were stopped for any delay. A door would pop open, and all the young people would quickly hop out, race around the car or van, and reboard before the light turned or the obstruction was removed.

Returning from Yosemite, we were waiting for a drawbridge to rise over the Sacramento River. A door opened in one of the vans behind me, and Phil, the driver, assumed that a drill was about to commence. Instead, Marnie, a five-foot blond firecracker, hopped out, ran around to the front of the van, unbuttoned her pants, bent over, and provided all the riders with a full moon. She quickly hiked up her pants, ran back to her door, and hopped in. Like many events in the class, I was oblivious. When we returned, Phil casually mentioned the event. I didn't know whether to laugh or curse. It would have been funny, except that I needed school board approval for every Biodesign trip. For many years, one board member was vehemently opposed to the program and lobbied vigorously to have all trips cancelled. I pictured him addressing the board: "He has brought disgrace to our schools by allowing girls to drop their pants in public!" I recalled Gibran describing joy and sorrow being like a lute that was hollowed out with knives. He didn't mention that the strings had to be stretched tightly in order to produce a pure note. I wasn't always able to handle the stress in silence and tranquility.

In Margery Williams's classic, *The Velveteen Rabbit*, the skin horse informed the Velveteen Rabbit that becoming real "doesn't often happen to those who break easily, have sharp edges, or have to be carefully kept." This was not a metaphor but a reality for the Biodesign classes. If Mother Nature could polish granite, carve out the Grand Canyon, and shape continental shorelines, could she not break people, dull their sharp edges, and remove them from their comfort zone? Both in the classroom and on the trips, we were all vulnerable to pain. If the chapter title is correct, I was uniquely and blessedly positioned in a nearly constant state of vulnerability. The lead goose had to bear the brunt of the storms.

I often mentioned to Christie that I would love to go on one of the trips as a dishwasher and not the leader. Before each trip, the tension would build. A chaperone backed out, a car broke down, my substitute teacher got sick, a mechanic cross-wired the trailer lights and burned up the van's wiring system; our septic tank backed up. The strain on Christie and our kids was palpable and often led to an outburst: "I hate this goddamned work; this is the last trip I am going to lead!" Sometimes I would remember Maria, our Lamaze teacher, and guess that I was dilated six centimeters and better start breathing to get through the phase. The tension usually continued into each trip, and like the Californian who moved to Alaska, I would have to adjust, quit, or die. Often this was painful and resulted in an, "I've been tested enough moment."

It was usually not unlike a father turning to his misbehaving kids in the backseat and yelling, "If you don't behave, I'm turning around and we're going home!" It was far more intense, however, and publicly humiliating. Those who understood what I was going through offered compassionate support; those who did not were disappointed that I was not perfect. I was well aware of Plato's warning, "If you doubt the power of evil, try to do something good and see what happens." Although I was never exactly sure of what good we were doing, I was aware that at some point on each trip someone or something would bang on a hornet's nest and all hell would break lose. The trip results were not measurable, and when students returned home with comments like, "life-changing experience," they were often greeted with doubt, skepticism, or dull glances.

Early in the 1980s, Victoria announced that she wanted to invite her dad, our local superintendent of schools, to help chaperone the Yosemite trip. I was put in the awkward position of telling my boss that the students had the privilege of selecting chaperones that they thought would be a good match. He laughed and said that winning a popularity contest with students was not in his job description. Surprisingly, the class agreed to invite him. He was a wonderful addition and blended in so well that I completely forgot that my boss was watching my every move for six days. Shortly after we returned to school, he visited the class. He shared that he was deeply grateful for being treated as a fellow learner and not rejected as an unwanted authority figure.

The class responded with applause and loud cheers. It was a supreme moment that left him speechless and embarrassed. He lingered after they left to thank me personally and share some thoughts. "You have enemies," he said. "Some of them want the Biodesign class cancelled, and some want you fired. I don't think it was an accident that I was selected to go along. John Muir was right; six days in the mountains with those kids has changed my life. I now have a newly discovered 'bag of tools' that I will be able to use to defend your program at future school board meetings."

I deeply appreciated his support, although his message was not new.

Galileo was put on trial and could have been executed for creative thinking. During his trial he said, "Despite what most people think, they are not really looking for truth, they are looking for information that harmonizes with what they already believe." Four hundred years later, in a country founded on freedom of expression, I naïvely assumed that we had overcome the ideological and liturgical diseases of bias, bitterness, and bickering. At first, I thought it was a huge mistake, then I recalled Shakespeare: "Assume the virtue though you have it not." This is exactly what the ballplayer had done years earlier. Countless times I reluctantly smiled, rubbed my chest, and said, "Ummmm, good." If I was going to play the game, I had to pay a price. Taking Maslow's advice, I was allowing, even encouraging, students to question the normal boundaries of science, religion, and education. As a result, I was considered dangerous by some parents, some administrators, some clergy, and especially the secular humanists.

Over the years, after returning from a field trip, several parents/ chaperones confided that their sole purpose of volunteering was to gather information to get me fired. All of the ones that I became aware of became our most ardent supporters. There were also critics, if not enemies, within the school. Some teachers questioned the "scientific validity" of the class. Some thought that I was going on three glorious vacations each year. Shortly after I retired, I was informed that a skeptical superintendent had hired a private investigator, hoping to gather evidence that would allow him to fire me. I laughed and thought, "God was playing with me."

One evening, after 10 years of leading the program, while resting in my recliner, I noticed my right hand was twitching. Our family doctor referred me to a neurologist. After a thorough exam, he sat down with me and said, "You may have noticed that on the information sheet, I did not ask you for your career. I didn't want that to influence my diagnosis. I am now prepared to guess that you are either in the military, law enforcement, or a high school teacher."

I started laughing, and he said, "That's just what I thought. Sixty percent of the high school teachers who have taught 20 or more years frequently have some of the symptoms of battle fatigue. My advice is that you find ways to make teaching less stressful."

The single-largest stress remover would be to cancel the Biodesign program, but that hardly seemed like an option. If all this sounds self-piteous it is not. It is an honest assessment of the fact that there was a physical, mental, and spiritual price to be paid for each trip. Anyone doubting this is respectfully invited to take a group of 30 teenagers into the wilderness, invite them to look for truth, beauty, and goodness, and see what happens. For 24 glorious years, Christie and I drank from the cup of joy and sorrow, and while most of our memories are joyful, there were moments on nearly every trip that were absolutely horrible.

It wasn't just Mother Nature that was busy reshaping us. I don't remember why, but in the early years of Biodesign, I was allowed to attend an Alcoholics Anonymous meeting. I was shocked by what I perceived as the brutal honesty of the members. I discovered they had to be; they were facing life-and-death issues. Although our class discussions rarely (if ever) reached that level of intensity, student comments and opinions, as well as mine, were held to a high level of accountability. ("What the hell do we believe anyway?")

All metaphors fail or else they wouldn't be metaphors. When the vessel that Sasha was crafting failed, it was both a cathartic and instructional moment. It illustrated that even experts can experience failure. Sasha and the clay had failed, and so had the metaphor, but not entirely. It revealed that clay, like people, can be overstressed to the breaking point. Unlike clay, however, people who are broken cannot be gathered up, patted into a ball, and reformed into a totally new being.

My reality was that some relationships that failed could not be repaired, and sometimes it was humanly impossible to "let go gently." The Biodesign dropout rate, over 24 years, was less that 2 percent. Nevertheless, when someone dropped out, I felt devastated and that somehow I should have known better or tried harder. I envied Sasha's ability to correct his errors, or the flaws in the clay, and wished that human relationships were that simple.

For some, the Biodesign concept was too physically, mentally, or spiritually demanding. I didn't blame them. I would not have considered taking a class like it in high school or college. For those who survived, their accomplishments would be theirs and theirs alone. Whatever they did with them was of their own choosing. Nevertheless, I was amazed by how many Biodesigners, like the baseball player, learned how to handle physical, mental, and spiritual pain so well that they could smile, rub their chest, and say, "Ummmm good!"

Throughout the 24-year class history, there were countless wonder-filled moments. Nevertheless, I had recurring doubts as to whether I had truly discovered what Lettie was wondering about. There were heartbreaking defeats, obstacles, and setbacks; however, even more important than the incomparable scenery, were the student observations that made the pain not only endurable, but essential. Joy and sorrow truly flowed from the same cup.

During a final circle in Mendocino, students were sharing their reflections. Amy condensed four days and thousands of images into one word: *Perfection*. She was not only alluding to an incomparable biological wonderland, but an extraordinary group of students who had truly done their homework. They gathered the tools that were offered the first week of school; listened to Maria, the nurse/midwife; and prepared, concentrated, and communicated. They explored one of Mother Nature's most biologically diverse systems with wide-open eyes and, more important, wide-open hearts. Using their invisible flashlights, they saw movements, shapes, and colors rarely seen by humans. If Emerson is correct, Amy was seeing herself as a being of perfection. *Perfection* is not a word that is often used by mortals, and so I wandered down to the beach to contemplate her word. I had always thought that Walt Whitman must have used mind-altering drugs to arrive at his motto:

> "To me, every hour of the day and night
> is an unspeakably perfect miracle."

It only took Amy one word to show me how foolish I had been.

"What shall we sing while the fire burns down?
We can sing only specifics, time's rambling tune,
the places we have seen, the faces we have known.
I will sing you the Galapagos Islands, the sea lions
soft on the rocks. It's all still happening there,
in real light, the cool currents upwelling, the finches
falling on the wind, the shearwaters looping on the waves.
I could go back, or I could go on; or I could sit down
like Kubla Khan:

Weave a circle round him thrice,
And close your eyes with holy dread,
For he on honey-dew hath fed,
And drunk the milk of Paradise."

Teaching a Stone to Talk, Annie Dillard

28: Amazing Faith

FOR THE CURIOUS mind, Mendocino was a wonderland of delight, with lessons that were learned to the rhythm of the nearby surf. It lacked the stunning height of Half Dome and the boggling depths of the Grand Canyon; instead, it offered gentle activities that, to some, were nothing short of mystical. They would form a living montage which would be incomplete without each component picture. The brightest pictures were those that reflected the magical wonder of the evening campfire ceremonies. The meetings were both literally and figuratively the end of the day. They provided an opportunity for students to share excerpts from their journals or from unrecorded reflections or observations gathered throughout the day. But the biggest unspoken advantage of the circular meetings was the fire itself.

In Edward Farrell's book *celtic meditations*, he presents wonderful directions for contemplating many examples of the wonders of nature. He properly suggests that fire is such a powerful dynamic, that no direction is necessary. Students were asked to quietly focus on the fire for a predetermined time period, and then asked to describe their thoughts and feelings. The fire often had magical, mesmerizing, even hypnotic powers that enhanced and transported conversations to a higher level of passion and sensitivity. Over the course of 24 years of traveling to Yosemite and Mendocino, I probably participated in over 200 campfire ceremonies. The magic of campfire circles was enhanced by singing traditional folk songs such as "Country Roads," "Cotton Fields," "Worried Man Blues," "Crawdad Song," "This Land Is Your Land," "Blowin' in the Wind," "Circle Be Unbroken," and many more. Although each ceremony was unscripted, unique, and most were special, one totally surprised me and transformed my thought process.

If spiritual gifts could appear in an instant, so too could spiritual traps. Knowing what to say, and sometimes more important, what *not* to say, was an ever-present challenge. Students and usually chaperones were rarely aware of the inner battles that were pitched behind the scene. One of these battles curiously erupted while we were snuggled within the serenity of an evening campfire in Mendocino. The waves were gently rolling in on the nearby beach, and the fire crackled quietly. We were singing out of our songbooks, and, as was the custom, students were invited to make selections that they deemed appropriate. I was quietly strumming my guitar, waiting for the next song selection when someone suggested, "Amazing Grace."

Dianna was at my left, and she leaned over and quietly said, "I hate that song."

I was shocked, not only by her acrimony, but by her courage to express her anguish. I asked her why, and she whispered, "I realize that I am not saved; that I cannot see spiritually, and my parents are wealthy so I am probably doomed."

I was dumbfounded. I was suddenly in the wilderness with no map, guide, or lesson plan. I saw no way out. My heart began to pound. If we sang the song it would add to her sense of alienation and contempt. If we didn't sing the song, without some explanation, her classmates would be curious or confused. If I explained the situation, I would betray her confidence and possibly jeopardize the circle. I flinched mentally and wondered how such a perfectly beautiful setting could instantly become so dreadful.

My mind did a flash, paragraph-cut, and paste. In her book, *I Heard the Owl Call My Name*, Margaret Craven describes a scene in a Canadian Indian village involving an exchange between a priest and a teacher.

The teacher said:

There was one more thing he felt it his duty to inform the vicar. The vicar might as well know right now that for himself, he was an atheist; he considered Christianity a calamity. He believed that any man who professed it must be incredibly naïve.

The young vicar grinned and agreed. There were two kinds of naïveté, he said, quoting Schweitzer; one not even aware of the problems, and another which has knocked on all the doors of knowledge and knows that man can explain little, and he is still willing to follow his convictions into the unknown.

"This takes courage," he said, and thanked the teacher, and returned to the vicarage.

The story was instructive and similar, yet with a striking disconnect. Craven's teacher was an insensitive lout. I had grown to love Dianna as a caring, compassionate individual. What she believed or didn't believe was her business, but she raised a haunting dilemma. On several occasions, I encountered students, like her, who were thoughtful, caring, and loving, and claimed to be nonreligious. On the other hand, I encountered students who were not so thoughtful, caring, or compassionate, who openly claimed to be religious. What did it all mean? My mind flashed back to the "Words have no meaning," speaker, and then Gibran offered help: "Your daily life is your temple and your religion."

I took a deep, cleansing breath, gathered myself, and began:

The song "Amazing Grace" has its origin in the sea. John Newton was a sailor returning from the United States to England on a sailing ship. They were caught in a North Atlantic storm off the coast of Ireland. He described their boat at 100 feet long, and he estimated the waves at nearly 90 feet high, which could have easily resulted in the total loss of life and property.

Newton was scared senseless and knelt down on a pitching deck and prayed to a god who may or may not exist. He assumed that his life was nearly over and did not pray for survival but for the peace of mind to face death with tranquility. Miraculously, he was engulfed in an aura of serenity. His ship survived the storm, and years later he became a priest. He had not forgotten his brush with death and was inspired to write a prayer of thanksgiving, describing his perilous journey. The prayer was actually a poem which he used as a basis for a sermon. It is unknown who later added the melody. The song "Amazing Grace" has spread worldwide and is considered to be one of the greatest spiritual songs written. However, the prayer is Newton's prayer, not your prayer and not my prayer.

If we were to sing it, I suspect that three groups would form. Some of you would connect with the song. Some of you would sing the song as a folk song without emotional attachment. And some of you may find the song irritating, even provocative, all, of which, I can fully understand.

Actually, I think the song should have been titled "Amazing Faith," because the act of faith had to occur before the experience of grace. Although I am intrigued with the courage it takes for men in foxholes and on pitching decks to pray to a god who may or may not exist, I am even more intrigued with the courage it takes for men and women to make the scary leap of faith, without the threat of impending doom.

If you recall, we began the year with the goal to explore Plato's triad of truth, beauty, and goodness and see where it takes us—discovering joy or sorrow and accepting the idea that stress and pain are common prerequisites to growth. This took an investment in courage that many people refuse to make.

Dianna slid her right arm alongside my left arm, gave me an arm-hug, leaned over, and whispered, "Thank you. I think we should sing the song."

The experience was surreal. I knew the story, but it seemed as though my mind and mouth were on autopilot. There was a cathartic release as we began to sing. By the third verse, I realized that I would never sing the song again in a more perfect setting. By some mysterious power, the circle deciphered, and then amplified the poignancy that Dianna and I were feeling. The sacred tears that glistened around the campfire light dripped on sand that had been a million years in the making. What happened could not be predicted or reproduced and can only be described as a mandorla between heaven and Earth. Or, perhaps, it was the mandorla between science and religion that prophets, poets, sages, and scientists, who are aware that miracles still happen, can celebrate vicariously.

After the last reflection was shared and the last song was sung, students drifted down to the beach or off to bed. I lingered, alone, listening to the ancient rhythm of the sea and basking in the after-glow of revelation, flames, and fellowship. The slowly flickering fire gently conjured up an image of an earlier ceremony around the same fire ring. This time, Ingrid sat alone by the fire, crying quietly. I approached and sat beside her without speaking.

After awhile, she said, "I don't believe this."

I had no idea of what she didn't believe, but guessed that she would tell me if she wanted to.

After a long pause she continued, "I can't believe I am alive, sitting here, in this place, 7,000 miles from Yugoslavia. I could have been born, grown up, grown old, and died without having any idea what life was all about." I reached over, gently took her hand and gave it a little squeeze of affirmation.

"Oh Great Spirit, whose voice I hear in the winds
and whose breath gives life to all the world,
hear me! I am small and weak, I need your wisdom.
Let me walk in beauty, and make my eyes ever behold
the red and purple sunset ...
Let me learn the lesson that you have hidden
in every leaf and rock ..."

Native American

29: Wayne

THE FACT THAT Matt could even ask the question, "What do we be-lieve?" is astounding when you put it in historical context. It took 4.5 billion Earth years for him to be able to ask it. He is a member of the only species out of 1,000,000 animals which has developed written and spoken language. He is arguably in an extremely small group of people, living or dead, who could contemplate and properly phrase the question about evolution.

The fact that he posed the question seems to validate the assumption that he has free will, or nothing else makes any sense. But whether he knew it or not, his question addressed, not just physical evolution, but what we believe relative to race, family, tribe, gender, politics, sexuality, religion, money, career, marriage, alcohol, narcotics, and countless other issues. Each of us is an individual, yet part of a society which is intertwined with all of humanity, which is evolving. Did the Biodesign class sessions and field trips conjure up thoughts, ideas, and discussions about any or all of these topics? Yes. Were the unscripted topics premeditated, planned, or predictable? No more so than planning to conjure up a rainbow at will. The reality is that I was probably unaware of most of what students were discovering and learning. I was responsible for guided discussions focusing on the biology of the area, but there were thousands of moments of quiet reflection or conversation which I was understandably unaware of. These occurred along Yosemite trails, in the tents, in the canyon, or along the Mendocino beaches. Many of these were shared at circles (especially during campfires); many that were too personal were not.

It was during one of these moments that an event occurred that was so extraordinary that I hesitate to record it. In fact, I would not have included it were it not for Eiseley's story titled, "The Dancing Frogs."

The story is found in Eiseley's book, *The Star Thrower*, a book that Christie found for me while we were on a brief vacation in Mendocino. I read the story to her that night while we were in bed, and her response was, "Don't ever read a story like that to me again just before I am going to sleep."

It involved an interview that Eiseley had with Dr. Albert Dreyer, who was doing research on amphibians. If truth is stranger than fiction, then it is understandable that this story about Dreyer's encounter with huge dancing frogs has left brilliant men scratching their heads in disbelief.

"… but in that final frenzy of terror before the water
below engulfed me I shrieked, Help! In the name of
God,

help me! In the name of Jesus, stop!
I was not, I suppose, a particularly religious man,
and the cries merely revealed the extremity of my terror.
Nevertheless this is a strange thing, and whether it involves the crossed beam, or an appeal to a Christian deity, I will not attempt to answer."

The Star Thrower, Loren Eiseley

The interfaces between land and air, water and air, and land and water often provide great opportunities for life-forms. They also provide a rich source for metaphors. After reading Eiseley's story, I was reminded about Wayne and his experience with such an interface. I suspect that this story, like the hymn "Amazing Grace," will produce three responses. One group will shout hallelujah. One group will find it an interesting, but a nonengaging tale. The third group will react with anger, hostility, and be "highly offended." Strangely, I can identify with all three groups.

Every time I find an arrowhead on our property, I pause to pay homage to the people who lived here 12,000 years before me. They lived at peace with nature and left no scars or evidence of their existence except for a few arrowheads and an occasional mortar and/or pestle. The great ironies, tragedies, and incongruities of our sociocultural evolution are that our forefathers came here seeking religious and political freedom and promptly enslaved people from Africa and systematically destroyed the Native American tribes. I received more than one reprimand from principals who demanded that I leave social study issues to the social study teachers. Up until the early 1990s, high school history books in the United States reduced the history of 500 Native American tribes to half a page titled, "Cowboys and Indians." I not only admired Native Americans for their ecological knowledge, but for their wisdom and rich tradition of storytelling.

The school district where I was teaching had 1,500 students, and

I think only three had Indian ancestry, Wayne and his two brothers. I met Wayne when he entered my biology class. He was bright, curious, and eager to learn. I usually included at least one essay question on every exam that invited students to discuss items that I had omitted or that they thought were relevant to our studies.

It was there that I learned that Wayne was part Cherokee, very proud of his heritage, and that he came pre-wired with an interest in his own spirituality. I felt honored to have him in class and was eager to learn from him. He was keenly interested in reconciling his native sense of spirituality with that of "the white man." At the end of the year, he elected to enroll in the Biodesign class for the next year. This was the first class to make it to the top of Half Dome and spend the night.

Unfortunately, Wayne would not be there. Before the trip, the football coach had given his approval for the four or five ballplayers to attend the trip. We delayed the trip to accommodate his demands. Unfortunately, he changed his mind on Friday night and at 4 a.m. the next morning, the boys arrived and sadly announced that they would be staying home. In a strange way, it would prove to be a blessing, because Wayne volunteered to be a chaperone the next year and was a principal player in Cindy's story.

During the year, he had mentioned that he had started to read the Bible and was interested in the similarities between the God of the Old Testament and The Great Spirit of the Cherokee. I assured him that I was not a Bible scholar and would be of little assistance as a reference. As I recall, he was amused over the spats between the Bible-thumpers and secularists, but was not involved. In the meantime, he started visiting our home and was welcomed as a quasi member of the family.

That spring, he graduated and attended a nearby community college where an English professor quoted Charles Dickens, "The New Testament is the best book the world has ever known or ever will know." By then, Wayne had discovered that although I was not a biblical scholar, Christie was. Wayne had worked his way through the Old Testament, but the New Testament was giving him no small amount of grief. The concept of the Christian Trinity was confusing, and as for Jesus being the son of God, that was absolutely "illogical." When he came to our home to discuss his dilemma with Christie, I watched a ball game or read a book. By the time I got home in the evening, I was exhausted and participating in biblical analysis was beyond me.

The year passed with little resolution and finally Christie said, "Wayne, sooner or later, you are going to have to ask Jesus if he is real or not."

Later, she said, "I remember thinking after he left our home, I can't believe I told him that. What if he asks and gets no response?" I shrugged my shoulders.

The next semester, Wayne headed north to Arcata, California, to attend Humboldt State University. Nevertheless, he wanted to chaperone the Mendocino trip, and we agreed on the time, date, and meeting place. He would drive 200 miles south, and we would drive 90 miles north.

The time arrived, and we met at Mendocino and proceeded to set up our campsite. I don't recall which day, but one afternoon during some free time, a group went to the beach to play the human destruction derby/hacky-sack version of the game I had seen played at Yosemite. Dinner was prepared and dishes were cleared, cleaned, and stored. We decided to drive up to the headlands, about three-quarters of a mile away, to watch the sunset.

I had just settled down to watch when Wayne came to me and said that he just discovered that he had lost his keys. I suggested that they were probably in his tent and he would find them. He was adamant that he had lost them on the beach and asked if I would give him a ride back to camp. I surprised myself by refusing. He was equally surprised but said that he would run back to camp and begin the search. I felt slightly guilty but thought my place was with the class. Thirty minutes later, the golden sun dropped below the horizon and the seagulls headed for their nightly roosts. We watched the sea settle down and darkness settle in, then boarded our vehicle and headed back to camp.

When we arrived at camp, my headlights revealed that Wayne was up in an alder tree with his hands tucked up under his armpits, flapping his arms and croaking like a raven. I had no clue what he was up to. As soon as I parked, he "flew" down from the tree, pulled my door open, yanked me out of the van, and said, "We have to talk!"

He dragged me toward a trail while I protested, saying I had to get the campfire started. He yelled to one of the other chaperones to start the fire; we would be back in 10 minutes. Then he hustled me up the trail and told me this story:

> When I got back to camp, I searched the tent and found no keys. I was certain that I had lost them on the beach and headed out to search. I methodically divided the area into a grid and covered the area one way and then at right angles. The beach was torn up with a thousand footprints in the sand which made searching impossible. Meanwhile, it was getting darker, and the tide was coming in. I realized that at high tide, the beach would be covered with water and erase all signs of our activity and probably further bury the keys. The thought of losing them was horrifying. I guessed that the closest locksmith would be in Fort Bragg or maybe even in distant Ukiah. It would cost $100 to have a key made for my car, which was $100 I didn't have. I also knew that my dorm key, as well as the key to the classrooms that I would have to clean on Sunday evening, were lost. All of this converged to create a terrifying moment. I felt like a caged animal. The tension was so great that I dropped to my knees, with tears streaming down my face. I decided I had only one option. I looked around and found a beach stone, held it firmly in my hand, and said, "Jesus, if

you are the Son of God, I am going to throw this rock, and my keys better be under where it lands."

I interrupted and grabbed him by the arm and shook him. "You *didn't* do that!" I gasped. "That is the stuff you read about but is never believable."

He grinned widely, pulled the keys out of his pocket, and dangled them in my face. There was a moment of profound silence.

On the way back, I said, "Wayne, you know that the campfire is a time for sharing, but—"

"Yea," he interrupted, "this is probably kinda heavy-duty."

"That's an understatement!" I gasped.

When we returned, the campfire was burning brightly, and everyone was present, waiting for us. I got out my guitar and found a place in the circle.

One of the girls said, "You two look like you have a secret." I faltered for a moment and recovered by saying that Wayne had lost his keys but found them.

Over the next 20 years, I only shared Wayne's story once, and I think it was a mistake. We were in Mendocino, sitting around a campfire, and I thought that the mystery of the story was timely. It was not. Did the students think the story was inappropriate? No one objected. Did they distrust my motives? No one questioned me, and they knew that they could. Did they think that I was suggesting that when they had a crisis, they should run to a beach and throw a stone? That was ridiculous. But looking at their eyes, I realized that they were deeply troubled by the story. I was sorry that I told them. It dawned on me too late that they might dread the possibility that one day they, too, could have to face a terrifying moment.

Actually, the story would have been an excellent ghost story to tell by campfire light, except that kids always suspected that the ghost stories were probably not true. Wayne's story was potentially far scarier, because it probably was true. How or why would anyone make up a story like that? As for me, I agreed with Albert Dreyer. Was

Wayne's terrified plea answered by a Christian deity? I don't know. Would I have done the same thing in a similar situation? Probably not, which is why it was a good thing that I did not give him a ride back to camp. Wasn't it a bit like saying, "C'mon, jump, God, jump"? Ironically, it brought me full circle back to Wayne's original premise, that "God was not logical." He certainly did not belong in a biology class, but what was I to do?

Wayne, apparently, had a close encounter with his "Great Spirit," and I had nothing to do with it. The experience happened during the formative years of Biodesign, and the results could have been explosive. Had the local newspaper printed his story, I am convinced that the class would have been cancelled, and I would have been reprimanded, censured, or fired. I suspect that some of the members of the firing squad would have been some of the local clergy. I was lucky; many fared far worse.

The previous summer was the summer of my discontent. Now I wondered how it was possible that, 400 years later, I would experience a reverse form of the same bigotry that Galileo experienced. After all, was this not America, the land of freedom? I was happy for Wayne, but not so happy to be teetering on the brink of losing my job and reputation. I had a wife and four children. Maslow was right. "Sooner or later we shall have to redefine both religion and science."

After completing the tenth draft of the story, I sent Wayne a copy and asked him to edit it for accuracy. He graciously complied with the following illuminations:

1. I don't remember the raven in the tree. (I thought that was funny because it was my most vivid and bizarre image.)
2. I am afraid that you may have caused my grandma to roll over in her grave. We are Choctaw not Cherokee. LOL
3. You failed to note that Christie's final challenge was uttered in frustration and that every time I left your house I thought she was a tad nuts. However, even though her faith was misplaced, it was impressive.

4. There was a lot more going on emotionally than just the keys. They were just the tip of a huge pyramid of inner turmoil, which included a religious and, therefore, a personal identity crisis.

5. When I threw the stone, I was certain that I would be able to tell Christie that the plan was nuts and that she was wrong. I even started to walk back to camp. Then I realized that I could not honestly tell her without looking. I also realized that if I did not look, she would surely yell, "Wayne, why didn't you?"(I thought that was funny. My response was, "How could you?")

6. I wasn't aware that you were walking a very narrow, and possibly dangerous, path by encouraging me to think. It's 30 years late, but I am sorry if I was a pain in the butt. LOL

Critics and skeptics will ask, so why tell Wayne's story now? There are several reasons. First of all, it is a great story. It's Wayne's story, so my ego is not involved. Next, the class has ended and is no longer in danger of being cancelled. Now, I am retired and not in danger of being fired. But most important, if one person reads this story and gains the courage to confront The Great Mystery, then all the blood, sweat, and tears will have not have been shed in vain. Wayne graduated from college, attended seminary, and became a pastor where he tends to people's spiritual needs.

Thanks, Wayne; you changed my life, even if you were a pain in the butt.

"Then I was standing on the highest mountain
of them all, and round about beneath me was
the whole hoop of the world. And while I stood
there I saw more than I can tell and understood
more than I saw; for I was seeing in a sacred manner.

Black Elk

30: Moses Appears

THE FINAL CLASS that would ascend and sleep on top of Half Dome
arrived in midafternoon. As we rounded the top, I noticed an old man
with a big bushy beard off to the right, writing in his journal. This would
be only the second time in 20 years that we would share the Dome. A
pang of anxiety shot through my body as I assumed that he would be
devastated to learn that his night of solitude would be ruined by a mob
of teens. I faced a chronic dilemma of leading a large group into the
wilderness, while trying not to disturb others' solitude.

After a group hug and cheer, we made the requisite pilgrimage
to the Diving Board and Eyebrow. After a suitable adjustment period,
we began to erect our tents in a widely scattered pattern. I noticed,
without concern, the old man was talking to some of the students. We
had often noticed that the farther away we were from the Ahwahnee
Hotel, the friendlier the hikers became.

When the tents were all erected and the cooking center established, I wandered over to the edge to gaze at The Incomparable Valley below. The old man approached and began to talk. He introduced himself as a mountain man from Santa Cruz, California; he didn't have to. I had seen his eyes before, dancing and sparkling in a potter in Mendocino. I had often wondered if Thoreau were correct in stating: "The mass of men lead lives of quiet desperation."

Still, it was heartbreaking to realize that the number of men that I had found with sparkling eyes, like Sasha and the Mountain Man, were few and very widely scattered. Obviously, like C. S. Lewis, I must have been missing something.

When I apologized to the old man about ruining his solitude, he reacted with shock and said, "My home may be in Santa Cruz, but my spirit dwells here. I have spent many nights alone out here, and God willing, I still have a few left. When you arrived up here, I was elated beyond belief. I can always spend a night alone, but how many chances will I have to greet a wonderful group of seekers like this? Once in a lifetime." He answered his own question. "I hope you don't mind, but I have greeted them all and given them my blessing."

My heart sank, and my mind raced. What had he said to them? Was he planning his own version of a Chautauqua celebration on top of Half Dome? I knew that in many indigenous cultures it was a high honor to receive a blessing from a tribal elder. Even so, that was then, and this is now, and these kids knew nothing about that honor and probably thought this guy was a Jesus freak. I didn't know if he read the fear in my eyes or not, but he gently took my right hand with both of his, shook it warmly, boldly looked into my eyes, and offered his eight-word blessing. I thanked him, and he returned to his campsite.

Everyone knows that lightning never strikes twice in the same place. Everyone would be wrong. For the second time on Half Dome, I was struck and lived to celebrate the event. Of course, it helped that the lightning was of a spiritual nature. I was a "C" student in college and was either an underachiever or a slow learner. In spiritual matters, either would describe my Biodesign experience. Twenty-four years after Lettie asked her fateful question, I received an answer. The old man's blessing was, "What you are doing here is very important."

With 30 teenagers we had 60 eyes that rarely missed a trick. Early the next morning, when we got up, someone yelled, "Moses is gone."

Those who were awake looked over at the empty campsite and murmured. We packed up and began what would be a long day returning to base camp.

Six weeks later, the Yosemite enthusiasm had been slacked by a six-period school day and the demands of civilization. The class was in a lowered state of energy. We were knee-deep studying Eiseley, preparing for our distant trip to the Grand Canyon. I stopped by my mailbox before class and saw a letter addressed to the class, with a name and address that I didn't recognize. We started each day with "news and notes," and I began with the letter. There was a note and three Kodak color slides within. The note read:

> Thank you for making my trip to Half Dome an unexpected treasure. I got up early because I knew there was a place down the trail that offered a great view of the cables. I got out my telephoto lens and waited for you to descend. The morning light could not have been more perfect. You will never know the joy I received watching you come down the cables. It made me wish I were 50 years younger so I could go around twice.
> I hope you enjoy the slides.
>
> The Mountain Man

I loaded the slides into the projector, turned off the lights, and we saw three of the most beautiful rainbows that we will ever see. He was right. The morning light was perfect and illuminated a row of multicolored jackets and backpacks descending the cables—frozen in three perfect Kodak moments. I turned off the projector, and we sat in the quiet darkness. No one moved.

I wondered if they sensed that:

> The circle had been completed.
> The question had been answered.
> I had received the message.
> It would soon be time for me to retire.

"Men go abroad to wonder at the heights of mountains,
At the huge waves of the sea, at the long courses of the rivers,
At the vast compass of the ocean, at the circular motions of the stars,
And they pass by themselves without wondering."

Saint Augustine

31: The Final Circle

CURRENTLY, THERE IS much squawking and wing-flapping over how
and when modern man evolved. What is not debatable, however,
is that millions of people have died from stones, clubs, spears, ar-
rows, famine, disease, and natural catastrophes. Ingrid, the exchange
student from Yugoslavia, was aware of this. Perhaps she was more
sensitive because she came from a war-torn area.

She did not verbalize a personal mystical encounter; however,
she did acknowledge that she was part of an experience involving
impossible odds that could not be described in any earthly language.
This left her with the haunting, yet exhilarating dilemma, "Why me?"
Her response was to feel privileged beyond belief.

Ingrid expressed my feelings precisely. Unlike those who lived
and died in silent or nonsilent desperation, I was singled out to lead a
life of unfathomable privilege. Unlike Buddha, who found the human
condition inherently miserable, I found life to be inherently joyful,

with a little misery. My experiences exceeded my wildest imagination, against unbelievable odds, and I have absolutely no idea why. After all, this class was conceived in mystery and would end in mystery. St. Paul chose his triad and suggested that the greatest of his three was love. Of the three seeds that were planted and grew into Biodesign, the greatest was planted by Lettie when she asked, "Is this really important?" The obvious reason is that without her seed, the other two could not have germinated. But, equally important, her question became a focus of the class and one that C. S. Lewis confronted and Matthew and hundreds of students pondered.

Over the 15 trips to the Grand Canyon, I got to know some of the staff members at Phantom Ranch. The manager always welcomed us warmly. On our last morning it was my custom to see that all the students were on the trail up to the South Rim, and then I would relax in the dining hall and enjoy a final cup of coffee. This year was no exception. However, what happened was unique. The manager brought his coffee over, joined me, and shared this story:

> For several years, I have been meaning to thank you for bringing your class here, but something always got in the way. I have worked here for eight years and enjoy it very much. The scenery is fantastic, and the people I work with are great. Sometimes, however, visitors are rude and obnoxious. Getting up at 4 a.m. to prepare food can be a drag. Changing sheets and scrubbing toilets gets tiresome. When I get discouraged, however, I pause and look forward to the annual visit of the magical group of students from the Catholic high school in Northern California; somehow, they offer meaning to my life.

I didn't tell him that our school was a public school named after an obscure Russian saint; I didn't think it was relevant. I don't know if he had a premonition or not, but as it turned out, that was his last chance to share his story. Fifteen minutes later, walking alone across the Silver Bridge over the Colorado River, I paused, took a deep breath, exhaled slowly, and realized that the Biodesign experience was ending. This would be my final trip to the Grand Canyon. I didn't know why, it just would be. Like a ghost that appears and disappears, Biodesign was created behind a shroud and was disappearing behind a shroud.

Four months later, the class graduated. The day after graduation, I was in a melancholic mood. I arrived at school late, but it didn't matter. Entering the empty room, I decided I needed some carnival. I arranged the desks in a circle for the final time, cued up Judy Collins's version of "Send in the Clowns," and turned off the lights.

As I sat in the dark, listening to the music, I pictured a little boy going to the circus for the first time. It was a three-ring extravaganza, and he was lucky to be attending the final performance. The next morning, he woke early, dressed quickly, and hopped on his bike and headed for the fairgrounds. He wanted to say good-bye to a clown or acrobat or maybe a magician. When he arrived, there was only an empty lot with a few empty popcorn bags rustling in the morning breeze.

The song ended, and I was magically transported back to the memory-filled recreation hall at Russian Gulch State Park. The class was sitting in a circle in the wonderfully rustic building that smelled of thousand-year-old incense cedar. The room was dark except for 30 brightly shining votive candles, each adding its unique color to the twinkling rainbow. This was their moment. They had traveled thousands of miles together; they had walked over 100 miles together. They sang, slept, and broke bread together. They had seen some of Earth's most beautiful scenery, matched with some of man's greatest thoughts. They had been encouraged to write their own bible. The time had arrived for them to gather the tools they had selected, pick up their candles, and head out into the darkness, alone.

Sean Gagne, a local folk singer, stood by, poised, ready to offer his musical benediction. The six strings on his guitar were perfectly tuned and came softly to life. His eyes sparkled like Sasha's, the Mountain Man's, and the Mule Skinner's, only they reflected the brilliance of 30 twinkling lights.

His final selection was not only appropriate for the evening, but the school year, the Biodesign experience, and my career.

He began with the chorus: "May the circle be unbroken."

"The clearest way into the Universe is through a forest wilderness."

John Muir

Afterword

Thirty years after I first stood in the shadow of Half Dome, I was standing in a circle of students for the last time. As I gazed up at my altar in the sky, I offered a prayer of thanksgiving:

> "When I think of all the things that could have gone
>   wrong, but didn't,
> I am amazed."
> In a perfectly timed antiphon, Erich offered:
> "When I think of all the things that could have gone
>   right and did,
> I am amazed."

A Very Slow Epiphany

During the entire journey, I thought I was in school. Years after I retired, I realized that I was really participating in a 24-year worship service. The word derives from *worth-ship*; things that we do to improve our worth.

Lettie offered the invocation, and every student was an exquisite living sermon on the creative power of God through evolution. Erich's benediction was an epigram for the 24-year odyssey.

We only went out for a walk, and ended up sauntering among the stars.

My cup overflowed.

Accident Report

63 Trips involving over 1,000 students and chaperones.

1. One entire class with blistered feet due to a badly planned 19-mile hike up and over El Capitan. Trip # 2.

2. Gina: Sprained ankle descending Half Dome.

3. Laurie: Lost all toenails due to ill-fitting boots.

4. Kelly: Broken fingertip due to 13 girls trying to crowd into two bathroom stalls at McDonald's.

5. Amy: One chipped tooth due to rock-climbing fall in Mendocino.

6. Eric: Banged knee in Nevada Falls pool.

7. Hamilton: Cactus spines in butt. The girls gladly removed.

8. Nikolai: One nearly ruptured appendix on Half Dome.

9. Pam: Blistered thigh by spilling hot water.

10. Author: Happy but mental wreck after each trip.

Acknowledgments

"God and the fairies …" Louise Townsend Nicholl, Silver Pennies, 1964, Macmillan.

"And all shall be well …" Four Quartets, by T. S. Eliot, copyright 1943, Harvest/HBJ Book.

"For the scientist …" Until The Sun Dies, by Robert Jastrow, W. W. Norton. XXXXXXX.

"You gotta smile …" Crystal Gayle song. Crystal Gayle Enterprises.

"I want to demonstrate …" Religions, Values, and Peak-Experiences, by Abraham Maslow, copyright 1964, Viking Press.

"They point their mysterious light …" Hunting The Divine Fox, by Robert Capon, copyright 1974, Seabury Press.

"i thank you God …" Copyright 1950, (c) 1978, 1991, by the Trustees for the E. E. Cummings Trust. Copyright (c) 1979 by George James Firmage, from Complete Poems: 1904–1962 by E. E. Cummings,

"Prevalent people believed ..." *The Outline Of History*, by H. G. Wells, copyright 1919, Garden City Books.

"Perhaps there also ..." *The Immense Journey*, by Loren Eiseley, copyright 1946, 1950, 1951, 1953, 1955, 1956, 1957, by Loren Eiseley. Used by permission of Random House Inc.

"And where better to grasp ..." *The Thread Of Life*, by Roger Lewin, copyright 1982, Smithsonian Books.

The Holy Bible, paraphrased references from Genesis.

"One of the great unresolved ..." *Omni* Magazine (out of print) article by Roger Sperry.

"Some molecules reproduced themselves ..." *Cosmos*, by Carl Sagan, copyright 1980, Carl Sagan Productions.

"It involves one of the most ..." *The Immense Journey*, by Loren Eiseley, copyright 1946, 1950, 1951, 1953, 1955, 1956, 1957, by Loren Eiseley. Used by permission of Random House Inc.

The Landlord's Slime, by Art Hoppe. Used by permission from the *San Francisco Chronicle*.

"It is a commonplace ..." *The Immense Journey*, by Loren Eiseley, copyright 1946, 1950, 1951, 1953, 1955, 1956, 1957, by Loren Eiseley. Used by permission of Random House Inc.

"Delaying gratification ..." *The Road Less Traveled*, by Scott Peck, copyright 1978, Simon & Schuster.

"To see from an inverted angle ..." *The Immense Journey*, by Loren

Call My Name, by Margaret Craven, copyright 1973. Used by written permission from Random House Inc.

"Oh Great Spirit whose voice I hear ..." Native American Prayer.

"but in the final frenzy ..." *The Star Thrower*, by Loren Eiseley, copyright 1978, Times Books.

"We shall not cease from exploration ..." *Four Quartets*, by T. S. Eliot, copyright 1943, Harvest/HBJ Book.

References

An incomplete list of references that contributed to the class.

John Muir: Many titles by him and about him.
By him:
All The World Over
John Of The Mountains
My First Summer in the Sierra
The Mountains of California
The Yosemite
Stickeen: An Adventure with a Dog and a Glacier
Travels in Alaska

About him:
The Wilderness World of John Muir, edited by Teale
John Muir: In His Own Words, edited by Browning
The Life of John Muir, Linnie Marsh Wolfe
John Muir: Nature's Visionary, Ehrlich
John Muir's America, Jones/Watkins
John Muir's Last Journey, edited by Branch
Muir Among the Animals, edited by Mighetto
Rediscovering America: John Muir in His Time and Ours. Turner
South Of Yosemite, edited by Gunsky
The Life and Adventures of John Muir, Clarke

Loren Eiseley: Many titles by and about him.
By him:
  The Immense Journey
  Darwin's Century
  The Firmament Of Time
  The Mind As Nature
  Man, Time, and Prophecy
  The Unexpected Universe
  The Invisible Pyramid
  The Night Country
  Notes Of An Alchemist
  The Man Who Saw Through Time
  The Innocent Assassins
  Another Kind Of Autumn
  The Star Thrower

About him:
  The Lost Notebooks of Loren Eiseley, edited by Heuer
  The Loren Eiseley Reader: Nebraska Book Source

A few references helpful in deciphering the Grand Canyon
  A Field Guide To The Grand Canyon, Whitney
  A Sand County Almanac, Leopold
  Desert Solitaire, Abbey
  Grand Canyon: Today and All Its Yesterdays, Krutch
  On Foot in the Grand Canyon, Spangler
  On the Edge of Splendor; Exploring Grand Canyon's Human Past, Schwartz
  The Grand Canyon Of The Colorado, Wild
  The Exploration Of The Colorado River And Its Canyons, Powell
  The Man Who Walked Through Time, Fletcher

A few references about the ocean and intertidal community

> *Beautiful Swimmers,* Warner
> *Between Pacific Tides,* Rickets and Calvin
> *Introduction to Seashore Life of the San Francisco Bay Region and Coast of Northern*
> *California,* Hedgpeth. Practical, easily carried into tide pools.
> *The Log of the Sea of Cortez,* Steinbeck
> *The Sea Around Us,* Rachel Carson
> *Whale Nation,* Williams

Although *Fearfully and Wonderfully Made* (Brand/Yancey) is Christian-based, it demonstrates how a medical doctor found it impossible to separate man's body from his mind and spirit. Man's awareness of this phenomenon is probably over 100,000 years old and is demonstrated in many forms of worship and celebration. The following list was helpful in creating the Biodesign experience.

> Adams, Ansel; selected photography
> *A Grief Observed,* C. S. Lewis
> Angelou, selected poems
> *A Natural History Of Love,* Ackerman
> *A Natural History Of The Senses,* Ackerman
> *Art Of Loving, The;* Fromm
> *As A Man Thinketh,* Allen
> *Black Elk Speaks,* Neihardt
> Celtic Meditations, Farrell
> *Civil Disobedience,* Thoreau
> *Cloud of Unknowing, The,* Unknown
> *Clowns,* Towsen
> *Cosmos,* Sagan
> Cummings, E. E., selected poems
> *Descent Of Man, The,* Darwin
> *Earth Speaks, The,* Matre/Weiler
> *Education of Little Tree, The,* Carter

Essential Rumi, The, Barks
Fearfully and Wonderfully Made, Brand/Yancey
Female Brain, The, Brizendine
Four Quartets, T. S. Eliot
Goodall, Jane, selected references
Gratefulness The Heart Of Prayer, Steindl-Rast
Great Evolution Mystery, The, Taylor
Huckleberry Finn, Twain
Hughes, Langston, selected poetry
Human Destiny, Lecomte du Nouy
Human Physiology, Silverthorn
Hunting The Divine Fox, Capon
I Heard The Owl Call My Name, Craven
Jeffers, Robinson, selected poems
Last Child In The Woods, Louv
Little Prince, The, de Saint Exupery
Lives of a Cell, The, Thomas
Living, Loving, and Learning, Buscaglia
Longfellow, selected poems
Male Brain, The, Brizendine
Meditations with Meister Eckhart, Fox
Men Are From Mars, Women Are From Venus, Gray
Oliver, Mary; selected poems
On Death And Dying, Kübler-Ross
On The Loose, T&R Russell
Origin Of Species, Darwin
Out Of Africa, Dinesen
Owning Your Own Shadow, Johnson
Pathway In The Sky: The story of the John Muir Trail, Roth
Personhood, Buscaglia
Prayers from the Ark, de Gasztold
Religions, Values, and Peak-Experiences, Maslow
Road Less Traveled, The, Peck
Rowell, Galen; selected photography

Sandburg, selected poems

Science and Moral Priority: Merging Mind, Brain, and Human Values, Sperry

Self-reliance, Emerson

Siddhartha, Hesse

Sierra Nevada Natural History: Storer and Usinger

Soul Of The World, Cousineau/Lawton

Tagore, Rabindranath, poems celebrating nature and spirituality

Teaching a Stone to Talk, Dillard

Tao of Pooh, The, Hoff

Tao Te Ching, Lao Tzu

The Prophet, Gibran

The Road Not Taken, Frost

Thread of Life, The, Lewin

Touching, Montagu

Unconditional Love, Powell

Until The Sun Dies, Jastrow

Van Dyke, selected poems

Voyage Of The Beagle, The, Darwin

Velveteen Rabbit, Williams

Vertical World Of Yosemite, The, Rowell

Walden, Thoreau

Walking, Thoreau

Whitman, selected poems

Wildlife Country: How to Enjoy It, National Wildlife Federation

CPSIA information can be obtained at www.ICGtesting.com
Printed in the USA
265665BV00002BA/2/P